AN ENGLISH HANDBOOK

AN ENGLISH HANDBOOK

by

W. G. BEBBINGTON, M.A. (Oxon.)

SCHOFIELD & SIMS LTD.
HUDDERSFIELD

0 7217 0061 6

This Edition revised and reprinted 1970
Reprinted 1974
Reprinted 1977
Reprinted 1978
Reprinted 1981

PRINTED IN GREAT BRITAIN BY
FLETCHER AND SON LTD.
NORWICH

Acknowledgements

WE are indebted to the following authors, executors and publishers, who so readily gave permission to include copyright material in this book:

Messrs. Faber & Faber and the authors for 'The Sleeper' by Walter de la Mare, 'Sunday Morning' by Louis MacNeice, the villanelle from 'The Sea and The Mirror' by W. H. Auden, lines from 'The Waste Land' by T. S. Eliot, lines from 'The Express' by Stephen Spender.

The Clarendon Press, Oxford, for 'When First we Met' from 'The Shorter Poems' of Robert Bridges.

Messrs. Kegan Paul, Trench, Trubner & Co., and the author for 'Above the Dock' by T. E. Hulme.

Messrs. J. M. Dent and the author for lines from 'The Conversation of Prayer' by Dylan Thomas, from 'Deaths and Entrances'.

Messrs. Chatto & Windus and the author for an extract from 'Along the Road' by Aldous Huxley.

Messrs. George Allen & Unwin for lines from 'Finale' by Alun Lewis from 'Raiders' Dawn'.

Messrs. Jonathan Cape and the author for lines from 'Ode to Fear' by C. Day Lewis, from 'Word over All', and Mrs. W. H. Davies for 'Killed in Action' from the 'Collected Poems' of W. H. Davies.

Messrs. A. P. Watt, Messrs. Methuen, and the executrix of the late G. K. Chesterton for 'Lucasta Replies to Lovelace' from 'Collected Poems' by G. K. Chesterton.

Messrs. New Directions, Connecticut, and the author for 'Francesca' by Ezra Pound.

Mr. Herbert Read for extracts from 'Summer Rain' and 'A Short Poem for Armistice Day'.

The Controller of Her Majesty's Stationery Office for an extract from Winston Churchill's speech, from the Official Report of the Parliamentary Debates, House of Commons.

The Public Trustee for 'There was a young man of Montrose' by Arnold Bennett.

The proprietors of 'Punch' for 'In Flanders Fields' by John McCrae.

Contents

CONTENTS

viii

Preface

THIS book is meant to be only a record of what has been and, by and large, still is. The words 'by common consent' or 'by established agreement' or 'by tradition' should be understood before most of the statements and read between most of the lines. The book is, in short, for reference, a sort of small encyclopedia to be kept ready to hand by the student of what is comprehensively called *English*. It does not contain any programme of study or sets of exercises at the ends of chapters and sections. It is not without shape, nevertheless, but keeps most of the subject-matter in place and in either a linguistic or a literary order.

It was written out of, and continues to serve, my own need—and that of my pupils—for such a record, a collection of definitions, accounts and illustrations freed from the confusions and repetitions of the typical school and college 'grammar book' or 'English course'. And I have no doubt that other teachers and other pupils feel the same need.

Like a dictionary, however, it can never be up-to-date in all its parts. Much of the grammar and syntax, for example, is bound to be hereditary, or even old-fashioned, and the latest movements, ideas and authors cannot be included until they are no longer news. History moves faster than editions. But such a book is not supposed to be primarily prescriptive or proscriptive; there should be little theory in it, a minimum of subjective criticism. Ideally there should be none.

Nor is anyone going to become an original writer or a profound expert on anything because he has and uses a copy.

Here and there, too, there must be items with which readers will disagree or about which argument is possible. In so much detail, I am sure, there must be some oversimplification, probably some error; from so much detail there must be some omission. I have long been aware of these dangers, however, above all of the risk of the book being, or becoming, a museum, a reliquary, or a storehouse, some of whose contents may be thought irrelevant to our revolutionary and rushing days when *English* seems to be in a state of greater uncertainty than ever before.

I still think that the risk was worth taking. For there is a mysterious but definite validity in the contention—which can be tested by anyone of serious disposition—that if you understand the phenomenon of, say, the verb then you will also understand Milton. And perhaps no age before our own has been in more need of such understanding. It is a truism to say that too many people today—and especially the young—have no 'sense of history' and are suffering from the loss.

So, although there are immediate and practical uses for such a book as this, in and out of school, it may—precisely because it is a 'handbook'—also have a bigger role to play than they can justify. I hope so. After all, the use of English should be concerned with the misuse.

WINDSOR. September 1969.   W. G. BEBBINGTON

1

The Parts of Speech

THERE are eight parts of speech: *noun, pronoun, adjective, verb, adverb, conjunction, preposition* and *interjection*.

Every word in the English language is one or other of these.

1. Noun

The word *noun* comes from the Latin *nomen* (=name) and means the name by which one thing is distinguished from another: thus all tables are distinguished in our minds from all elephants, the name for the one thing being *table*, the name for the other *elephant*. Both words are therefore nouns.

There are four kinds of nouns: *common, abstract, collective* and *proper*.

Common

Every physical object, living or dead, animal or human, is a common noun:

e.g. cow, lion, giraffe, raven, cuckoo, adder, salmon, bee, ant, man, woman, boy, girl, giant, dwarf, policeman, conductor, king, soldier, nurse, maid, scout, dancer, tree, flower, oak, rose, grass, radio, piano, car, trombone, rock, hill, mountain, aluminium, phosphorus, air, sky, sun, moon, star, world, earth, universe.

Abstract

No physical thing is abstract, and abstract nouns are all those things which we cannot sense externally (see, hear, touch, etc.), which are, in other words, abstracted from the world of matter. They are qualities, states of mind, attitudes, ideas:

e.g. apathy, arrogance, beauty, brightness, comfort, duty, eagerness, faith, greed, height, individuality, joy, kindness, love, mirth, novelty, opinion, pride, quietude, reality, suspicion, truth, unity, virtue, work, xenophobia, youth, zeal.

Collective

Any single word which means a collection of things is a collective noun. Apart from such general examples as *crowd* and the word *collection* itself, there are many special ones meaning collections of special things, such as a *covey* of partridges and a *pride* of lions. The following are representative collective nouns:

army, audience, bevy, chorus, duet, flock, gaggle, jury, multitude, party, queue, regiment, score, team.

All collective nouns are singular words and should therefore be followed by singular verbs, pronouns, etc.:

e.g. The crowd *roars*. The congregation *is* asleep. An army *marches* on *its* stomach.

But there is no hard-and-fast rule about this, and many people (including the Civil Service) prefer to say:

The Cabinet *are* aware of the situation or The Government *do* not hold *themselves* responsible for the crisis

and so on; though it must be noted that these collective nouns are the names of official, and usually governmental, institutions. Unofficial collective nouns are usually considered to be singular:

e.g. The orchestra *is* now going to play Tchaikovsky's Fifth Symphony.

2

Proper

The individual names of people, countries, towns, places, streets, houses, books, commercial articles, etc., are proper nouns; it is conventional to spell them with an initial capital letter:

e.g. George, Margaret, Williams, Homer's 'Iliad', Churchill, Napoleon, The Gables, Paris, London, Covent Garden, The Hippodrome, High Street, Embassy, Persil.

Also: whereas ranks and titles are common nouns spelt with initial small letters when they are generally applied, they become proper nouns with initial capital letters when they accompany names:

e.g. Queen Elizabeth, Inspector Hornleigh, Corporal Robins, Lady Oxford.

And many common and collective nouns become proper, at least in that they are spelt with initial capital letters, when they are the names of special, individual organizations:

e.g. The Windsor Town Council; The County Boys' School.

2. Pronoun

Pronouns are words which are substituted for nouns (Latin *pro*=instead of). They must not be confused with such noun-equivalents as the gerund (*q.v. infra*). For instance, instead of saying:

John picked up the ball and kicked the ball

we say: John picked up the ball and kicked *it*.

The word *ball* is a noun and so the word *it*, which is used to avoid a repetition of the noun, is a pronoun. Instead of saying:

My name is George; George lives in London

we say: My name is George; *I* live in London.

I is a pronoun.

The following words are known as *personal pronouns*:

3

I, me, thou, thee, he, him, she, her, it, we, us, you, they, them.

There are certain special pronouns:

Idiomatic

This pronoun appears to flaunt the laws of grammar:

e.g. It is *me*.

The grammatical rule would demand that this should be: It is *I*, *I* being in the nominative case after the verb *to be*. But our idiom is paralleled by the French expression, *c'est moi* (not *c'est je*), *moi* in French and *me* in English being the special idiomatic (sometimes called 'disjunctive') use of the pronoun. So we say: It is *him, her, us, them*. (*It is I* is nevertheless commonly used, even if it is now somewhat archaic: cf. *It is I: be not afraid*.) This pronoun is also used after conjunctions, again in an idiomatic and not a strictly grammatical way:

e.g. He is taller than *me*.

Relative

These are the words: *Who, whom, whose, which, what* and *that* (plus their *-ever* or *-soever* forms sometimes). All introduce *relative clauses* and are called *relative* because they relate their clauses to antecedents (v. next page) and join one sentence to another, because, in other words, they combine separate sentences into one. The sentence *The dog, which ate my dinner, is ill* is composed of two separate sentences: *The dog ate my dinner* and *The dog is ill*. The second of these is unchanged in vocabulary but its subject, *The dog*, is separated from its predicate, *is ill*, by the insertion of the first sentence in a new form. The noun *dog* and its accompanying article *the* have been replaced by *which*; *which* is therefore a relative pronoun because it has related 'ate my dinner' to 'dog' and joined the two sentences. It can also be seen that the relative

4

pronoun is used to avoid a clumsy repetition of the same noun and a succession of short sentences. This uniting of sentences is called *synthesis*.

It is not necessary, however, for the noun instead of whose repetition it is used to be written down even once. In the sentence *I will see who is there*, the noun is understood:

e.g. *person*. The two separate sentences would be: *I will see the person* and *The person is there*.

The following diagram shows how the relative pronoun and the clause it introduces perform their syntactical function:

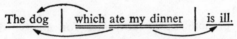

The noun instead of whose repetition this pronoun is used is called the 'antecedent'.

Interrogative

All the words listed above as relative pronouns except *that* automatically become interrogative pronouns when they introduce, not relative clauses, but questions.

e.g. *Who* is there? (The noun is understood: e.g. What *person* is there?); *Which* do you mean?; *Whatever*'s the matter?; *What* do you want?

Reflexive

These words refer back to and, as it were, reflect the nouns they replace. They are:

myself, thyself, himself, herself, itself, ourselves, yourself, yourselves, themselves.

In the sentence 'Red Indians painted *themselves*', the word *themselves* stands in place of a repetition of *Red Indians* and also reflects them or refers back to them. Syntactically it is the object of *painted*, but it still means the *Red Indians*, i.e. subject and object are the same thing.

5

These pronouns can also be used in an emphasizing capacity. In the sentence 'I'll have that *myself*' the word *myself* not only refers back to *I* (for one pronoun can be a substitute for another since both are substitutes for the same noun) but also emphasizes it: *I'll have that—I*.

The form *ourself* is now obsolete except as the royal plural (*v. infra*): e.g.

> Ourself will mingle with society,
> And play the humble host.
> ('Macbeth', III. 4. 3-4.)

Indefinite

These pronouns are substitutes for nouns whose own identity is vague and general and which are seldom, if ever, used:

e.g. one, anyone, anybody, anything, someone, somebody, something, no one, nobody, none, any, all, some, nothing, everything, everyone, everybody.

Some of the personal pronouns can also be used indefinitely:

e.g. *You* never know your luck; *they* say the ration is to be increased; why doesn't the government tell *us* the truth?

Sometimes *a man*, *a woman*, *a body*, *a citizen*, *people*, etc., are used in an indefinite capacity, *a man*, for example, meaning the same as *one*:

e.g. *A man* can stand up here and look about him.

Such words are nouns, of course, but are temporarily doing the work of indefinite pronouns.

Distributive

These are the words *either*, *neither* and *each* used without nouns; all of them are grammatically singular:

e.g. Neither of them *was* keen to go (the noun, which is understood, might be *boy* or *woman*).

6

Possessive

These pronouns denote possession. They are the words: *mine, thine, his, hers, its, ours, yours, theirs.*

e.g. This book is mine (=This book is my book); That coat is *his* (=That coat is his coat).

Only *his* and *its* are the same in form as the possessive adjectives (q.v.). Both are possessive adjectives in the following sentences because they accompany nouns:

He heard *his* name called;
They like *its* cover;

both are possessive pronouns, however, in these sentences:

He said he did not hear *his* called out (no noun);
That dog does not seem to like *its* (no noun).

Thus *his* and *its*, possessive pronouns, correspond to *his* and *its*, possessive adjectives, as *mine, thine, hers, ours, yours, theirs*, possessive pronouns, correspond to *my, thy, her, our, your, their*, possessive adjectives.

It should be noted that there is no use of the apostrophe with these words.

Impersonal

This is the single pronoun *it* when used in such idioms as '*It* is raining', '*It* is very cold out today'.

Reciprocal

These are the expressions *each other* (of two things or persons only) and *one another* (of more than two):

e.g. in the sentence 'The two men resembled *each other* closely', the two words *each other*, which are taken as tantamount to one word, stand reciprocally for each man in turn.

7

Demonstrative

These are the four words *this, that, these, those.* In the sentence 'I don't want *that* cake, I'll have *this*' the word *that* is an adjective (also called demonstrative—q.v.) accompanying the noun *cake*, but the word *this* is a pronoun because it is substituted for *this cake*. It is a one-word substitute for the demonstrative adjective and its noun. The function of the four words, whether they are used as adjectives or pronouns, is the same: to demonstrate, to point out in order to distinguish.

The Special Plural

A special use of the first person plural pronouns—*we, us,* etc.—followed by plural verbs and by *our* and *ours,* is made by kings and editors—i.e. 'the Royal *We*' and 'the Editorial *We*'. In both cases the individual speaker or writer is representing more than himself.

A development of this use has been the exaltation of themselves by some sportsmen—and by boxers in particular —to the ranks of monarchs and editors:

e.g. 'We've trained hard for this fight, and we think we'll win.'

3. Adjective

Those words are adjectives which, not themselves being things, tell us about things (i.e. nouns). If we read only the noun *hat* we do not know anything about it; but if we read *large hat* we have a clearer picture of the particular hat in question; and this picture can be made still clearer if the hat is said to be *black* or *dusty* or *old.* Adjectives, therefore, give information about nouns (or their equivalents—e.g. pronouns): about size, condition, colour, etc.:

e.g. awful, brilliant, charming, dubious, easy, fair, green, horrible, idiotic, jolly, kingly, likeable, marvellous, nice, old, pure, quick, red, sweet, tough, unkind, vicious, wonderful, young, zealous.

There are, in addition, certain special adjectives:

Numerical

These are the numbers accompanying nouns: (cardinal) *one* book, *three* children, *twenty-six* cars, *a thousand* men; (ordinal) the *sixth* day, the *fourth* commandment.

Demonstrative

The four words *this, that, these, those* are, when used with nouns, demonstrative adjectives (cf. their use as demonstrative pronouns):

e.g. I want *this* cake (=this one here) rather than *that* cake (=that one over there); Hand me *that* file, will you?

Indefinite

Any word qualifying a noun which does not say anything definite about it is an indefinite adjective:

e.g. any, some, no. Are there *any* boys present? There will be *no* holidays this year.

We can gather no information about the boys or the holidays themselves.

Interrogative

These are the words *which* and *what* accompanying nouns and introducing questions:

e.g. *Which* course do you want, sir?

Possessive

These are the words *my, thy, his, her, its, our, your, their* qualifying nouns. This is *my* pencil. The dog was wagging *its* tail.

Comparative

These are the four words *less, least, more, most* used with nouns. There was *less* sickness there than we had expected.

Distributive

These are the four words *each, every, either, neither* qualifying nouns. They can qualify only singular nouns. *Each* boy did his best. *Neither* hat suits me.

Emphasizing

When the words *the* and *very* are used with nouns in an emphasizing capacity they are classed as emphasizing adjectives. It is *the* solution. That's the *very* book I've been looking for.

Relative

These are the two words *which* and *what* accompanying nouns in a relative position:

e.g. 'I agree,' he said; with *which* statement the conversation ended.

The definite article *the* and the indefinite articles *a* and *an* are classed as adjectives since they are always used with nouns and state whether or not a particular object is being discussed. *The* book means one special book, *a* book does not refer to any special book.

NOTE.—It can be seen that on many occasions a word which is an adjective when it is accompanying a noun automatically becomes a pronoun when it stands alone.

4. Verb

All those words are verbs which express what action has taken, is taking or will take place, or what state has been, is being or will be arrived at:

e.g. (to) accept, burn, come, do, eat, fight, give, hunt, invade, jump, knit, love, marry, nominate, open, push, quieten, run, sleep, teach, unite, vacate, worship, yawn, zoom.

In the sentence *I answered his question*, the action which took place was that of answering: *answered* is therefore a verb.

Transitive and Intransitive Verbs

All those verbs are called transitive which need objects to complete their sense. The action of eating, for instance, must be done at the expense of something other than the person or thing performing the action: it is impossible to eat without eating something—that *something* is the object. So all transitive verbs must, in technical language, *take objects* (which may or may not be written down). The following are all transitive:

advise, buy, cook, do, encourage, fetch, give, hold, imagine, join, kick, love, meet, open, place, quit, rap, see, touch, untie, verify, write, yoke.

All verbs are intransitive which, so far from not needing objects to complete their meaning, cannot *take objects* except in very special circumstances (as explained later). For instance, the action of walking cannot be done at the expense of another person or thing—it is an action performed independently by the subject. So in such a sentence as *He walked four miles* the words *four miles* are not the object of *walked* since he did not in any way affect those miles by his walking. The sentence means that he walked *for* four miles. The following verbs are intransitive:

appear, become, crawl, dawdle, escape, fly, go, hasten, interfere, look, peer, run, yawn.

But whereas all transitive verbs are always transitive, some intransitive verbs can assume a temporarily transitive role and, so far as grammatical function is concerned, take objects.

11

In the sentence *She ran the duster over the top of the table*, *she* is apparently doing the running to *the duster*, which is therefore the object of the verb *ran*. Thus an intransitive verb is taking an object. Yet it is still intransitive, for the true meaning of the sentence is revealed if it is paraphrased as 'She *made* the duster *run* over the top of the table', in which *the duster* is the object of the transitive verb *made* and *run* remains as its intransitive self. Similarly, *walk* can mean *made to walk* in such a sentence as 'The policeman *walked* the prisoner down the street'. Compare 'He *sailed* his boat on the lake', 'He *was flying* a kite', 'She *boiled* the water for tea'. In all these cases the intransitive verbs are taking objects only because they are condensed forms of the transitive verb *to make* plus themselves, i.e. they are used *causatively* or *factitively*.

In slang almost anything can happen to grammatical rules and even so obviously an intransitive verb as *to yawn* can at least appear to have an object: *I yawned my head off*. The anarchy of slang apart, however, *To yawn* can never be anything else but intransitive. Yet even the slang expression can be defended, on the ground that *my head* is *cognate* with *yawned*, i.e. is really part of the verb, is qualifying it rather than is its direct object. cf. He looked *daggers* at me; She lived *a happy life*.

Tense

For our general purposes in our own language it is perhaps sufficient to know that there are three main tenses, the past, the present and the future.

The word *tense* comes from the Latin *tempus* (=time), and so the tense of a verb tells when the action specified takes place: the action happened in the past, is happening now, or will happen in the future. So of the verb *to take*:

the past tense is: I took, used to take, did take, have taken, etc.;

12

the present tense is: I take, do take, am taking;
the future tense is: I shall (or will) take (or be taking).

These three main tenses are subdivisible into several special forms, which are enumerated in the chapter on syntax.

Some Special Parts of the Verb

The Infinitive. The present infinitive of the active voice is the name of the verb: to be, to do.

There are four true infinitives:

Active voice: past (or perfect) infinitive: *to have done;* present: *to do;*
Passive voice: past (or perfect) infinitive: *to have been done;* present: *to be done.*

The infinitive need not always include the word *to* (which is not the preposition but an old prefix). For instance, in the sentence *Can that be done?* the present infinitive of the passive voice is used, *be done;* that it is so can be proved if the sentence is paraphrased as 'Is it possible for that *to be done?*'

A form of future infinitive in both voices can be composed by using the word *about* before the present infinitive: *about to do, about to be done.*

To place any words between the *to* of the infinitive and the name of the verb is to write what is called a *split infinitive:*

e.g. It was his habit *to gracefully decline* all invitations.

Sometimes this is unavoidable, but every effort should be made to avoid it as it is clumsy and ugly, an unnatural separation of two words which are in effect one and in many old verbs were actually written together as one. When it is unavoidable, i.e. when any other word-order would create ambiguity, it must be used if there is no convenient way of totally rewording the sentence. In his popular book, 'Modern

13

English Usage', H. W. Fowler cites the following instance: 'Our object is *to further cement* trade relations', in which any replacing of *further* to avoid splitting *to cement* would either give the sentence a different meaning or at least leave its meaning in doubt.

The Imperative. This is used when a command is directly uttered (Latin *imperare*=to order); the subject of the verb is the pronoun *you* understood:

e.g. *Halt! Come here!*

The Participles. These parts of the verb are used adjectivally (v. infra, p. 29), in the construction of subordinate phrases, and in the formation of tenses. They exist in the two voices, active and passive. The following table, using *to make*, shows their forms:

Active voice:	present participle:	*making;*
	perfect participle:	*having made;*
Passive voice:	present participle:	*being made;*
	perfect participle:	*having been made;*
	past participle:	*made*

The present participle of the active voice ends in *-ing*: *being, going, measuring.* So in the sentence, *John, being the oldest, was chosen,* it is the use of the participle which makes the three words *being the oldest* a subordinate phrase: those three words could not stand alone.

This participle is very widely used in the formation of tenses: *I am going, he will be starting, she will have been doing that.* . . . The participle is preceded by some part of the auxiliary verbs *to be* and *to have.* It is also used in the formation of all the other participles except the past: *having been made* is composed of the present participle of *to have* and the past participles of *to be* and *to make.*

The perfect participle of the active voice is made up of the present participle of *to have* and the past participle of the

14

verb in question. The following sentence shows how it too is used in the formation of subordinate phrases: '*Having* at last *decided* what action to take, they adjourned the meeting'.

The present and perfect participles of the passive voice are now self-explanatory. The past participle, which except in the composition of tenses is always passive in meaning, often takes the same form as the past tense: e.g. *made*. But the forms differ in such verbs as *to see*: the past tense is *saw*, the past participle *seen*. It has the same subordinating function as the other participles: '*Struck* down a third time, he lay motionless'. And it is also widely used in the formation of tenses: *I have been, he had caught, you should have known*. It is present in all tenses of the passive voice (q.v.): *I am surprised, they were trapped, you will be met*. Standing alone it always has a passive meaning.

The Gerund

This has the same form as the present participle, and is the 'verbal noun'. As such it may be the subject or object of another verb, or be governed by a preposition, or be qualified by adjectives. Yet simultaneously it can retain its character as a verb and have its own object. In the sentence *Their violently attacking the bridge at that moment spoilt our plans* the word *attacking* is the gerund: it is the subject of the verb *spoilt* and is thus doing the work of a noun, but it has its own object *the bridge* and so retains its verbal function, which is also shown by the qualifying adverb *violently*. Cf. *Parting is such sweet sorrow*: *Parting* is the subject of *is*.

Since the gerund is a noun it must, whenever necessary, be accompanied by the possessive adjective and not by the personal pronoun (the use of this is a common mistake). So: 'We were shocked by *his* interfering like that' is correct: 'We were shocked by *him* interfering like that' is wrong.

15

The Active and Passive Voices

A verb is in the active voice when its subject is responsible for the action specified:

> The boy kicked the ball; the cow chews the cud; the policeman arrested the thief.

In each of those sentences the subjects, *the boy*, *the cow* and *the policeman*, are all actively engaged (or were or will be—the tense of the verb does not matter) in the actions of kicking, chewing and arresting. The verbs—*kicked*, *chews* and *arrested*—are therefore in the active voice.

A verb is in the passive voice when its subject is not responsible for the action specified but has that action done to it: i.e. the subject is the receiver of the action:

> The ball was kicked by the boy; the cud is (being) chewed by the cow; the thief was arrested by the policeman.

Now the subjects, *the ball*, *the cud* and *the thief*, are not actively engaged.

It can be seen that the passive voice is composed of the verb *to be* in any of its parts and the past participle of the verb in question.

Normally, only transitive verbs can be changed from the active to the passive voice since, as can be seen in the sentences above, it is the object of the active verb which becomes the subject of the passive verb.
Example:

> Active: *The boy kicked the ball;*
>
> Passive: *The ball was kicked by the boy.*

Intransitive verbs, therefore, which have objects only when they are used in a quasi-transitive sense (as explained earlier),

cannot change into the passive voice since there is no object of the active form to become the subject of the passive. When they are used quasi-transitively the usual changes occur.
Example:

Active: She boiled *the water* (=she made the water boil);

Passive: *The water* was boiled by her (=the water was made to boil. . . .).

The subject of the active voice is known as *the agent* of the passive and is always preceded by the preposition *by*.
Example:

Active: *The policeman* arrested the thief;

Passive: The thief was arrested by *the policeman*.

Thus, when the change from active voice to passive is made, the subject and object of the verb become the agent and the subject respectively.
Example:

Active: *The soldiers* attacked *the fort*;

Passive: *The fort* was attacked by *the soldiers*.

It can be stated as a rule, therefore, that there is no object of a verb in the passive voice. But there is one exception to this rule. For if the sentence whose verb is in the active voice includes an indirect object and it is that indirect voice which becomes the subject of the passive verb, the direct (or ordinary) object of the active is left over to remain as object even though the verb is in the passive voice.

17

Example:

Active: *Mr. Jones* first showed me that book.

Passive: *I* was first shown *that book* by *Mr. Jones.*

The indirect object always has either *to* or *for* understood (never written down) before and governing it. Whenever, therefore, this indirect object becomes the subject of the passive verb the direct object (it is so distinguished when an indirect object is being discussed) remains the direct object and is grammatically known as either *the retained object* or *the retained accusative* (since all direct objects are in the accusative case—*v.* chapter on syntax).

But the direct object of the active verb can still become the subject of the passive in the normal way, in which case the indirect object remains itself.

Example:

Active: Mr. Jones first showed *me that book.*

Passive: *That* book was first shown *me* by Mr. Jones.

One further example may help to make this alternative method of change from active to passive perfectly clear:

Active: *I* gave *that man a penny.*

Passive: (either.) *A penny* was given *that* man by *me.*

(or) *The man* was given *a penny* by *me.*
(*a penny* is the retained accusative.)

18

The Quasi-Passive Voice is the name given to the active voice when it has a passive meaning. In the sentence 'The cushions *felt* soft' the verb is in the active voice (the passive would be *were felt*), but the cushions—i.e. the subject—are not responsible for the action of feeling, they are being subjected to that action (they should properly be the object, therefore). So in the following sentences none of the subjects is responsible for the action named in the active form of its verb, and all the verbs have a passive meaning:

> This house is to let; this egg smells bad; this book reads very well; the soup tasted like dish-water.

Auxiliary Verbs

Certain verbs are called auxiliary because they help other verbs in the formation of their various parts (tenses, participles, etc.). The two most common are *to be* and *to have* (cf. the use of *être* and *avoir* in French), which accompany the present and past participles of other verbs: 'I *am* doing; he *will be* coming; he *was* wounded; I *have been* told; they *had* done'.

All the other auxiliary verbs are followed by the infinitive of the other verb; they have no infinitives of their own and no independent existence, for even if they are not followed by an infinitive it is understood:

e.g. *But you must*=you must . . . do whatever is being referred to.

These are the auxiliary verbs in question: *can, could, must, will, would, shall, should, may, might*. The verb *to do* is also used as an auxiliary verb, but only for the sake of emphasis: *I do like that*.

NOTE.—When the verb *to be* stands alone (i.e. followed by a complement) it is known as the *copula* (such verbs as *to become* and *to grow*, intransitive, are known as *copulative* verbs).

19

Mood

The grammatical word *mood* has nothing to do with the word meaning *state of mind or feeling* but is a form of *mode* (cf. that word in music and logic). It is a technical word, therefore, and serves to show the function of a verb.

There are five moods of the verb: the infinitive, the imperative, the indicative, the subjunctive and the conditional. The first two have already been discussed.

The indicative: this is the mood of definite statement, of fact, of actual event:

e.g. The clock *struck* twelve; *I am* determined; He *will be* here soon.

No matter what tense or voice a verb is in, it is in the indicative mood if it states fact.

The subjunctive: this is the mood of hypothesis, supposition, wish, likelihood:

e.g. God *save* the Queen; If that *were* true, it would solve all our troubles; In order that he *might* not *be heard*, he wore rubber-soled boots (*wore* is indicative because it states fact).

Conditional: this is the mood of condition, and the verbal form is a combination of the words *should* and *would* and the infinitive:

e.g. If that were true, it *would solve* all our troubles.

Like the subjunctive it does not state fact.

There is a special use of the subjunctive known as the *jussive subjunctive* (Latin *jubeo*=command) in which the mood includes the element of command. This is frequently met in prayers. *Save* in 'God *save* the Queen' is an example.

Finite and Non-Finite Verbs

All parts of the verb except the infinitives and participles are called finite: the infinitives and participles are called non-finite. As the word *finite* implies (Latin *finio*=end, complete, finish), the infinitives and participles are not finished: they need the help of the auxiliary verbs to complete them. It is the absence of a finite verb from a phrase that makes it incomplete and distinguishes it from a sentence; and it is the presence of a finite verb that gives the subordinate clause its peculiar character (q.v.). A phrase is definable as a group of words not containing a finite verb. It may not contain any verb, but such verb as it does contain is always either an infinitive or a participle. A sentence, on the other hand, is a group of words which does contain a finite verb (and, of course, is complete sense in itself).

The following groups of words are phrases: *Having seen* them; at the bottom of the hill; *walking* down the street; *to be* or not *to be* (non-finite verbs are in italics).

The following groups are sentences: I *had seen* them; The car *stopped* at the bottom of the hill; He *was walking* down the street; To be or not to be, that *is* the question (finite verbs are shown in italics).

The following sentence shows the use of the two parts in conjunction: He *felt* (finite) able *to walk* (non-finite) in spite of his accident.

The finite verb is, therefore, the most important word in any sentence: that is why it is sometimes called the *main* verb.

Strong and Weak Verbs

Verbs are said to be strong if they undergo a change of internal vowel in the past tense and past participle, and weak if they form their past tense and past participle merely by the addition of -ed, -d or -t. So *to walk* (walked), *to love* (loved), *to sleep* (slept) are weak verbs, but *to swim* (swam, swum), *to break* (broke, broken), *to teach* (taught) are strong.

21

5. Adverb

The main function of the adverb is to state in a single word how, where or when the action named in a verb takes place. In the sentence 'He ran *swiftly* down the street' it is the word *swiftly* which tells *how* he ran: it is therefore an adverb.

All adverbs which state *how* an action is done are called adverbs of *manner*:

e.g. admirably, beautifully, eagerly, fast, openly, well.

In the sentence 'She stood *there* for an hour' it is the word *there* which is adding information to, or, in grammatical terms, qualifying, the verb *stood*: it is stating *where* she stood. It is therefore an adverb.

All adverbs which state *where* an action takes place are called adverbs of *place*:

e.g. anywhere, everywhere, hence, here, nowhere, out, thither.

Many prepositions (q.v.) automatically assume the role of adverbs of place when they stand alone, i.e. without the nouns which they would govern. In the sentence 'I met him *outside*' the name of the place is understood (say, the house), but since it is not written down and there is therefore no noun to be governed by the preposition *outside*, *outside* is performing the function of an adverb of place, stating where I met him. Similarly, such prepositions as *inside*, *near*, *around* can become adverbs of place.

Adverbs of *time* state *when* the action of a verb takes place. In the sentence 'I knew him *then*' the word *then* tells when it was that I knew him and is therefore an adverb of time. Other such adverbs are:

again, ago, daily, hourly, lately, meanwhile, never, now, soon, today, tomorrow, yesterday.

A special adverb is that of *degree*. This does not qualify verbs but other adverbs or adjectives. In the sentence 'He played *rather* badly' the word *rather* qualifies the adverb *badly* by stating the degree of badness: it is therefore an adverb of degree. cf. the use of *very* in *I am very tired*, qualifying the adjective *tired*. Other such adverbs are:

any (Is it any better?), more, much, less, no (It is no better), so, somewhat, even, only.

The four words *where, when, why, how* are adverbs able to play three different parts, each with its own special name:

Interrogative Adverbs: i.e. they introduce questions. Examples:

Where are you going? *How* are you today?

Conjunctive Adverbs: i.e. doing the work of conjunctions (q.v.).
Examples:

I don't know *how* he does it; *When* the war ended I was ill; I asked him *why* he did it;

(i.e. they introduce subordinate clauses).

Relative Adverbs: i.e. they are substitutes for relative pronouns governed by prepositions.
Examples:

The house *where* (=in which) they live is haunted; Let's find out the time *when* (=at which) it's due.

There are some words which are to be classed as adverbs even though they are not strictly adverbs of place or time or manner or degree. They are free-lance adverbs which may become any of these at any time but may be simply associable in a vague way with either a verb, another adverb or an adjective. So in the sentence *I have just told you* the word *just* can be taken as an adverb of time, but in another context it might be one of degree. Other such adverbs are:

only, however, merely, perhaps, thus, also, besides, not, doubtless, still, therefore.

23

6. Conjunction

The conjunction is the word which joins together, makes a junction between, either one word and another or one group of words and another. *And* is the most common conjunction. In the phrase *You and I* it joins *you* to *I*; in the sentence *You will come here and you will write what I say* it joins one simple sentence *You will come here* to one complex sentence *You will write what I say*. It is a sort of bridge connecting the two: without it they would be entirely separate.

The following words are all conjunctions:

after, although, as, because, but, since, till, until, before, either . . . or, neither . . . nor, for, if, than, unless, while, whilst, that, lest, whether . . . or.

Several of them appear elsewhere as pronouns or prepositions: *that*, for instance, is also a demonstrative pronoun (and adjective), *after* is a preposition. The only way of knowing when the same word is a conjunction and not another part of speech is to understand its function. In the following sentence the word *that* cannot be any other part of speech than a conjunction:

I have told them that you cannot come.

Certain small phrases which do the work of conjunctions and are in effect single words are also classed as conjunctions:

e.g. *in order to* (or *that*), *so that*.

Conjunctions do not qualify or govern words, they merely act as links between words; but although that is all they do, the importance of such a function cannot be overestimated, as a study of the part played in a sentence by those conjunctions which introduce subordinate clauses (i.e. subordinating conjunctions) will prove. (*V.* chapter on analysis into clauses.)

7. Preposition

The preposition names a special relationship between one word and another, where one thing is in relationship to another: it is always followed—grammatically, though not necessarily in order of words—by a noun or its equivalent (pronoun, gerund, etc.), which it is said to *govern*. So in the sentence *He placed his hat on the table* it is the word *on* which states the relationship between the hat and the table, the position of the one as it affected the other. *On* is therefore a preposition; and in that sentence it governs the word *table*. The following words are common prepositions:

after, around, beside, between, by, from, in, off, over, through, to, under, up, with.

As has already been observed, many of these words become adverbs if the nouns or noun-equivalents which they govern are not written down: they are, that is, prepositions temporarily being denied their full grammatical role and playing only the false part of adverb: to play their proper part they must be accompanied by the words which they govern.

One should also be careful to avoid confusing such a word as *after* as a conjunction and as a preposition. In the following sentence it is a conjunction: *He arrived after we had finished*—for it joins *He arrived* to *we had finished* and subordinates the latter sentence to the former; but in this next sentence it is a preposition as it governs a noun: *They all walked after the band*.

8. Interjection

The word itself comes from Latin and means something thrown among other things: this literal meaning is the clue to its function, or lack of function. For it is any word which is thrown among other words so that it remains aloof from the syntactical arrangement and has no grammatical relationship with any of those other words. Often it is separated from them by an exclamation-mark.

What may be called pure interjections are such exclamations as: *ah, bosh, coo, golly, hurrah, oh, phew, shush, tut.* But almost any word can be used in a similarly exclamatory manner and so play the temporary part of an interjection:

e.g. '*Well*, fancy that,' he said: '*Confound!*' he shouted; '*My, my*,' she murmured.

Few interjections are appropriate in writing except when conversation is being quoted; and even in speech a distinction must be made between such of them as are old euphemisms—e.g. *By jiminy!* which means *By Jesus!*— and such as are permissible in good talking—e.g. *Well* and *Oh*. Many interjections occur in swearing, of course, and in the colloquial language of childhood (*Crikey!*); and it would seem that they find their home in slang.

2

The Parts of Speech Continued

How One Part of Speech Can Become Another

A WORD does not effectively become a part of speech until it is used with other words; and in the last analysis every word is only one part of speech. But, as we have already seen, a word can assume the character of another part according to its function in different contexts, and so, for the moment, be classed as that other part. The essential meaning of the word does not change—we are not concerned here with a word like *that* which changes its part of speech with its meaning.

Thus every part of speech can temporarily change to one or other of the remaining seven.

Noun

Nouns can be used as adjectives: e.g. *Cabinet* minister: the noun *Cabinet* is qualifying the noun 'minister'; cf. the use of nouns in this way in hyphenated words: *farm*-labourer, *record-player*. And cf. the modern use of 'home' in *home* town.

Christian names—i.e. proper nouns—may also be said to be used adjectivally, qualifying the surnames: *George Brown*, *George* qualifying *Brown*.

A noun can also become an adverb. In the sentence *I went home then* the noun *home* has become an adverb of place.

27

Almost any noun can become a verb. In *They chaired him off the field* the word *chaired* is the past tense of a verb *to chair* which has been adapted from the noun *chair*. cf. *Uncle me no uncle* (Shakespeare: 'Richard II').

Pronoun

Pronouns are used adjectivally in hyphenated words: e.g. *he-man*. Shakespeare used 'she' as a noun in 'Twelfth Night': 'Lady, you are the cruell'st she alive'.

Adjective

The title of one of Edmund Burke's books, 'The Sublime and Beautiful', shows the use of two adjectives as nouns. By placing the article before them they have assumed the character of qualities, i.e. of abstract nouns. cf. The *red* of the sunset; The *green* of the countryside; He is obsessed by the *ugly* in life. (This is known as the *absolute* use of an adjective.)

In compound or hyphenated words adjectives may also become adverbs. So in *happy*-looking the adjective *happy* is qualifying the present participle 'looking' and thus has an adverbial function.

Verb

The infinitives can be used as nouns, i.e. they become 'verbal nouns'. In the sentence '*To hear* is to obey' the infinitive *To hear* is the subject of *is* and so is a noun-equivalent. In 'I don't want *to know*' the infinitive *to know* is the object of *don't want* and so is being used as a noun.

Probably, in such a sentence as 'He likes *being fussed*' it is wrong to say that *being fussed* is the participle used as a noun, since it should be called the gerund. In English, however, there is really no telling the difference, and we may as

28

well say that when the present participle is used as a noun it is called the gerund.

Just as nouns can be made into verbs, so verbs can be turned into nouns and have plurals, apostrophes, etc. In 'They took two *runs*' the word *runs* is a noun adapted from the infinitive *to run*. cf. They made their *stand* there.

The present and past participles are frequently used as adjectives:

e.g. I have a *splitting* headache; The *wounded* man died. (The participle is also called the 'verbal adjective'.)

Other parts of the verb, but especially the infinitive, can be used in hyphenated expressions in an adjectival function:

e.g. He is not the *do*-or-*die* type; He had a *go*-as-you-*please* attitude.

Adverb

Occasionally an adverb is used as an adjective:

e.g. It was a *daily* occurrence.

Nightly, weekly, monthly, quarterly and *yearly* are also used in this way:

e.g. The *Quarterly* Review.

A recent development has been the use as adjectives of such adverbs of time as *now* and *then*:

e.g. . . . the *then* state of affairs.

Occasionally, too, an adverb can be used as a noun:

e.g. The *why* and the *wherefore* of the matter . . .; That is the difference between *now* and *then*.

Conjunction

In an artificial way conjunctions also can become nouns:

e.g. There are too many *but's* in your writing; It's all a question of *if*.

Some conjunctions can become adverbs:

e.g. I'd never seen him *before*; Have you met him *since*?

That these two words are conjunctions only acting as adverbs can be seen when it is realized that they would normally introduce subordinate adverbial clauses were it good style to write those clauses: *I'd never seen him before I saw him then* and *Have you met him since you met him last?*

Preposition

We have already seen how prepositions can become adverbs of place. They can also become adjectives. In 'The *outside* walls were scarred' the preposition *outside* is qualifying the noun *walls* and so is temporarily an adjective. Cf. this use of the preposition in hyphenated words: *Over*-arm; The soft *under*-belly of Europe.

Prepositions can also become nouns:

e.g. He knows all the *ins* and *outs* of this subject.

Interjection

Even interjections can become nouns. In the sentence 'They all shouted *hurrah*' the interjection *hurrah* is the object of *shouted* and so is acting the part of a noun. In the form *huzza* it can be a verb also (intransitive) with all the tenses, etc.

Once one part of speech has come into being by adaptation from another (as *to chair* originated from the noun), it often happens that the new part becomes an entirely new word, existing in its own right as that new part. In a sense, the noun *chair* has no longer any connection with the verb *to chair*, which of course has all the distinctive verbal parts. So conjunctions and prepositions can, as nouns, be in the plural, as we have seen. And so an adverb can give birth to an adjective which then lives its own life, having its own degrees of comparison. The word *out* for instance is originally an adverb of place. But in hyphenated words it has an adjectival function:

e.g. the *out*-house (qualifying the noun 'house'); and this new role gave birth in its turn to the comparative adjective *outer* or *utter* and the superlative *outermost* or *utmost*. Similarly, the preposition *in* became the true adjectives *inner* and *innermost* or *inmost*.

The Homograph

A homograph is a word which has the same spelling as another but has a different meaning and pronunciation. Sometimes it may remain the same part of speech:

e.g. *bow* (=weapon for shooting arrows), *bow* (=fore-end of boat or ship from where it begins to arch inwards).

But change in part of speech often accompanies change in meaning. The word *tear*, for example, is a verb if it means *pull apart*, *rend*, *lacerate*; but it is a noun if it means *drop of saline liquid ordinarily serving to moisten and wash the eye*.

Other examples of the homograph are:

Row: propel boat (verb); disturbance, dispute (noun);

Wind: go in circular course (verb); breeze (noun);

Sow; buffet;

reading—Reading; scone—Scone; slough—Slough.

(V. reference in section on the homonym, p. 36.)

Corresponding Parts of Speech

In the same way that the word *lovely* is the adjective which corresponds to the noun *love*, so the word *quickly* is the adverb corresponding to the adjective *quick*, *to defy* is the verb corresponding to the noun *defiance*, and *afterwards* is the adverb corresponding to the preposition or conjunction

31

after. So innumerable words change as they change from one part of speech to another.

Examples:

noun	adjective	adverb	verb
gold	golden		gild
beauty	beautiful	beautifully	beautify
revolution	revolutionary		revolutionize
nation(ality)	national	nationally	nationalize
period	periodical	periodically	
presumption	presumptive	presumptuously	
	presumptuous	presumably	presume
joy	joyful, joyous	joyfully	
	enjoyable	joyously	enjoy
		enjoyably	
abundance	abundant	abundantly	abound
simplicity	simple	simply	simplify
derision	derisive	derisively	deride
cleanliness	clean, cleanly	cleanly	cleanse, clean
secret	secret(ive)	secretly	secrete
repetition	repetitive	repetitively	repeat
tyrant	tyrannical	tyrannically	
	tyrannous	tyrannously	tyrannize

Many proper nouns have their corresponding adjectives: *Shakespearian, Baconian, Jacobean, Caroline, Shavian, Lancastrian;* and all countries: *English, Gallic, Icelandic, Singalese.* cf. *Mancunian* (of Manchester), *Cestrian* (of Chester), *Brummagem* (of Birmingham).

Parts of Speech Phrases

With the exception of the verb every part of speech is a single word. If, therefore, a group of words which does not contain a finite verb—i.e. a phrase—is doing the work of a single-word part of speech it is called by the name of that part.

There are thirteen parts of speech phrases: one adjectival, eight adverbial and four noun.

Adjectival

Any phrase which qualifies a noun or noun-equivalent is performing the function of the adjective and so is called an adjectival phrase. In the sentence 'A boy *with fair hair* sat next to me' it is the phrase *with fair hair* which is describing, i.e. qualifying, the noun *boy*: it is therefore an adjectival phrase. cf.:

The house *standing at the corner of the street* was hit;
The man, *struck dumb with fright*, gaped at it;
The aeroplane, *with two of its engines on fire*, landed safely;
They met in the wood *at the bottom of the hill*.

Adverbial

The eight adverbial phrases are:

Place. Any phrase which states *where* the action named in a verb occurs is an adverbial phrase of place:

e.g. A boy with fair hair sat *next to me.*

Time. Any phrase which states *when* the action named in a verb occurs is an adverbial phrase of time:

e.g. I'll see you *at seven o'clock.*

Manner. Any phrase which states *how* the action named in a verb occurs, or which qualifies an adjective, is an adverbial phrase of manner:

e.g. He plays golf *like a professional*; He was handsome *in an unusual sort of way.*

Reason. Any phrase which states *why* an action named in a verb occurs is an adverbial phrase of reason:

e.g. They ran away *for fear of being punished.*

Concession. Any phrase which states a concession is an adverbial phrase of concession:

e.g. *While agreeing with you in principle*, I must go my

33

own way. (cf. the adverbial clause of concession.)

Condition. Any phrase which states the condition affecting the action named in a verb is an adverbial phrase of condition:

e.g. *Regulations permitting,* I shall visit Paris next year.

Purpose. Any phrase which states the purpose with which an action is performed is an adverbial phrase of purpose:

e.g. He went first *in order to prove his courage* (=reason+ purpose: cf. the adverbial clause of reason).

Comparison-degree. The conjunction *than* followed by the idiomatic or disjunctive pronoun and itself following some comparative adjective or adverb constitutes an adverbial phrase of comparison-degree (cf. the adverbial clause of this name):

e.g. He is a better player *than me.*

Noun

The four noun phrases are: *subject, object, in apposition* and *complement.*

Subject. Any phrase which is the subject of a verb is a noun phrase subject:

e.g. *To be able to say that* is a great privilege (subject of *is*); *Telling funny stories* is his hobby.

Object. Any phrase which is the object of a verb is a noun phrase object:

e.g. He likes *being read to* (objects of *likes*); I would have preferred *to stay there for ever.*

In Apposition. Any phrase in apposition to a noun or noun-equivalent is a noun phrase in apposition:

e.g. Winston Churchill, *Prime Minister during the war,* wrote many books.

It is a great privilege *to be able to say that.*

In the first sentence the phrase is in apposition to *Winston Churchill,* in the second it is in apposition to *It.* A phrase or a word which is in apposition (for the noun or noun-equivalent is also in apposition to the phrase) amplifies the meaning of the word or words to which it is in apposition and could, if necessary, take the place of that word or those words without altering the structure of the sentence. So in the first sentence, *Winston Churchill, Prime Minister during the war, wrote many books*, the phrase could replace *Winston Churchill* as the subject of *wrote* (the article would have to be added): *The Prime Minister during the war, Winston Churchill, wrote many books.* Now the phrase is a noun phrase subject. If necessary, too, the word or words to which the phrase is in apposition could be removed, the phrase be substituted, and still the structure of the sentence would be unimpaired. If *It* is removed from the second sentence and the phrase is put in its place, the phrase becomes the subject of *is* as above.

Complement. Any phrase which acts as a complement referring back to a subject or an object is a noun phrase complement. (The nature of the complement is explained in a later chapter.)

E.g. He was elected *to be the new captain of the team.*

These parts of speech phrases are an elaboration of the single-word parts of speech; the next, and final, elaboration is the parts of speech clauses. And just as these phrases cannot be understood without a sure knowledge of the adjective, the adverb and the noun, so the clauses cannot be understood without a sure knowledge of these phrases.

The Antonym

An antonym is a word with the directly opposite meaning of another: it must therefore be the same part of speech as that other word. So the antonym of the adjective *good* is the adjective *bad*; the antonym of the adverb *slowly* is the adverb *quickly*; the antonym of the noun *sympathy* is the

35

noun *antipathy*; and the antonym of the verb *to live* is the verb *to die*.

There are certain common methods of *making opposites* such as the prefixing of *in-* and the suffixing of *-less* to adjectives; but in the main antonyms can be learnt only as vocabulary is mastered. For an antonym is the direct opposite of another word: thus the antonym of *failure* is *success* and not, say, *victory*, which is the antonym of *defeat*.

The Synonym

The word *synonym* is the antonym of *antonym*, since it means a word with the same meaning as another. It too must be the same part of speech as the other word. Dr. Johnson insisted that there is no such thing, and it is perhaps true that there are no two words which are always interchangeable. But there are some words which approximate in meaning so closely to others as to be called synonymous with them:

e.g. *stockings* and *nylons*, *intent* and *purpose*, *shape* and *form*, *hamlet* and *village*, *ponderous* and *heavy*.

The Homophone and Homonym

A *homophone* is a word which is always pronounced in the same way as another but is spelt differently and has a different meaning:

e.g. *see* is a homophone of *sea*. cf. *know—no*; *knew—gnu*; *rough—ruff*.

A word is a *homonym* when it is simultaneously a homograph and a homophone: i.e. its spelling and sound remain constant but its meaning changes:

e.g. hoop, swift, lay, founder, sack.

3

The Sentence and its Analysis—
The Parts of Speech Clauses

THERE are four kinds of sentences: *simple, complex, double* and *multiple* (sometimes called *compound*).

Simple

A sentence, as distinct from a phrase or a subordinate clause, is a group of words which makes complete sense and can stand alone: it must, therefore, as we have already seen, contain a finite verb. Any sentence which contains only one finite verb is called a simple sentence (it may contain any number of non-finite verbs):

e.g. At dawn the German soldiers chose one of their company as leader. (The single finite verb is *chose*.)

The first stage in the analysis of a simple sentence is to divide it into *subject* and *predicate*.

The subject of a group of words is responsible for the action named in the verb when the verb is in the active voice and is the receiver of the action when the verb is in the passive voice. In the sentence *The cow jumped over the moon*, whose verb, *jumped*, is active, the subject is *the cow*; and in *The dog was whipped by the cruel boy*, whose verb, *was whipped*, is passive, the subject is *the dog*.

A predicate is anything predicated about a subject, and

37

so the predicate of a sentence is all the rest of it when the subject and any qualifying words (called the *extension* or *limitation of the subject*) have been removed. So in the two sentences above the predicates are: *jumped over the moon* and *was whipped by the cruel boy*.

The analysis then proceeds to separating from one another the various constituents of the predicate. The finite verb is already known, and any words qualifying it, i.e. in an adverbial capacity, are then isolated and called the *extension* or *limitation of the verb*.

The *object* is then dealt with, if there is one. The object receives the action named in the verb when the verb is active and transitive (or intransitive in the special usage explained in Chapter 1); but except as the retained accusative it does not exist when the verb is passive. In the two sentences above there are no objects, but in *The cow was eating the grass* the object is *the grass*. (We are speaking now of the *direct* as distinct from the *indirect* object—q.v. Chapter 1.)

Any word or group of words qualifying the object is called the *extension* or *limitation of the object*.

The *complement* is any word or group of words which refers back to a subject or object and completes the meaning of a verb (the complement is therefore either a noun, noun-equivalent or adjective). It states what the person or thing named is, becomes or is made or chosen to be: i.e. the complement is used with, or after, either *copulative* or *factitive* verbs. The verb *to be* is always followed by the complement: 'He is *captain*.' In *She became angry with me* the complement is *angry*. cf. 'They chose him *to be their representative*' (noun phrase complement referring back to the object *him*).

Thus the simple sentence is analysed into: subject, extension of subject, predicate, finite verb, extension of verb, object, extension of object and complement. The analysis is usually set down as follows:

38

Subject	Predicate					
	Extension of subject	Finite verb	Extension of verb	Object	Extension of object	Complement
soldiers	the German	chose	at dawn	one	of their number	(as) leader

It can be seen, therefore, that in the predicate most adverbial phrases and the indirect object are extensions of the verb, and all adjectival phrases, some adverbial phrases of manner, and noun phrases in apposition, are extensions of the object or parts of the complement.

A simple method of determining the subject and direct object of any transitive verb is as follows:

Ask the question *who or what?* before the verb and the answer is the subject.

Ask the question *whom or what?* after the verb and the answer is the object.

i.e.:

SUBJECT		OBJECT
who or what?	VERB	whom or what?

Complex

A complex sentence contains two or more finite verbs and is analysable into a single main clause and one or more subordinate clauses. The individual clauses may be analysed in the same way as the simple sentence, but the complex, double and multiple sentences taken in their entirety are analysed only into clauses.

There are two kinds of clauses, *main* and *subordinate*.

In most cases main clauses could stand alone as simple sentences; but no subordinate clause could ever stand alone since it depends for its own existence on the existence of the main clause to which it is subordinate. The main clause is therefore the most important group of words in a complex sentence.

He ran down the street is a simple sentence since it contains only the one finite verb *ran*. But in this sentence: *He ran down the street when he heard the siren*, there are two finite verbs, *ran* and *heard*. *He ran down the street* can stand alone, but *when he heard the siren* cannot; it is, therefore, dependent upon *He ran down the street* for its own existence as part of the whole sentence: it is therefore a subordinate clause. *He ran down the street* is the main clause.

This example shows that the subordinate clauses are at once like and unlike phrases: for they too cannot stand alone as they do not make complete sense, yet they do contain a finite verb. It shows also how they resemble yet differ from sentences: for they do contain a finite verb but they are incomplete.

The example shows, thirdly, that there is only one finite verb to a clause, whether the clause is main or subordinate.

Analysis into clauses is the separation of the clause-groups which compose complex, double and multiple sentences. It shows how sentences are constructed; a thorough understanding of it is one of the indispensable media towards an appreciation of the elements of written style, not least among which is a judicious mixture of the different kinds of clauses.

There is only one kind of main clause; the subordinate clause, like the phrase, may have an adverbial, an adjectival or a noun character.

The Parts of Speech Clauses

Adverbial

There are eight kinds of subordinate adverbial clauses.

Time. In the sentence above: *He ran down the street when he heard the siren*, the group of words *when he heard the siren* states when he ran; it tells the time of his running. *Ran* is a verb and so the group has an adverbial function; it contains the finite verb *heard* and so it is more than a phrase; but it could not stand alone, it is dependent upon the other groups of words, *He ran down the street*; it is therefore a subordinate adverbial clause of time qualifying *ran* in the main clause.

Such conjunctive adverbs as *when*, *while* and *whilst*, or any adverbs standing in place of them (e.g. *directly* or *immediately=as soon as*), will normally introduce this type of subordinate clause.

Place. In the sentence *Let's meet where we met before* the main clause is *Let's meet* and the group of words *where we met before* (finite verb *met*) states where, in what place, we should *meet* (a verb): it is therefore a subordinate adverbial clause of place qualifying *meet* in the main clause.

The conjunctive adverb *where* usually introduces this clause.

Cause or reason. In the sentence *He missed the train because he refused to run* the main clause is *He missed the train*, and *because he refused to run* (finite verb *refused*) states why it was that he missed the train. *Missed* is a verb, and so *because he refused to run* is a subordinate adverbial clause of reason qualifying *missed* in the main clause. Such conjunctions as *because*, *as*, *since*, *for* (=because) introduce this clause.

Purpose. In *They went to the circus in order that they might see the elephants* the main clause is *They went to the circus*, and *in order that they might see the elephants* (finite verb *might see*) states, not merely why they went, but the purpose with which they went: the group of words is therefore a subordinate adverbial clause of purpose qualifying *went* in the main clause.

The difference between the clause of reason and the clause

41

of purpose is simply that the former states only reason and the latter states reason plus purpose, the emphasis being on the purpose.

Such conjunctive expressions as *in order that* and *so that*, and the conjunction *lest*, introduce clauses of purpose. *In order* cannot introduce a clause since it must be followed by an infinitive: 'They went to the circus in order *to see* the elephants' (=a simple sentence). It is the presence of the conjunction *that* in *in order that* which makes the following verb finite.

Condition. The main clause of the complex sentence, *If you can't come the meeting will be postponed*, is *the meeting will be postponed* (the main clause need not be written first), and the group of words, *If you can't come* (finite verb *can't come*), states the condition on which the action of postponing depends. *Will be postponed* is a verb, and so the group is a subordinate adverbial clause of condition qualifying *will be postponed* in the main clause.

Such conjunctions as *if* and *unless* introduce this clause.

Concession. In the sentence *Although he is a better player than me, I have occasionally beaten him* the main clause is *I have occasionally beaten him*, and *Although he is a better player than me* states the concession which the statement in the main clause—that 'I *have beaten* him'—makes: i.e. in spite of the fact that he is the better player, nevertheless I have beaten him; although I admit, or concede, that he is better . . . etc. The finite verb in the concession is *is,* and so the group of words is a subordinate adverbial clause of concession qualifying *have beaten* in the main clause.

Usually the conjunctions *although* and *though*, and the conjunctive expression *even if* (never *if* alone), introduce this clause.

Result. In the sentence *He worked so hard that he passed the examination easily* the two finite verbs are *worked* and *passed.* The main clause is *He worked so hard* and the rest of the sentence states the result of his working so hard: it therefore qualifies all three words *worked so hard,* but especially *hard* (which is an adjective being used as an adverb), and so is a subordinate adverbial clause of result qualifying *hard* (or the three words) in the main clause.

Most clauses of result will be introduced by the conjunction *that* following *so* in another clause (not immediately following *so* but separated from it by an adverb or adjective).

Comparison. This clause may take two forms:

(*a*) MANNER. In *You should act as if you meant it* the main clause is *You should act* and *as if you meant it* states how you should act, the manner in which you should act: the group of words is therefore a subordinate adverbial clause of comparison-manner qualifying *should act* in the main clause. The finite verb is *meant.* Such conjunctive expressions as *as if* and *as though,* and the conjunction *as,* introduce this clause (but never *as*=because).

(*b*) DEGREE. In *He is a better player than I am,* whose finite verbs are *is* and *am,* the main clause is *He is a better player,* and the group of words *than I am* states the comparison in degree (in *how much* and not in *how*) between his *playing* and mine: it is therefore a subordinate adverbial clause of comparison-degree qualifying *is a better player* (or, since only *he* is omitted, the whole of the main clause). The conjunction *than* usually introduces this clause.

Two Notes

(i) It is a mistake to think that every time the conjunctions quoted above are met they introduce the same type of subordinate clause. If no finite verb follows, there will be no clause of any kind; and, secondly, even though a finite verb

43

does follow, the clause may not always be of the same type. The conjunctive adverb *where*, for instance, commonly introduces subordinate adverbial clauses of place, but the relative adverb *where* (=relative pronoun governed by a preposition, e.g. *in which*) introduces subordinate adjectival clauses. The function of the clause introduced must be understood before the clause can be correctly named.

(ii) All subordinate adverbial clauses begin, or are introduced by, either conjunctions, conjunction-equivalents or conjunctive expressions. The only conjunctions to which this rule does not apply are *and, but, yet, either, whether, or, neither* and *nor*. These are not, like all the others, *subordinating conjunctions*. They merely join words or groups of words, they do not subordinate one word or group of words to another: i.e. they are *co-ordinating conjunctions*, or *correlatives*.

Adjectival

A subordinate adjectival clause is any group of words containing a finite verb which qualifies a noun or noun-equivalent. In the sentence *This is the house that Jack built* the main clause is *This is the house* and the words *that Jack built* give information about the noun *house*; they contain the finite verb *built*, they have a subordinate role since they could not stand alone, and so they constitute a subordinate adjectival clause qualifying *house* in the main clause. In *I saw the place where it happened* the clause *where it happened* (finite verb *happened*) qualifies the noun *place* in the main clause and so is a subordinate adjectival clause. *Where* in this context means *at* (or *in*) *which*.

Adjectival clauses are always introduced by relative pronouns or their equivalents. If a preposition is governing the pronoun it is actually the first word in the clause, although the operative word is still the pronoun:

44

e.g. This is the man *by whom the book in question was written.*

Noun

There are the same four noun clauses as noun phrases.

Subject. Any group of words containing a finite verb and constituting the subject of a verb is a subordinate noun clause subject. Thus in the sentence *That you are ignorant makes matters very difficult* there are two finite verbs, *are* and *makes.* The subject of *are* is *you*, but there is no single-word subject of *makes*, and if we ask the question for the subject, *Who or what makes?*, the answer is *That you are ignorant*, a group of words which is therefore a subordinate noun clause subject of *makes.* The main clause is *makes matters very difficult*, which could not stand alone. When there is a noun clause subject, therefore, the main clause is as dependent upon the subordinate as the subordinate is upon it: it is distinguishable as the main clause, however, since it is making use of the subordinate clause and does not need any subordinating word to introduce it.

Object. Similarly, any group of words including a finite verb and constituting the object of a verb is a subordinate noun clause object. So in *Do you think that it is true?* the transitive verb *think* needs an object: *Do you think whom or what?* Answer: *that it is true* (finite verb *is*). The main clause, therefore, is *Do you think* and *that it is true* is a subordinate noun clause object of *think.*

In this instance the main clause could stand alone, even if not very satisfactorily. Being a main clause it is not introduced by any subordinating word as the object-clause is (*that*). The subordinating word may not be written down:

e.g. *Do you think it is true? That* is understood, and the analysis is unaffected.

The subordinating word which introduces noun clauses

45

subject and object may be either a conjunction (or its equivalent) or a relative pronoun (or its equivalent):

e.g. Tell me *what* (relative pronoun) you mean; I know *when* (conjunctive adverb) you were there; *Who* you are is no concern of ours; *Because* you can't do it does not mean *that* I can't.

The first two sentences contain noun clauses object, the third and fourth noun clauses subject, and the fourth also a noun clause object.

The conjunctive or relative adverb *where* can introduce either adverbial clauses of place or adjectival clauses: it can also introduce noun clauses:

e.g. *I saw where it happened*, in which *where it happened* is a subordinate noun clause object of *saw*. *When* may also introduce three types of clauses, adverbial of time, adjectival and noun.

In Apposition. Any group of words with a finite verb in it and acting in apposition is a subordinate noun clause in apposition. In the sentence *It is no laughing matter that you should say that* there are the two finite verbs, *is* and *should say*. Both have single-word subjects, *It* and *you*; there can be no object of *is*, and the object of *should say* is *that*. The group of words, *that you should say that*, therefore, whose first word, *that*, a subordinating conjunction, proves that it is a subordinate clause, cannot be a noun clause subject or object. We must search elsewhere for its function. What, then, is *it*? *That you should say that*. The sentence could be rewritten: *That you should say that is no laughing matter*, and the subordinate group of words would be a noun clause subject of *is*. It can, therefore, take the place of *it*; and since it amplifies the meaning of *it* it must be a subordinate noun clause in apposition

In *He was compelled to state the reason why he had left* there are also two finite verbs, *was compelled* and *had left*, *he* being the subject of both. There are no objects of these two verbs; but the non-finite verb, *to state*, is transitive and active and so needs an object—*the reason*. What, then, of the group of words *why he had left*, which, beginning with the subordinating conjunctive adverb *why*, and containing the finite verb *had left*, must be a subordinate clause? It is giving information about the noun *reason*, in whose place it could also stand as a noun clause object of *to state*, and so it is a subordinate noun clause in apposition to *reason*. The main clause is *He was compelled to state the reason*.

The subordinate noun clause in apposition is always in apposition to a noun or noun-equivalent which is either the subject or the object of a verb in another clause. And it can always be substituted for the word to which it is in apposition, thus becoming automatically either a noun clause subject or a noun clause object. The following clauses are all in apposition:

> The fact *that he was ill* did not worry him (to *fact*);
> Never ask me the question *who I am* (to *question*);
> It is obvious *that he is the best* (to *it*).

This clause also is always introduced by either a subordinating conjunction (or its equivalent) or a relative pronoun.

Complement. A group of words containing a finite verb and performing the same function as the single-word complement is a subordinate noun clause complement. It may, therefore, be complement to either a subject or an object. In the sentence *He will soon become what he has always wanted to be* the main clause is *He will soon become* and the words *what he has always wanted to be*, introduced by the subordinating relative pronoun *what* and including the finite verb *has wanted*, state what he will *become* (an intransitive, copulative verb). They are therefore a subordinate noun

47

clause complement of *he will become*. They could not, like the clause in apposition, be substituted for *he*.

So in *They made him what he had always wished to be* the words *what he had always wished to be* are the complement to the object *him* and, since they contain the finite verb *had wished*, are a subordinate clause. The main clause is *They made him*.

cf. He is *what you would expect him to be* (complement of *he is*).

There are thus thirteen subordinate parts of speech clauses:

8 adverbial: of TIME (when?);
              of PLACE (where?);
              of REASON (why?);
              of PURPOSE (with what intention?);
              of CONDITION (on what condition?);
              of CONCESSION (in spite of what?);
              of RESULT (with what result?);
              of COMPARISON (in what way? or to what extent?);
1 adjectival;
4 noun: SUBJECT, OBJECT, IN APPOSITION, COMPLEMENT.

When two or more clauses perform the same function they are said to be *co-ordinate with* each other or one another. In the sentence *I have now read the book which you found and lent to me a fortnight ago* the main clause is *I have now read the book*; and the two groups of words, *which you found* (finite verb *found*), and *lent to me a fortnight ago* (relative pronoun *which* and *you* understood before *lent*, the finite verb), are qualifying the noun *book* and so are both subordinate adjectival clauses, co-ordinate with each other.

All subordinate clauses are subordinate to main clauses, but they may qualify etc. words in other subordinate clauses. So in *He told me that he had given away the money he had inherited*, whose three finite verbs are *told*, *had given* and *had inherited*, the words *he had inherited* (=which he had inherited, *which* being understood) are a subordinate adjec-
48

tival clause qualifying the noun *money* in the subordinate noun clause object of *told* in the main clause.

As the notes above show, words introducing subordinate clauses may be understood. So in *I wonder can you come* the conjunction *if* or *whether* is understood before *can*, introducing the subordinate noun clause object of *wonder*. Such omission of conjunctions (whether co-ordinating or subordinating) is called *asyndeton*.

A *complex* sentence, then, is composed of one main clause and any mixture of these subordinate clauses (or only one). The actual tabulating of the analysis is best done in two columns, using capital letters for the main clauses and the same letters in small for their subordinate clauses, each of them numbered. The main clause is isolated first, then each group of words introduced by a subordinating conjunction (or its equivalent) or relative pronoun (or its equivalent) is separated in turn and named according to its function.
Example:

Here is the house about which I spoke to you when we last met.

The finite verbs are *is*, *spoke* and *met*, and so there are three clauses. There are two subordinating words, *which* (governed by the preposition *about*) and *when*, and so two subordinate clauses. The function of the group of words *about which I spoke to you* is to qualify the noun *house*, i.e. it is an adjectival function, and *when we last met* states the time at which I performed the action of speaking, i.e. the group has an adverbial function. The analysis can, therefore, be tabulated as follows:

A Here is the house	main clause
a1 about which I spoke to you	subordinate adjectival clause qualifying *house* in A
a2 when we last met	subordinate adverbial clause of time qualifying *spoke* in a1.

49

Double

As its name implies, a double sentence combines two sentences in one. They are either joined by a conjunction, though not a subordinating conjunction, or are separated by such punctuation-marks as the colon and semi-colon. Thus there are always two main clauses in a double sentence. The two sentences may be: both simple, both complex, or one of each kind.

Two Simple

He was enjoying himself but I was bored. The sentences are *He was enjoying himself* and *I was bored*, and they are merely joined together by *but*. They are both main clauses, and the analysis of the sentence would be as follows:

A He was enjoying himself	main clause
B (but) I was bored	main clause.

Two Complex

This is the house which pleases me most, and I think I shall buy it. The first complex sentence is *This is the house which pleases me most*, the second *I think I shall buy it* (subordinating conjunction *that* understood). The analysis is:

A This is the house	main clause
a1 which pleases me most	subordinate adjectival clause qualifying *house* in A
B (and) I think	main clause
b1 I shall buy it	subordinate noun clause object of *think* in B.

One Simple and one Complex

This is the house, and I think I shall buy it. The analysis is:

A This is the house	main clause
B (and) I think	main clause
b1 I shall buy it	subordinate noun clause object of *think* in **B**.

Multiple

A multiple sentence is one in which are combined three or more sentences, either all simple, or all complex, or a mixture of both kinds.

Three Simple

I came, I saw, I conquered. That sentence would be analysed as three co-ordinate main clauses, A, B and C.

Three Complex

The car raced down the hill out of control when the chauffeur collapsed; but a farmer who was working in a nearby field saw it and raced to the wreck to see if he could rescue anyone. Analysis:

A The car raced down the hill out of control	main clause
a1 when the chauffeur collapsed	subordinate adverbial clause of time qualifying *raced . . .* in A
B (but) a farmer saw it	main clause
b1 who was working in a nearby field	subordinate adjectival clause qualifying *farmer* in **B**
C (and) raced to the wreck to see	main clause coordinate with **B**
c1 if he could rescue anyone	subordinate noun clause object of *to see* in C.

Since the main clauses B and C are in the same sentence as A they may be called co-ordinate with A, but, strictly, only those main clauses whose finite verbs share the same subject are co-ordinate (so *a farmer* is subject of *saw* in B and *raced* in C).

Two Simple and one Complex

Tom was happy, and so was Jim, but Eric, who felt ill, could not share their happiness. Analysis:

A Tom was happy	main clause
B (and) so was Jim	main clause
C (but) Eric could not share their happiness	main clause
c1 who felt ill	subordinate adjectival clause qualifying *Eric* in C.

It will be noted that it is customary to put the merely co-ordinating conjunctions between brackets.

Appendix A. The *periodic* and the *loose* sentence.

A sentence is called *periodic* if it does not make completed sense until its end: i.e. it opens with some subordinate words, a phrase or a clause.

Example:

> Simple Sentence: And so, after the longest journey of my life, I reached home.
>
> Complex Sentence: If I were you, I would answer it immediately.

But that sentence is called *loose* which could end earlier than it does because it makes completed sense inside itself: i.e. it opens with the main statement.

Example:

> Simple: I reached home | after the longest journey of my life.
>
> Complex: I would answer it immediately | if I were you.

It is, therefore, the periodic sentence which creates suspense. A mixture of the two gives variety to style, together with the alternation of simple and complex sentences, double and multiple, short and long, and so forth.

Appendix B. *Apodosis* and *protasis*.

These are the technical names of, in the first place, the main clause and any subordinate adverbial clause of condition, whether the latter precedes or follows the former:

$$\overset{A}{\text{I shall be there}} \mid \overset{P}{\text{if it doesn't rain;}}$$

$$\overset{P}{\text{If you join the committee}} \mid \overset{A}{\text{we may get something done.}}$$

But the terms may also be applied to other forms of the complex sentence, so that every main clause is the apodosis, and every subordinate clause is a protasis.

4

Syntax

MUCH that is covered by the word *syntax* has already been discussed in previous chapters: in this chapter the gaps are filled in. The word means a multitude of things, great and small, including the whole range of what is commonly called *grammar*; but it may be generally defined as *the grammatical arrangement of words in speech or writing, set of rules governing this* (Concise Oxford Dictionary). Knowing it in all its departments we can understand the functions of words, when they are performing those functions correctly and when they are being made to perform functions unnatural to them. For writing is an artificial technique and has to be learnt and practised: it therefore has its rules, and these must be respected. We are at liberty to ignore them and write in our own way; but the chief purpose of writing is to express in this form what we have in our minds, and usually so that it makes sense to other minds. But we cannot expect other people to pay attention if they either cannot understand what we are saying or are offended by our manner of saying it. We cannot be either intelligible or commanding unless we write with due observance of the rules and conventions of established syntax.

In this chapter, then, the remaining grammatical gaps are filled in, certain common mistakes are analysed and corrected according to these rules, and, finally, individual words are studied so that their syntactical function may be realized.

(This definition of the syntactical function of a word is known as *parsing*.)

Cases

There is small point in talking about 'cases' in English, but, if we must, there are five: *nominative, vocative, accusative, genitive* and *dative*. (The ablative, familiar in Latin, is not used in English).

Nominative

All subjects and all words associated with them, i.e. qualifying or in apposition or as complements, are in this case:

e.g. *John, the captain,* issued his orders. *I* will go. *Who* is *he*? *She* was elected *secretary*.

The *Nominative Absolute* is a special syntactical construction analogous to the Latin ablative absolute, when the subject of a non-finite verb is different from the finite verb to which the non-finite verb is subordinate. For it is normal —and logical—that the subject of the main, i.e. finite, verb should also be the subject of any subordinate non-finite verb:

e.g. *Having walked for two miles, I was glad of the rest,* in which *I* is the subject of *having walked* as well as of *was*.

But in the nominative absolute this logical process is abandoned:

e.g. *The rain having stopped, we continued the game,* in which *we*, the subject of the finite verb *continued*, is not the subject of *having stopped*.

The separate subject of the non-finite verb is, as in this example, always written down: in the normal process the subject of the non-finite verb, being the same as that of the main verb, is, of course, understood.

55

Vocative

All names of people directly addressed are in this case:
e.g. I say, *you*, come here; *Peter*, do you want this?

Accusative

All direct objects and all words associated with them are in this case:

e.g. He planted *carrots* yesterday; They made *him leader*; *Whom* do you wish to see?

All prepositions are followed by nouns or their equivalents in the accusative: i.e. the act of governing these nouns puts them in this case:

e.g. She gave it to *her brother*; I stood beside *him*; Between *you* and *me* and *the gate-post*, it's untrue.

The *Retained Accusative* has already been explained.

Genitive

This is the case which shows possession and is the only one in which English nouns take on a different form, i.e. inflect. In early English the suffix *-es* was added to the nominative form, and it is for this *e* in the singular that our modern apostrophe before the *s* stands:

e.g. That is a man*'s* job.

The genitive singular is, therefore, the nominative form plus *'s*. The genitive plural is the nominative plural followed by the apostrophe when the nominative plural already ends with *s*:

e.g. All ships' crews will stand by;

when the nominative plural does not already end with *s*, *s* is added as in the singular:

e.g. The children*'s* clothes were wet.

All pronouns inflect into the genitive as into the accusative (*v. infra*).

The *group genitive* is the inflecting of the last word in a group, and is idiomatic rather than in accordance with the logic of grammar:

e.g. The *Queen of England's* name is Elizabeth; . . . and so is *everyone else's*.

Dative

All indirect objects are in this case:

e.g. I gave *them* all I had (=to them); I'll change it *you* (=for you); Will you lend *me* your bike? (=to me).

The prepositions *to* and *for* are never written down before indirect objects. If they were, the following words would be in the accusative case.

The so-called *Ethic Dative* is now obsolete. It was the use of a personal pronoun as though it were an indirect object, but only to emphasize a point; unlike the indirect object, however, it could be omitted from the sentence with no loss of syntactical sense. It is frequently seen in Shakespeare's plays:

e.g. Mark *me* with what violence she first loved the Moor.

The following table shows how the personal and relative pronouns inflect in the various cases:

Nominative	Vocative	Accusative	Genitive	Dative
I		me	my, mine	me
thou	thou	thee	thy, thine	thee
he		him	his	him
she		her	her(s)	her
it		it	its	it
we		us	our(s)	us
you	you	you	your(s)	you
they		them	their(s)	them
who		whom	whose	whom
which		which	whose	which

Verbs

The Tenses

As has been observed, the three main divisions of present, past and future are subdivisible into a number of separate forms. These are:

Present	I make
Continuous present	I am making
Future	I shall (will) make
Continuous future	I shall (will) be making
Imperfect	I was making, I used to make
Perfect	I have made
Continuous perfect	I have been making
Past (also called *preterite*)	I made
Pluperfect	I had made
Continuous pluperfect	I had been making
Future perfect	I shall (will) have made
Continuous future perfect	I shall (will) have been making

All those examples are in the active voice. In the passive voice the forms are:

Present	I am taught
Continuous present	I am being taught
Future	I shall (will) be taught
Imperfect	I was being taught, I used to be taught
Perfect	I have been taught
Past	I was taught
Pluperfect	I had been taught
Future perfect	I shall (will) have been taught

Some of the other continuous forms are possible in the passive voice, but rarely.

Shall and Will

The difference between these two auxiliary verbs is fast diminishing, but, for what it is worth, is as follows: when mere futurity is involved, *shall* is used with the first person only, singular and plural, *will* with the second and third persons, singular and plural; but when futurity is reinforced by determination or command, exactly the opposite happens, *shall* being used with the second and third persons and *will* with the first.

Examples:

> I think I shall go (=mere futurity);
> Yes, we certainly will do it (=futurity+determination);
> Do you think they will come? (=mere futurity);
> They shall sign, or else . . . (=futurity+determination or command);
> You shall go (=futurity+command).

Historic Present

This is a special and now largely archaic use of the present tense, once used in historical novels, for instance. Thus in 'Henry Esmond' Thackeray used the past tense to set the scene but the present tense when making his characters speak:

> e.g. *Mr. Addison said his own lodgings were hard by* . . . (past tense) . . . 'I shall get credit with my landlady,' *says* he, with a smile.

Though it is archaic in such a context, however, we still use the present tense in a historical way, when speaking of writers and paraphrasing their work:

> e.g. In his 'Phaedo' Plato *says* that the soul . . .; The third witch *prophesies* that Macbeth *is* to be the future king of Scotland.

It is still used also in certain forms of colloquial narration:

> e.g. And I *says* to him, I *says* . . .

Some contemporary writers, notably American, also use it in fiction:

> e.g. Damon Runyon in 'A Piece of Pie': I *am* in Mindy's Restaurant one day when who *walks* in but . . .

Number and Inflexion (i.e. Accidence)

There are two numbers, *singular* and *plural*, and all nouns and pronouns and the finite parts of verbs are said to inflect from one to the other. Thus *I* is singular and inflects to *we* in the plural; *he is running*, singular, inflects to *they are running*, plural. The pronouns, as we have seen, inflect according to case also, as do nouns in the genitive case. The reflexive pronouns inflect from *-self* in the singular to *-selves* in the plural.

There is a variety of ways in which nouns change from singular to plural:

(*a*) simply by the addition of *s*: *hat—hats; piano—pianos;*

(*b*) by the addition of *-es*: *class—classes; tomato—tomatoes;*

(*c*) by the addition of *-en*: *ox—oxen; child—child(r)en; brother—brethren;*[1]

(*d*) by changing the final *y* to *ies*: *lady—ladies;*

(*e*) by changing *fe* to *ves*: *wife—wives;*

(*f*) by changing the internal vowels: *goose—geese.*

Certain words, however, do not change:
e.g. sheep, species, deer, grouse, salmon.

Other words, which can inflect into a plural form, often retain their singular form while yet having a plural meaning:
e.g. *cannon* as in *The Germans had over a thousand cannon*; *dozen*, as in *I'll take two dozen, please*; *potato* as in *Would you like some potato with it?*

Many words have come into English from other languages and retained their original forms both in the singular and

---

[1] The original plurals of *child* and *brother* were *childer* and *brether*. The suffix *-en* was added later and in the process the *e* preceding the *r* was omitted.

when inflected in the plural:

e.g. *hippopotamus—hippopotami* (though *hippopota-muses* is also common); *addendum—addenda*; *crisis—crises*; *formula—formulæ* (*formulas* is also used); *phenomenon—phenomena*; *octopus—octopodes* (or, anglicized, *octopuses*); *index—indices* (simple English form, *indexes*, also used).

Hyphenated or *double-barrelled* words inflect into the plural in three different ways:

Sometimes only the first word changes:

e.g. *courts-martial* (the second word being an adjective in this case); *mothers-in-law*.

Sometimes both words change:

e.g. *men-servants*;

Sometimes only the second word changes:

e.g. *fighter-bombers*.

One has to learn the inflexion in each particular instance. Where proper names are concerned after *Mr.* and *Miss*, the name does not inflect but the titles do:

e.g. *Mr. Brown* becomes *Messrs.* (=French *messieurs*) *Brown*; *Miss Smith* becomes *The Misses Smith* with the definite article.

The use of *Mesdames* from French for the plural of *Mrs.* (which is an abbreviation of the now-obsolete *Mistress*) is still met with, but less frequently than *Messrs.*, which is, of course, used a great deal in business, commerce, etc.

Person

There are three persons, singular and plural: first (*I*, *me*, *we*, *us*, etc.); second (*thou*, *you*, etc.) and third (*he*, *she*, *it*, *they*, etc.). The finite verbal forms inflect as the number changes. So the present tense of *to be* is conjugated:

	singular	*plural*
1	I am	we are
2	thou art, you are	you are
3	he, she, it is	they are

The finite verb must always agree with its subject in both number and person. If two or more separate singulars are the joint subject, then the verb is in the plural:

e.g. Tom, Dick and Harry *were* there.

Relative pronouns are identical in number and person with their antecedents, i.e. the nouns or noun-equivalents whose substitutes they are, so that when they are subjects their verbs inflect accordingly:

e.g. I who am . . .

Gender

There are four genders: *masculine, feminine, neuter* and *common*.

All male words are masculine: *man, boy, stallion, bull, fox;* all female words are feminine: *woman, girl, mare, cow, vixen;* and all sexless, i.e. inanimate, things are neuter: *pen, paper, sea, earth*. The common gender embraces all those words which may be either masculine or feminine: *child, adult, relation, employee, student*.

All male words naturally have their female counterparts: *Jew—Jewess, tiger—tigress, lord—lady, marquis—marchioness*.

Degrees of Comparison

There are three degrees or stages of comparison: *positive, comparative* and *superlative*.

Positive. This is simply the ordinary adjective or adverb

(the only parts of speech concerned here): *good, sweet, quickly.*

Comparative. This expresses comparison: *better, sweeter, more quickly.*

Superlative. This expresses perfection: *best, sweetest, most quickly.*

With the exception of irregular words like *fast,* adverbs take the words *more* and *most* before them for their comparative and superlative degrees. But adjectives vary. Some change completely, as *good* changes to *better* and *best.* Others merely assume the suffixes *-er* and *-est*: *sweeter—sweetest.* Others take *more* and *most* before them: *beautiful—more beautiful —most beautiful.*

A few adjectives exist only in the positive form:

e.g. *unique.*

It is a common solecism to say *more* (or *most*) *unique.* (Probably *more perfect* and *most perfect* are also philosophically impossible.) *Most excellent,* which is often heard and seen, is also a solecism.

Prepositions

Certain prepositions must follow certain verbs. *To compare,* for example, must be followed by either *with* or *to.* Since its first syllable, *com,* is the Latin *cum* (=with), the former is historically the more correct, but *to* has a long idiomatic existence. So we can have *Do not compare me with him* and *Shall I compare thee to a summer's day?*

To discriminate must be followed by *between* or *against.* *To differ* is followed by *from* or *with* according to its meaning: if it means *to be different, from* must always be used (as it is after the adjective *different*), but if it means *to have a difference of opinion, to dispute,* then it is normally followed by *with*: e.g. *He had a difference with her, and they parted.*

63

The noun *difference* may also be followed by *between*:

e.g. *There is all the difference in the world between them.*

To sympathize should be followed by *with* (*sym* is from the Greek preposition meaning *with*); but idiom has often favoured the use of *for* after the noun *sympathy* and *to* after the adjective *sympathetic*.

To contrast and *to correspond*, whose first syllables both equal *cum* (=with), should strictly be followed by *with*, but again idiom has taken another course and *to* is sometimes used after both verbs.

Certain adjectives and nouns are also followed by special prepositions, and the use of any others after them would be wrong. So *averse* must be followed by either *from* or *to*, *indifferent* by *to*, *authority* by *over* or *on*.

While on the subject of prepositions it may as well be asserted that the idea that it is wrong to end a sentence with a preposition is no more than, in Fowler's words, 'a cherished superstition'. One is at liberty to begin and end a sentence how one likes, and it is wrong to end a sentence with a preposition only when to do so would make the whole sentence clumsy and ugly. As Fowler says: 'almost all our great writers have allowed themselves to end a sentence or a clause with a preposition.' No good writer would say *What did you choose that book to read to me from for?*

Explaining Common Mistakes

The following sentences contain mistakes, some of which, however, can be (indeed, must be) defended as idiomatically established though all are syntactically or grammatically indefensible.

    (i) There is the man who I mentioned to you.

    (ii) Who do you think you are staring at?

    (iii) Each of them stated their case as best they could.

(iv) Does your family enjoy the food they eat?

(v) Neither John nor Susan were able to come.

(vi) Walking down the street yesterday the bus sped past me.

(vii) Those kind of men are useless.

(viii) He is as good if not better than you.

(ix) I can neither find it here nor there.

(x) The government have not and do not intend to agree to that.

(xi) He was one of the few men who was able to do it.

(xii) Everybody was enjoying themselves.

(xiii) The most successful example of dramatic collaboration are Beaumont and Fletcher.

(xiv) Among the champions of the poor is Mr. Lyons, who, if he is not a philanthropist, then, we may wonder, what is philanthropy?

(i) *There is the man who I mentioned to you.*

As the sentence now stands the relative pronoun *who* is in the nominative case and so must be the subject of a verb. But there is no verb of which it can be the subject: the subjects of *is* and *mentioned* are *the man* and *I*. But *mentioned* is a transitive verb and so needs an object. The relative pronoun joining the main clause to the subordinate is that object, and should therefore be in the accusative case. *Who*, then, should be *whom*.

(ii) *Who do you think you are staring at?*

Since it is a rule that all words governed by prepositions must inflect into the accusative case, *who* in this sentence, which is governed by *at* but is now in the nominative case, should, strictly, be *whom*.

(iii) *Each of them stated their case as best they could.*

The distributive pronoun *each* is singular, but in this sentence the possessive adjective *their* and the personal pronoun *they*, both of which refer back to the original subject of *stated*, i.e. *each*, are plural. Thus there is no

65

syntactical logic in the sentence, and it should be: *Each of them stated his case as best he could.*

(iv) *Does your family enjoy the food they eat?*

This sentence (which appeared in a popular daily newspaper) contains a common confusion. For although the collective noun *family* is correctly followed by the singular verb *does* (*enjoy*), the pronoun which takes its place in the second half of the sentence, *they*, is plural and is naturally followed by the plural verb *eat*. Either the strict grammatical rule should be followed so that the whole sentence is singular: *Does your family enjoy the food it eats?;* or the whole sentence should be plural: *Do* your family enjoy the food they eat?

(v) *Neither John nor Susan were able to come.*

The conjunctions *neither* and *nor* must correlate words in the same number, singular or plural, and the verbs which follow must be in that same number, since the correlated words are in turn the subjects of those verbs. Here the words are both in the singular, and so the verb should be *was* and not *were*. The opposite of *neither . . . nor* is *both . . . and*, which necessarily entails a verb in the plural: the sentence could therefore be alternatively worded as *Both John and Susan were unable to come.*

(vi) *Walking down the street yesterday the bus sped past me.*

As we have seen, it is a rule in syntax that the subject of a finite verb must also be the subject of all dependent non-finite verbs except in the special context of the nominative absolute. But in this sentence the subject of the finite verb *sped*, i.e. *the bus*, can be the subject of the non-finite verb *walking* only if the sentence is meant to be nonsensical. Presumably, however, it is meant to be sensible; and so it

66

must be reworded so that the non-finite verb becomes finite in a subordinate adverbial clause of time: *As I was walking down the street yesterday, the bus sped past me.*

This misuse of the participle is known as *the misrelated participle.*

(vii) *Those kind of men are useless.*

There is considerable grammatical confusion here. The subject of the sentence is the singular word *kind,* yet it has both a demonstrative adjective qualifying it in the plural and its verb is also plural. It must therefore be changed into the plural itself: *Those kinds of men are useless;* or else the whole sentence must be changed to the singular: *That kind of man is useless.*

(viii) *He is as good if not better than you.*

The second conjunction *as* is omitted from the expression *as good as* with the unfortunate result that *as good* is followed, along with *better*, by *than*. The sentence should read: *He is as good as if not better than you.*

Such omission of essential words is known as *ellipsis.* cf. (x).

(ix) *I can neither find it here nor there.*

Not only must *neither* and *nor* correlate words in the same number, those words must also be the same part of speech or its equivalent. But in this sentence *neither* is followed by the verb *find* and *nor* by the adverb of place *there*: it is a question of neither finding nor there—which is nonsense. The writer meant, and the sentence must be rearranged as: *I can find it neither here nor there*, in which the correlated words are both adverbs of place.

(x) *The government have not and do not intend to agree to that.*

Here the auxiliary verb *have* stands without the past

67

participle into which it is combined to make the perfect tense of *to intend*. *Intended* must therefore be inserted: *The government have not intended and do not intend to agree to that*. This is another example of *ellipsis*.

(xi) *He was one of the few men who was able to do it.*
The relative pronoun *who* is here standing for the plural noun *men* (its antecedent) and so is itself plural. But in this sentence it is followed by a singular verb *was*. Moreover, the sense alone demands that the verb be changed to *were*: he was not alone in being able to do it but was one of a few. The sentence should therefore be: *He was one of the few men who were able to do it.*

(xii) *Everybody was enjoying themselves.*
The indefinite pronoun *everybody*, which is composed of the distributive adjective *every* and the noun *body*, is singular (the plural of *body* is *bodies*). It is correctly followed here by the singular verb *was enjoying*, but the reflexive pronoun, which should agree with it in number, is in the plural. The sentence should be changed to: *Everybody was enjoying himself.*

This is a good example of how idiomatic usage ignores grammar, however. Nobody would dream of saying (or writing) *Everybody was enjoying himself*. For what about the ladies?

(xiii) *The most successful example of dramatic collaboration are Beaumont and Fletcher.*
The noun *example* is the subject of this sentence but is followed by the plural verb *are*. The mistake—an easy one to make—is due to the plurality of the complement *Beaumont and Fletcher* and the feeling one has that the verb should be *are*, as it would be if the order of words were inverted to: *Beaumont and Fletcher are the most successful example of*

dramatic collaboration. But as it now stands the sentence should read: *The most successful example of dramatic collaboration is Beaumont and Fletcher.*

(xiv) *Among the champions of the poor is Mr. Lyons, who, if he is not a philanthropist, then, we may wonder, what is philanthropy?*

Here the relative pronoun *who* is in the nominative case and so must be the subject of a finite verb in a subordinate adjectival clause. But neither verb nor clause exists. Instead, a subordinate adverbial clause of condition, *if he is not a philanthropist,* is immediately introduced and followed by a new main clause, *then, we may wonder* and its own subordinate noun clause object *what is philanthropy? Who,* therefore, is left alone with no work to do. It must be removed and the co-ordinating conjunction *and* put in to join the second main clause to the first: *Among the champions of the poor is Mr. Lyons, and if he is not a philanthropist, then, we may wonder, what is philanthropy?* This is an example of *anacoluthon* (q.v. in Chapter 15) and is specifically called *nominativus pendens* or *hanging nominative*—i.e. a subject without any syntactical function.

These sentences illustrate how vulnerable strict grammar can be; and the notes show how essential a knowledge of syntax is for understanding mistakes and why and how they can be corrected.

In the following sentences certain words are emphasized in italics, and all the departments of syntax are called upon to analyse their functions. One thing at least is revealed: the tremendous adaptability of words. But in such adaptability there is, besides the wonderful medium of expression, the constant danger of mistaken usage.

(i) I was given *that gramophone* by a friend.

These two words, a demonstrative adjective and its noun,

69

are the retained accusative, i.e. the object of a passive verb (*was given*). If the sentence were changed so that the verb were active we should get *A friend gave me that gramophone* and the normal change back into the passive would be for the direct object, *that gramophone*, to become the subject: *That gramophone was given me by a friend.* But it is the indirect object *me* which has become the subject of *was given*, and so *that gramophone* still is the direct object.

(ii) He overslept *himself.*

The verb *to sleep* is intransitive and so cannot have any object—it cannot have one even in the special way explained earlier. But if we ask the question *whom or what?* after *overslept* in this sentence we shall have to answer with the word *himself*, which is, therefore, the direct object. But *himself* is a reflexive pronoun, and though syntactically it must rank as a special kind of object in a context like this, it is being used only in an emphasizing capacity and could be omitted from the sentence: *He overslept.*

(iii) He takes an excessive delight in *talking.*

Talking is in the same form as the present participle of *to talk* and is being used as a noun governed by the preposition *in*: it is therefore a gerund.

(iv) I doubt if that is worth *doing.*

Doing is the present participle of *to do* in the active voice. But here it has a passive meaning: *I doubt if that is worth being done;* it is thus an example of the quasi-passive use of the active voice.

An alternative possibility is that *doing* is a gerund, the sentence being paraphrased: *I doubt if that is worth the doing of it.*

(v) *May* it *be* as you wish, my friend.

May be is in the subjunctive mood of the verb and here

70

has the sense of an indirect command, an earnest wish plus the element of an imperative: it is therefore an example of the jussive subjunctive.

(vi) I did not say *that* you could go.

That is a subordinating conjunction joining the main clause *I did not say* to the noun clause object *you could go*.

(vii) I saw him *immediately* he had finished.

Immediately is an adverb of time and is here doing the work of a conjunction subordinating *he had finished* to the main clause *I saw him*.

(viii) *Even* the best men make mistakes.

Even is an adverb of degree qualifying the adjective *best*. It equals the adverb of degree *very*: *The very best men make mistakes*.

(ix) There is *but* little to say.

But is normally a co-ordinating conjunction; here, however, it is being used in the sense of *only*, which is an adverb of degree, and qualifies *little*. *Little* is normally an adjective, of course, but here it is being used as a noun; *but* is therefore an adjective.

(x) They were all there *but* Jones.

Here the conjunction *but* is being used in place of the word *except*, which is variously either a conjunction itself or a preposition (here the latter, governing *Jones*).

(xi) He was ultimately elected *the new chairman*.

The new chairman is a noun phrase complement of the subject *he*; or, if the three words are taken as the single-word complement (*the*) *chairman* and its qualifying adjective *new*, they do not constitute a noun phrase but must be discussed as three separate words, definite article, qualifying adjective and complement.

(xii) It's a most *exciting* story.

Exciting is the present participle of *to excite* (active voice) being used as an adjective qualifying the noun *story*.

(xiii) He wore a *worried* expression.

Worried is the past participle of *to worry* being used as an adjective qualifying the noun *expression*.

(xiv) I won't do it any *more*.

The word *more* is an adjective, but very often it is made to do the work of an adverb (as in the formation of degrees of comparison). In this sentence it is doing the work of an adverb of time, standing as it does for the full expression *more times*, in which it is playing its original role as an adjective (qualifying the noun *times*).

(xv) *So* much do I read that I have almost become a book myself.

So is qualifying the word *much*, which, originally an adjective, is here being used either as an adverb (=frequently, extensively) or as a noun (=many books). *So* is therefore either an adverb of degree or an adjective.

(xvi) They searched around *to find* the treasure.

To find, the present active infinitive, is here being used to express purpose, standing in place of the words *in order that they might find*, which, including the finite verb *might find*, would—with *the treasure*—be an adverbial clause of purpose. *To find the treasure* is thus an adverbial phrase of purpose.

(xvii) I'll see you *outside*.

Outside, a preposition, is here being used as an adverb of place.

(xviii) He was shaving *his* chin.

His is a possessive adjective qualifying the noun *chin*.

(xix) The new secretary, *Mr. Williams*, made a brief reply.

Mr. Williams is in apposition to *the new secretary*, the subject of *made*, and could therefore take the place of those three words as subject. All five words are of course in the nominative case.

(xx) I wish *to go*.

To go is the present active infinitive being used as a noun, object of *wish* and therefore in the accusative case.

(xxi) *To hear* is *to obey*.

To hear is the present active infinitive being used as a noun, subject of *is*; and *to obey*, which is also a present active infinitive, is equivalent to a noun, being the complement of *is* and referring back to *to hear*.

(xxii) This is a discovery *which* will revolutionize science.

Which is a relative pronoun standing in place of a repetition of the noun *discovery* and joining together the otherwise separate simple sentences, *This is a discovery* and *This discovery will revolutionize science*. It therefore introduces a subordinate adjectival clause.

(xxiii) He ran *his fingers* over the surface of the picture.

These two words are the direct object of the intransitive verb *ran*, which is therefore being used in a special quasi-transitive, factitive way, meaning *made to run*.

(xxiv) This is the place *where* it happened.

The word *where* is the relative adverb (=*at which, in which* etc.) introducing the subordinate adjectival clause, *where it happened*, which qualifies the antecedent *place* in the main clause, *This is the place*.

(xxv) Such articles *as* he has written are difficult to understand.

As is a conjunction, but here it is doing the work of a

73

relative pronoun (*which*): *Those articles which he has written* . . . The subordinate clause which it introduces, *as he has written*, is therefore adjectival, qualifying *articles*.

(xxvi) It is not hard *to appreciate that*.

To appreciate that is a noun phrase, composed of the present active infinitive, *to appreciate*, and its object, the demonstrative pronoun *that*, in apposition to the subject *It*, in whose place as the subject of *is* it could therefore stand: *To appreciate that is not hard*.

Every word in a sentence can be syntactically discussed in this way. The discussion takes into account its original part of speech, whether it is being used as another part, and what is its relationship with the words about it (i.e. if it is a subject, an object, a complement, in apposition, qualifying and so on).

Thus in the sentence *Every word in a sentence can be syntactically discussed in this way*, the analysis of the function of each word is as follows:

Every:	distributive adjective qualifying the noun *word*;
word:	subject of *can be discussed*;
in:	preposition governing *a sentence*;
a:	indefinite article (=adjective qualifying *sentence*);
sentence:	noun governed by *in*, forming with *in a* an adjectival phrase qualifying *word*;
can:	auxiliary verb combining with the non-finite verb *be discussed* to make the finite verb *can be discussed*;
be:	auxiliary verb composing the present infinitive of the passive voice of *to discuss*;
syntactically:	adverb of manner qualifying *can be discussed*;
discussed:	past participle of *to discuss*, combining with *be* as part of the passive infinitive *be discussed*;
in:	preposition governing *this way*, with which it combines to compose the adverbial phrase of manner qualifying *can be discussed*;

this :   demonstrative adjective qualifying the noun
                  way;

way :   noun governed by *in*, qualified by *this* and part
                  of the adverbial phrase of manner, *in this way*.

5

Direct and Indirect Speech

WHEN the actual words spoken by a person are written down, either between inverted commas if they are being quoted by someone else or without inverted commas as in speeches, plays and autobiographies, they are said to be in *direct speech*. Examples:

(a) 'It must be a very pretty dance,' said Alice, timidly.
  'Would you like to see a little of it?' said the Mock Turtle.
  'Very much indeed,' said Alice.

(b) But in a larger sense we cannot dedicate, we cannot consecrate, we cannot hallow this ground. The brave men, living and dead, who struggled here, have consecrated it far above our power to add or detract.

  (Some of the actual words spoken by Lincoln at Gettysburg.)

(c) MAGNUS. Am I supposed to write these articles?
  NICOBAR. Your man Sempronius does. I can spot his fist out of fifty columns.
  CRASSUS. So can I. When he is getting at me he always begins the sentence with 'Singularly enough'.

  (From GEORGE BERNARD SHAW'S 'The Apple Cart'.)

(d) I was now in the last year of my apprenticeship, and was running a bit wild, taking no interest in my trade, and determined in a few months to throw off all restraint.

  (From W. H. DAVIES'S 'Autobiography of a Super-Tramp'.)

Words are in *indirect speech* (sometimes called *reported speech*) when they are not written down as they were originally

76

spoken (or written) but are reported by someone else who therefore speaks about the original speaker or writer in the third person and past tense. Such directly personal words as the first and second person pronouns—that is unless they are being used in an impersonal sense—are, as a rule, changed to third person pronouns; and words like *here, today* and *now* are changed to *there, on that day* and *then*. *Tomorrow* becomes *the next day*. Some of the original words may have to be omitted and other, new, words added.

So the four passages above become in indirect speech:

(*a*) Alice said timidly that it must be a very pretty dance. The Mock Turtle asked if she would like to see a little of it, and Alice said that she very much would.

NOTES.—The inverted commas have disappeared; the conjunctions *that* and *and* have been added; *indeed* has been omitted as not fitting the indirect speech.

(*b*) Lincoln said that in a larger sense they could not dedicate, they could not consecrate, they could not hallow that ground. The brave men, living and dead, who had struggled there had consecrated it far above their power to add or detract.

NOTES.—*Lincoln said* has been added; the existing past tenses, *struggled* and *have consecrated*, have been put a tense back into the pluperfect; *this ground* has become *that ground*.

(*c*) Magnus asked if he was supposed to write those articles. Nicobar replied that his man, Sempronius, did and he could spot Sempronius's fist out of fifty columns. Crassus said that he could too. When Sempronius was getting at him, he always began the sentence with 'Singularly enough'.

NOTES.—The names of the speakers have been incorporated into the text; *these* has become *those*; the name of Sempronius has been added to avoid confusion with the third person pronouns; the inverted commas around *Singularly enough* are retained because the words are still quoted.

> (d) W. H. Davies wrote that he was then in the last year of his apprenticeship and was running a bit wild, taking no interest in his trade, and determined in a few months to throw off all restraint.

NOTES.—Since the original is already in the past tense, as Davies was writing of his own youth, there is no need to make any change there; the words *W. H. Davies wrote that* are added to introduce the indirect speech.

Special Points:

The present tense may be retained in indirect speech when the contents of a book are being paraphrased (cf. note on the historic present):

e.g. In his book 'Critique of Poetry', Michael Roberts *gives* an account of . . .

The first person pronouns may also be used in indirect speech even though they do not have a general, impersonal meaning. If, for instance, a person is recounting an incident in which he himself took part, he will speak of himself in the first person.

Examples:

(i) Original conversation:
'Do you think you will be able to go?' X said.
'I doubt it very much,' Y answered.

(ii) As reported by X:
'I asked Y if he would be able to go and he said he doubted it very much.'

(iii) As reported by Y:
'X asked me if I would be able to go and I told him that I doubted it very much.'

Second person pronouns may be similarly retained.

Examples:
  (i) Original conversation:
        'I want you to come round and see my pictures some-
     time,' A said.
        'Yes, I'll be pleased to,' B replied.
  (ii) As reported later by A:
        'I told you that I wanted you to come round and see
     my pictures and you said you'd be pleased to.'
  (iii) As reported later by B:
        'When you asked me to come round and see your
     pictures I said I'd be pleased to.'

The examples given in this chapter show that in the
change from one kind of speech to the other, and when there
is a mixture of the two, there are also changes in the punctuation, the diction and the paragraphing.

We do not normally have to turn indirect speech into direct,
however; but we often have to turn direct into indirect: skill
at this is, indeed, essential to the quick and accurate writing
of summary and paraphrase.

6

Punctuation

THE words *punctuation* and *point* both come from the same Latin word, and punctuation is the practice of putting points among words: the art of punctuation lies in putting them in the correct places.

Without punctuation, the reader would be presented with a continuous stream of words, and the process of reading would be slow, laborious and very dull; and the writer would not be able to show his reader how he wanted his words to be understood. For punctuation splits words up into groups, both to make them readily intelligible and to show how they are to be understood. No more and no less punctuation than serves these two ends is necessary, although certain conventions have grown almost into rules which it is as well for us to observe. George Bernard Shaw did not use the apostrophe in the conventional places; but he was for long in the happy position of being able to do what he liked. Many, too, have been the experiments with punctuation and the absence of it, by the Irish novelist, James Joyce, for instance, and by several modern poets. But in this chapter all the conventional usages will be illustrated, and rules will be laid down. Punctuation, however, like the words whose servant it is, must be used to suit the writer's purpose and never allowed to dictate to him.

There are twelve different punctuation-marks, some of which are, however, interchangeable:

.	the full stop
,	the comma
;	the semi-colon
:	the colon
:—	the pointer
?	the question-mark
!	the exclamation-mark
" "	double inverted commas
' '	single inverted commas
—	the dash
( )	the round bracket
[ ]	the square bracket

It is conventional to call the hyphen (-) and the apostrophe (') punctuation-marks, and so they are discussed in this chapter; but they are really involved in spelling.

All the other symbols which are used—such as the asterisk *, the oblique stroke / and the omission-mark ∧ (i.e. the caret)— are not counted as ordinary punctuation-marks since they are used only in special circumstances.

The Full Stop

'The period (i.e. full stop) is the note of abruption and disjunction', Dr. Johnson wrote. So it is used at the end of all sentences that are not questions or exclamations:

e.g. The full stop is used at the end of all sentences that are not questions or exclamations.

It is also put at the end of all separate groups of words even though they are not sentences:

e.g. in notes, diaries, etc.:

9 a.m.	Meet Smith.
9.30.	Taxi.
10.	Telephone message expected from London.

It is, in other words, the point which shows that the end of a particular passage of writing—even if that passage consists of only one word—has been reached.

81

It is also used in abbreviations: *e.g.* (*exempli gratia*), *a.d.* (*anno domini*), *i.e.* (*id est*), *p.m.* (*post meridiem*), *D.S.O.* (*Distinguished Service Order*), *Hon. Sec.* (*Honorary Secretary*). cf. its use after initials: *G. K. Chesterton.*

There are some modern abbreviations which are so familiarly used and whose full forms are so seldom if ever spoken or written that it is not necessary to use the full stop in them: e.g. *BBC, ITV.* There are, also, many whose letters form words and which are therefore written as such with only initial capital letters: Naafi, Unesco, Seato, Balpa. There is, of course, nothing to prevent anyone from writing them as formal abbreviations with full stops.

The Comma

Dr. Johnson described this mark as being 'the note of connection and continuity of sentences', i.e. it does not symbolize an ending but a momentary interruption which occurs only to assist the onward movement of the sentence towards its ending.

It makes, therefore, a necessary brief pause between groups of words:

I'll show you the painting I was talking about, but don't expect too much.

Whether that sentence is read aloud or silently, the sense of the words demands the slight interval after *about*, and so the interval is marked by the comma. Certainly the sentence has not ended there. Such short breaks or intervals occur in almost every sentence of any length.

All the uses of the comma originate from this elementary function, even though some of them are by now only conventional.

(i) It is placed before and after small groups of words or single words that are interjected, whether as mere colloquialisms or as links with previous words:

   e.g. . . . and, by the way, . . . Well, to tell you the truth,
   . . . There is a difference, however, between . . .

   (ii) It is similarly used before and after any direct naming
of a person (i.e. the vocative case): *Yes, my dear, . . . Hello,
George, . . . No, sir, . . .*

   (iii) It is used to enclose as a separate group any words
in apposition: *The lion, king of the jungle, is . . . Mr.
R. G. Casey, the Governor of Bengal, said . . .*

   (iv) When a subordinate adjectival clause is an enlargement of an appositional phrase, it too is separated from the
rest of its sentence by commas: *Mr. R. G. Casey, who was
then Governor of Bengal, said . . .* But there is no need so
to separate all adjectival clauses. There need be no comma
in this sentence: *He rushed off to meet the brother whom
he had not seen for five years.* Whether or not any subordinate
clause should be separated by a comma or commas depends
on how it is to be read in relationship to the rest of its
sentence.

   (v) The comma is placed between all items in lists except
the last two, which are usually joined by the co-ordinating
conjunction *and*. These last two may also be separated by a
comma if the writer wants the different effect which that will
have, and all the other items may be joined by *and* instead
of being separated by commas. But the conventional method
is the use of the comma so that the items, considered as
numbers, go: *1, 2 and 3;* or *1, 2, 3 and 4;* and so on:

   e.g. Tom, Dick and Harry were there.

Sometimes the two methods may be combined, so that the
last two items are both separated by a comma and joined
by *and*:

   e.g. He smoked, walked up and down, smoked again, sat
   down, got up, and then lit another cigarette.

Thus the staccato effect is preserved throughout the list.

When two or more adjectives or adverbs qualify the same word, it is customary to separate them by commas:

e.g. He was a big, strong, handsome man; She danced gracefully, charmingly, wittily.

It is not customary to use *and* in lists of this kind.

(vi) The comma is put at the end of every unit and line of an address except the last, which is, of course, followed by a full stop.

Examples:

> A. B. Seaman, Esq.,
> 42, West Avenue,
> Southampton,
> Hants.

The use of the comma after the full stop as in *Esq.*, is one of the few occasions on which two punctuation-marks occur simultaneously.

(vii) The comma is also used in conjunction with inverted commas to separate the quoted words from the others (except, of course when the quoted words are questions or exclamations). If the quoted words come first, the comma is placed inside the inverted commas; if the other words come first, then the comma still comes first, outside the inverted commas.

Examples:

> Quoted words first: 'It must be a very pretty dance,' said Alice.
> Other words first: Alice said, 'It must be a very pretty dance.'
> Example of both: 'You shouldn't make jokes,' Alice said, 'if it makes you so unhappy.'

The misplacing of a comma can reduce what is intended to be sense to nonsense. For instance: *I think it was done by Mr. Jones, who is a communist, out of sheer devilment.* If the comma after *communist* is omitted, so that the adjectival clause is no longer *who is a communist* but all the words from

84

who to the end of the sentence, the original sense is altered completely and, so far as the writer's intention at least is concerned, has become nonsense. Similarly, the absence of the comma can make the meaning of a sentence very ambiguous:

e.g. This letter was written in response to an appeal by Mr. Jones.

That may or may not be ambiguous as it stands, but the writer meant that the letter was written by Mr. Jones: this meaning the sentence can have only if commas are used after *written* and *appeal*: *This letter was written, in response to an appeal, by Mr. Jones.* The ambiguity can of course be avoided—and the style improved—by changing the order of the words to *This letter was written by Mr. Jones in response to an appeal.*

The Semi-Colon

The symbol itself, a combination of the full stop and the comma, implies the function of this mark. For the semi-colon is a half-way house between the full stop and the comma, denoting neither a complete ending nor a momentary interruption but such an interval in the progress of a sentence as is not conclusive enough to warrant a full stop nor brief enough to justify a comma.

Example:

This punctuation-mark is used so often by some people that at first sight it would seem almost a hopeless task to define its chief purpose; but it does too easily lend itself to excessive usage and should therefore be treated with more than usual respect.

The writer of that had not completed what he wanted to say within the limits of a single sentence by the time he had reached *purpose*, since he wanted to write a second statement which would balance the first. He did not want to write a bold contradiction, which would have necessitated a new sentence, but a statement which, while contradicting, was a continuation

85

of the point made in the first statement. The break after *purpose*, then, is not big enough for a full stop or small enough for a comma but just of the correct duration for a semi-colon. The second half of the sentence is neither a mere contradiction nor a mere continuation.

Such is the chief purpose of this punctuation-mark. It is probably the most useful one of the twelve, since it enables a writer to build up long sentences and yet keep them in order.

It is also used, like the comma, to separate items in lists, items which are, however, bigger than those separated by commas, e.g. clauses and sentences inside which commas may already exist. The last two items may be joined by *and*, but the break between them is still large enough for the semi-colon. Example:

> By noon everyone was busy about the camp: the men were cleaning their equipment, oiling the guns and saddling the horses; cooks and orderlies were preparing the rations and collecting all the odds and ends that make up the stores of an army in the field; and the officers were making the final plans for the march.

The Colon and Pointer

These two marks perform the same function: they point forward to such a continuation of the sentence as will substantiate by example what has been already stated. The difference between them is that it is normal for the colon to be used in the middle of sentences and, with the single exception of quotations, for the continuation then to follow on the same line of writing; whereas the pointer, when used at all, introduces lists or examples which begin, each on a new line, like a new paragraph.

Thus in the sentence above about the camp the colon is placed after the word *camp* to introduce the details which show how *everyone was busy*. cf. *After he had turned out all his*

pockets the following articles lay on the table: penknife, watch,
pencil, string . . .

It is customary to introduce quotations by the colon, but
since they usually start on a new line the pointer may be used
instead.

Example:

> But, as usual, it is Shakespeare who has best expressed the
> sentiment: (or :—)
>> 'To be or not to be, that is the question:
>> Whether 'tis nobler in the mind . . .'

The following example shows the normal use of the pointer
introducing a list:

> The titles of the books in stock are:—
>> 'The Good Companions';
>> 'Pickwick Papers';
>> . . .

The pointer once had a much more vital role than it has
today, and was regularly used inside sentences; now, however, the colon is supplanting it everywhere.

The Question-Mark

There is only one use to which this mark is put: to denote
that the words which precede it are in the form of a question.
The order of words itself will often show when a question is
being asked, of course, but not always; the mere placing of a
question-mark after words, however, automatically transforms a statement into a question. *'I don't know,'* he said is
completely changed in meaning if it is punctuated *'I don't
know?'* he said. It will be seen that when it is used with
inverted commas in this way—that is when the quoted words
are a question—the question-mark is placed inside them.

The Exclamation-Mark

This is placed after any word or group of words which

is exclamatory, so that the reader may appreciate the force with which it should be spoken aloud:

e.g. 'Come here!' he shouted.

It is commonly used after interjections: *Hurray! Ouch! Dash!*

Double and Single Inverted Commas (or Quotation Marks)

Today these are interchangeable on all occasions; but the double ones are longer in the field and most writers still prefer to use them, reserving the single for the special function of signifying a quotation within a quotation. (It should be observed, however, that many printers have adopted the other method.)

The purpose of inverted commas is to show that words are being quoted as they were originally spoken or written:

'You shouldn't make jokes,' Alice said, 'if it makes you unhappy.'

Except in the specific context of drama, therefore, they are used in the recording of original conversation.

All quotations from books, speeches, etc., and all titles, are similarly separated from the words accompanying them. Examples:

(*a*) One is immediately reminded of Blake's lines:
'Tyger! Tyger! burning bright
In the forests of the night';
(*b*) Last night I went to see 'Gone with the Wind';
(*c*) He was reading Tolstoy's 'War and Peace';
(*d*) He first played Beethoven's 'Moonlight' Sonata.

When double inverted commas are already in use and a new quotation is made, the single commas have to be introduced to separate it from the words already being quoted. Example:

"She was reading Aldous Huxley's 'Brave New World'," he said.

Similarly, if the single commas are already being used the double ones must be introduced to separate any new quotation:

'Have you read "Brave New World"?' she asked.

It is advisable to avoid more than one such alternation.

All the punctuation-marks that logically go with the quoted words are placed inside the inverted commas, all the others are placed outside them.

Examples:

(a) 'Have you been to see him?' she asked.
(b) 'I don't think I'll have time to see "Fantasia",' he said.
(c) He was carrying a copy of 'Macbeth', but he obviously has not read it.
(d) He began his speech with the trite opening: 'Unaccustomed as I am to public speaking'.

If a quotation includes more than one paragraph, the opening set of inverted commas is repeated at the commencement of each new paragraph.

Example:

The following are the principal passages from his statement:
'About four o'clock in the morning I dictated my testament to my secretary, and this was witnessed by my personal deputy, Mr. Smith, Captain Bergen and Dr. Williams.
'Later that morning I planned my escape and . . .'

The Dash

The dash has a variety of uses. The first and most common is to mark a complete interruption of the onward flow of a sentence. One dash marks the beginning of the interruption and another its end, after which the original progress of the sentence is resumed. The words between the dashes remain syntactically apart from the rest of the sentence, whose structure is therefore unimpaired by the interruption. What

89

comes between the dashes is a sudden after-thought or remembrance which cannot wait until the sentence is completed but thrusts itself in there and then.

Example:

> He showed him the free dispensary and the clinic and the nurse—Scotch girl named Smith, she was—and the dental chair he'd rigged up . . .

This example also shows that other punctuation-marks can be used with the words between the dashes.

Brackets (q.v.) might have been used instead of dashes, but they have other uses to which the dash cannot be put, and most writers prefer the dash in such a context as this.

If the interruption occurs at the end of a sentence the introductory dash only is used:

> He showed him the free dispensary and the clinic and the nurse—Scotch girl named Smith, she was.

But the single dash has other functions:

(i) To show that either a word or a sentence is uncompleted.

Examples:

> 'Of course D— was there,' he said;
> 'Why, you wouldn't—' he gasped.

It is similarly used in plays and other records of conversation to show that one speaker is interrupted by another:

> BROADBENT. But don't you want to see your country again after eighteen years absence? to see your people? to be in the old home again? to—
> DOYLE (*interrupting him very impatiently*). Yes, yes . . .

(ii) To mark a sudden, dramatic end to a sentence, often in the form of an anticlimax:

> 'I'll tell you who the ghost was—me!'

(iii) To mark a sudden alteration in intention:

'All right, I'll tell you—no, I can't, I can't.'

The dash is so useful and so easy to use that all serious writers have to be on their guard against it. It can be employed most effectively as a stylistic device—as it was by Charles Lamb in his essays and by Byron in his journals—but it can be a dangerous tool in the wrong hands.

The Hyphen

As has been said, this is not really a punctuation-mark. So far, indeed, from separating words, it joins them together. It is used in two ways only, both with individual words:

(i) In compound words, i.e. words made up of two or more originally distinct words: *father-in-law; sea-girl; death-pale; commander-in-chief.*

(ii) To split into syllables words which cannot be written in the space left at the end of a line. It is placed at the end of the line:

It is, in other words, the point which shows that the end of a par-ticular passage of writing . . .

It is distinguishable from the dash in appearance by being shorter.

Round and Square Brackets

As was said earlier, round brackets can be used instead of dashes to separate from the syntactical progress of a sentence any afterthought or aside.
Example:

There was Phidias to whom tradition assigns the supervision (though not the execution) of the Parthenon carvings.

But brackets can also be used where dashes cannot. For whereas dashes separate only parts of sentences, brackets can separate from their context whole sentences, paragraphs or long passages containing several paragraphs. For these too may express the extra information of afterthought or sudden remembrance—information which needs more space than a few words within a sentence.

Brackets are also placed after abbreviations or words to add information about them:

e.g. (exempli gratia); the captain (Charles Smith); callisthenics (physical exercises).

It is the round bracket that is normally used in these contexts, and the square bracket is reserved to alternate with the round when it is desired to parenthesize words which are already between the round brackets.

Example:

He was talking about abbreviations (abbreviations [e.g., i.e., BBC, etc.] are his favourite topic) when . . .

The Apostrophe

(i) This mark is used in the genitive case of nouns to show possession. In the singular it precedes the addition of the letter *s* to the nominative form:

(*a*) I was using John's pencil;
(*b*) The dog's tail was wagging rapidly;
(*c*) He borrowed James's pencil.

There are occasions, however, when the additional *s* after the apostrophe makes the pronunciation of a word already containing several *s* sounds difficult for some people, who therefore—though wrongly—add only the apostrophe:

e.g. *Narcissus' face.*

But how do they pronounce the word? They can always use the preposition *of* instead, of course: *The face of Narcissus.*

When a noun is in the genitive plural two processes are involved:

(*a*) If the word already ends in *s* the apostrophe is placed after that *s* and no further *s* is added. *The boys' efforts; the trees' leaves.*

(*b*) But if the word does not already end in *s*, *'s* is added as though the word were in the singular: The children*'s* faces were dirty; he studied the women*'s* claims.

(ii) The apostrophe is also used to denote the omission of letters from words (in the genitive singular of nouns it stands for the old *e* of the original genitive form).
Examples:

> can't (no); they'd (woul, ha); mustn't (o); I'm (a); you're (a); appear'd (e); 'm (*mada*); goin' (g); 'im (h). So it's= it *is*, it *ha*s.

(iii) Sometimes the apostrophe is used before the letter *s* to make the plural form of words and letters which do not normally inflect into the plural.
Examples:

> mind your *p's* and *q's*;
> There are too many *but's* in your writing;
> There are two *l's* in usually;
> Three *3's* are 9.

It is however, the growing practice merely to add *s* without the apostrophe whenever it is desired to make an abnormal plural.

There are two other uses of the apostrophe, both of which are, however, fast falling into disrepute:

(i) In such expressions of time as *a two months' holiday, a three weeks' vacation.* In the singular the apostrophe is still respectfully retained: *one month's holiday, a week's holiday,* and so, to be logical, it should be retained in the plural also, since the meaning is still the same: a holiday of

93

two months, a vacation of three weeks. But it is becoming fashionable to omit the apostrophe in the plural forms, thus regarding *two months* and *three weeks* as equivalent to adjectival phrases.

(ii) Similarly, it is no longer as fashionable as it was to use the apostrophe in such phrases as *for goodness' sake* and *for conscience' sake*. The genitive form is required—for the meaning is that of *of goodness, of conscience*—but as the *s* which should go after the apostrophe is omitted in order to avoid too much sibilance, the feeling has grown that the use of the apostrophe itself is pedantic. When the word which precedes *sake* does not end with a sibilant sound, the (presumably) logical step of omitting both the apostrophe and the *s* has been taken, e.g. in *for fashion sake*.

The technical term for such pronouncing of the same sound (e.g. *s* and its equivalents) only once in preference to twice is *haplology*.

The Capital Letter and Punctuation

(*a*) The first word of every sentence begins with a capital letter.

(*b*) The first word inside a new set of inverted commas also begins with a capital letter:

> Then the Queen left off, quite out of breath, and said to Alice, '*H*ave you seen the Mock Turtle yet?'

If the inverted commas are only interrupted for a moment, the first word inside them when they are resumed does not begin with a capital letter:

> 'I've been to a day-school, too,' said Alice; 'you needn't be so proud as all that.'

But when the interruption of a quotation continues to a full stop so that the resumption itself begins a new sentence, the first word of the resumption naturally starts with a capital:

> 'Ah! then yours wasn't a really good school,' said the Mock Turtle in a tone of great relief. '*N*ow at ours they had . . .'

(*c*) It is not necessary to start the next word after either a question-mark or an exclamation-mark with a capital. If either mark ends a sentence, then the first word of the following sentence will commence with a capital in the usual way, but if they themselves come in the middle of a sentence, the next word starts with a small letter as it does when following a comma or semi-colon or colon.

Examples:

> 'What was that like?' *s*aid Alice.
> 'Ah! *t*hen yours wasn't a really good school . . .'

(*d*) All words in titles start with capital letters except short words like the articles, certain prepositions and conjunctions; and even those do if they are the first words.

Examples:

> Last night I went to see '*G*one with the *W*ind';
> I have just read John Steinbeck's '*O*f Mice and Men'.

7

The Paragraph

JUST as the divisions of a poem are its stanzas and of a book its chapters, so the divisions of a continuous passage of prose—an essay, article, letter or chapter—are its paragraphs. The divisional mark—the written indication that a new paragraph has commenced—is made by placing the first word of the first line slightly farther away from the left side of the page than are the first words of the succeeding lines in the paragraph.

Why, then, do these divisions exist?

It is obvious that in all but very short passages of writing we are bound to speak either of more things than one—i.e. different things—or of more than one aspect of the same thing. To make clear to our readers—as well as to ourselves—when we start to speak either of a new thing or of a new aspect of the thing already being discussed, we have at our disposal this device of the new paragraph. The reader is enabled to make the pause necessary to adjust his mind to the commencement of something different, and the presentation of the varying subjects or points is both easier and more memorable. If the passage is being read aloud, there should be a significant interval between the end of one paragraph and the beginning of the next.

The following examples illustrate these two main functions of the paragraph-division. The first shows how a new paragraph introduces a new subject:

. . . not so C. He referred to the attack as one might speak of catching a train, and in it a few hours later he showed such wonderful Saint Christopher spirit that he was expected to be awarded a posthumous Victoria Cross. Meanwhile all waited.

The cold disturbing air and the scent of the river must marked the approach of the morning. I got my . . .

In the first paragraph the writer is describing the time prior to the attack and brings his account to a laconic and sinister ending. He then moves on to the new subject of the atmosphere of the approaching daylight, and so begins a new paragraph for it.

Since the new paragraph introduces a new subject there is no verbal link between it and the preceding paragraph. The style demands that there should be no such link.

The second example shows a new paragraph introducing a new aspect of the same subject:

> Johnson used to say that he made it a constant rule to talk as well as he could, both as to sentiment and expression; by which means, what had been originally effort became familiar and easy. The consequence of this, Sir Joshua observed, was that his common conversation in all companies was such as to secure him universal attention, as something above the usual colloquial style was expected.
>
> Yet, though Johnson had this habit in company, when another mode was necessary, in order to investigate truth, he could descend to a language intelligible to the meanest capacity . . .

The single subject under discussion is Johnson's talking. In the first paragraph the point is made that he talked as well as he could on all occasions in company, having trained himself to do so, and thereby gained everyone's attention. The second paragraph then takes up the new point that, when he wanted, Johnson could also talk as simply as anyone could wish.

This time, the second paragraph is not left separate from

97

the first, since both are about the same subject. It is doubly linked to it, by its very first contradicting word *Yet*, which immediately announces something new about what has just been said, and by the reference-back to the matter of the first paragraph in *this habit*.

The style demands that such a link be made, and it is the presence or absence of this link which marks the stylistic difference between the two functions and purposes of the new paragraph. When a new subject is introduced, there must be no link; when a new aspect is being introduced, the link is essential.

There are also three more special uses of the paragraph, all based, however, on the same principle of the introduction of something new:

(i) To separate items, examples, etc. in books of this kind, in note-books and diaries;

(ii) When a quotation is introduced which one does not wish to stand as part of one's own sentence, and even though the words quoted do not begin a new paragraph in their original context:

> The unfavourable impression made on Charles Dickens's mind by wandering in and out of courts of law was imparted by him years after to Mr. Frederick Pollock:
> 'I have that high opinion of the law of England generally, which one is likely to derive from the impression that it puts all the honest men under the diabolical hoofs of all the scoundrels.'
> The cases Charles Dickens was called on to report were heard and argued in a large room . . .

It will be observed that the whole quotation is set farther in from the left-hand edge of the page than the rest of the passage.

(iii) In the recording of conversation a new paragraph must begin every time there is a change of speaker, even though all that the new speaker says is a single word. Both psychology and punctuation provide sound reasons why this arrangement has become established practice.

Example:

'Well, Sam,' said Mr. Pickwick, 'what's the matter now?'
'Here's rayther a rum go, sir,' replied Sam.
'What?' inquired Mr. Pickwick.
'This here, sir,' rejoined Sam. 'I'm wery much afeerd, sir, that the proprieator o' this here coach is a playin' some imperence with us.'

cf. the arrangement of dialogue in plays:

AUNT JUDY. Oh now what a shame. An I told Patsy Farrell to put a nail in it.
BROADBENT. He did, Miss Doyle. There was a nail, certainly.
AUNT JUDY. Dear oh dear.

NOTE.—The length of a paragraph depends solely upon the considerations discussed above. It may be very long or very short. In the recording of conversation it may, as has been observed, be a single word:

'What sort of communication do you want?—a written one?'
'Yes, I wish for a written one.'
'From any particular spirit?'
'Yes.'

The very short, single-sentence paragraph is most effective in swift narrative:

. . . In place of the hat and feathers, what dusky object was it that now hid his forehead, his eyes, his shaking hand?
Was the bed moving?
I turned on my back and looked up . . .
(WILKIE COLLINS: 'A Terribly Strange Bed'.)

8

Idiom—The Figures of Speech—Jargon

IDIOM is defined in the Concise Oxford Dictionary as a *form of expression peculiar to a language.* It is expression which is not literally translatable into any other language; which sometimes cannot be literally understood or analysed; and which sometimes disobeys the laws of syntax. English idiom—idiomatic English—is the language which is spoken and written natively by English people. A foreigner who came here and asked to be *put in the correct direction towards the post-office which is nearest* would make himself understood but would not be speaking idiomatic English: an Englishman would ask to be *shown the way to the nearest post-office.* It is idiomatic English to say that *it is raining cats and dogs,* but no Frenchman would think us French if we said *il pleut des chats et des chiens,* for the corresponding French idiom is *il pleut des cordes* (or *des hallebardes*), which literally means in English: *it is raining ropes* (or *halberds*).

An example of idiom flouting the strict law of syntax is its use of the disjunctive pronoun in expressions like *it is me.*

There are few people who do not speak idiomatically, since we all acquire colloquial idiom in infancy; but when it comes to writing idiomatically, as many people fail as succeed. An artificiality creeps in; the knowledge that written expression is different from oral becomes a desire to make that expression

100

as remote from speech as possible, and the result often is not English idiom at all but a mere sequence of English words: the reader can usually tell what the writer meant to say but is aware that he has not said it idiomatically.

All the following examples of unidiomatic expression are taken from essays by boys in the fourth form of a secondary-grammar school:

(a) Recollecting many thousands of years one thinks of Stonehenge.

(b) Even now people are pumped with falsities by political parties.

(c) When people are in captivity, such as many countries in the war, they are always rising to gain their freedom.

(d) Television-sets and the radio are useful instruments in case of anybody having nothing to do.

(e) Of course to the people that lived there, if you asked them what to them makes the Thames famous they will immediately tell you stories of the floods.

(f) All his life, every day he said his prayers.

(g) Time has brought about the main changes in buildings, but time has not done it with the modern ruins.

Examples of unidiomatic—though intelligible—English abound in foreign brochures, programmes, notices and so on. The following warning can be seen in a certain Italian camp-site: 'Campers are asked not to wear bath-robes that give offence to the morals'.

Besides idiom in this general sense, however, there are in English, as in every other language, hundreds of short figurative expressions each of which is known as *an idiom*. They are the very stuff of idiom, the most distinctive element in any language's personality. We all use them, of course, but not until we know their origins and true meanings can we use them correctly. The following list contains some of the more interesting of these *idioms*:

A storm in a teacup; the thin end of the wedge; rule of

thumb; to bell the cat; to show the cloven hoof; to draw a bow at a venture; the writing on the wall; to hitch one's wagon to a star; to cut your coat according to your cloth; a busman's holiday; to play to the gallery; the last straw; to play with fire; not the only pebble on the beach; to draw in one's horns; to flog a dead horse; a red herring; a white elephant; to send a person to Coventry; to temper the wind to the shorn lamb.

Dr. Brewer's 'Dictionary of Phrase and Fable' is the standard work to consult for the origins and definitions of these, often strange, expressions, many of which have an actual first use (e.g. *to bell the cat*), others of which were the inventions of individual writers (e.g. *God tempers the wind, said Maria, to the shorn lamb*—Laurence Sterne's version of a French proverb in 'A Sentimental Journey'), and others of which are occupational (e.g. *to play to the gallery*).

Slang

Slang is probably the most idiomatic form of a language, but although it is usually at home in speech it is seldom appropriate to written expression. Such idioms, for instance, as *to keep your shirt* (or *hair*) *on, to pull your socks up* and *to want jam on it* would reduce any serious passage of prose to the lowest level of bathos. If conversation is recorded, or original words quoted, then all the slang that the speakers used must be written down; but apart from that special context the presence of slang in writing depends on the spirit of the passage. It may be needed for a sensational or dramatic effect, and in a light-hearted, conversational piece it can be a most useful stylistic device. There is certainly no ban on slang in writing. But in any formal passage it will seldom find a suitable place. The following sentence illustrates how it can ruin a passage to which it is unsuited:

On this, one of the most dramatic occasions in English

history, great crowds had gathered to see the king bumped off.

But the following sentence shows it being effectively introduced:

G. K. Chesterton was a veritable block-buster of good humour.

The slang word *block-buster* is picturesquely appropriate to a criticism of the man, as all who know his size and the methods he employed against his enemies will realize.

There is, therefore, a right place and a wrong place for slang in writing; and only good sense can decide when the place is right and when it is wrong. (*V.* also Appendix B, 'The English Language'.)

The Figures of Speech

The figures discussed in this chapter do not include those more commonly found in verse, which are discussed in Chapter 14.

The Good

Simile. This is the name given to an expression in which things, actions, people etc. are compared with other things etc. of a totally different kind:

Australian Red, being the worse for drink, and forgetting that we had only to feign this part, began to roar *like a bull*, merry in earnest;

Tho' your sins be *as scarlet*, they shall be as white *as wool*; tho' they be red *like crimson*, they shall be as white *as snow*;

Her lips fluttered *like two leaves in a wind*, and her words crowded and rushed *like a flock of sheep at a gate*.

Metaphor. Metaphor is an expression in which one thing is said actually to be another thing which is of a totally different kind:

103

The handsome, charming youth had fascinated Elizabeth. The new star, rising with extraordinary swiftness, was suddenly seen to be shining alone in the firmament.

The handsome youth (Essex) is not compared with a star but is discussed as though he actually were one; and the court in which he had become so prominent is not likened to the firmament but actually named as such.

The sentence is actually an example of *sustained metaphor*, i.e. the picture or image is extended from the *star* to *rising*, *shining* and *firmament*. cf. Shakespeare's:

> This fell sergeant, death,
> Is strict in his arrest.
> ('Hamlet', v. 2. 350.)

Single words can be used metaphorically:

The car *sailed* along the road.

The car is made to do what only a ship can properly do. Had the sentence included a simile: *The car moved along the road as though it were sailing*, the concise effectiveness of the single metaphorically used word would have been lacking.

The following all contain examples of metaphor:

(*a*) The primrose path to the everlasting bonfire;
(*b*) The ship of state sails calmly on;
(*c*) The so-called civilized country was no more than a jungle;
(*d*) One of the twins was a lion, the other a lamb;
(*e*) The conference tried to hammer out a solution of the problem;
(*f*) He seemed able to leap easily over the difficulties of life;
(*g*) He put the company on its feet again;
(*h*) He made some very cutting remarks.

One has to be careful not to write what is called a *mixed*

metaphor. The following sentence, for example, contains a ludicrous mixture: *Having let loose the flood-tide of his oratory, he worked up his speech to a white heat.* One metaphor at a time is the rule.

Epigram (or *Aphorism*). An epigram is defined as a *pointed saying or mode of expression.* It is a short statement which sums up a point in a witty and striking manner:

> A perpetual holiday is a good definition of hell;
> A thing that nobody believes cannot be proved too often;
> It takes a thoroughly good woman to do a thoroughly stupid thing;
> To love oneself is the beginning of a life-long romance.

Writing that is continually epigrammatic (e.g. Oscar Wilde's) or full of maxims (e.g. Bacon's essays) is known as *gnomic* (*gnome*=epigram, aphorism).

Proverb. Examples:

> Rome was not built in a day;
> There's no smoke without fire;
> Where ignorance is bliss, 'tis folly to be wise;
> Charity begins at home;
> Self-praise is no recommendation.

Proverbs state briefly, and often illustrate, a general truth; but, unlike epigrams, they do not have to be witty. They are in a sense quotations, though there is no need to write them between inverted commas.
Example:

> The movements of the enemy were fully understood by our leaders: there's no smoke without fire.

Oxymoron. This is a statement in which antonyms are combined for the special effect:

> He was cruel only to be kind;
> All his remarks are most uncommonly common;
> It is by now an open secret.

105

cf. the title of Noel Coward's operetta, 'Bitter Sweet'.

Metonymy. It is metonymy when a detail is made to represent a whole: e.g. *the bottle* for drinking intoxicants, public-houses, etc.; *the press* for newspapers, journalists, etc.; *the Bench* for the legal system, judges, etc.; *the stage* for theatres, actors, etc.

Synecdoche. In this figure too a part stands for a whole, but this time part and whole are of the same kind. In metonymy a detail like the printing-press represents people (journalists) as well as things, but when *hands* represents the crew of a ship, i.e. only human beings, it is an example of synecdoche. Similarly, it is synecdoche when *guns* stands only for all armaments and *butter* represents only all food-stuffs in the famous war-cry: *Guns instead of butter.* cf. *I've seen forty springs* (=*years*).

Paradox. This is a statement which contains an essential contradiction; and because of this, it cannot be interpreted literally. Like oxymoron, which it closely resembles, it is used for its special effect.
Example:

You expect to have your cake and eat it.

cf. Wordsworth's *The child is father of the man.*

Litotes. This is a deliberate understatement to give a stronger indication of meaning than overstatement would give in the same context:

Well, I don't think much of that (=I think it very poor indeed);
He is not very popular (=he is very unpopular);
I am a citizen of no mean city (=of a magnificent city).

An alternative name for litotes is *meiosis*.

Hyperbole. This is the opposite of litotes, a deliberate exaggeration:

> That joke is as old as the hills;
> He had to make his way through mountains of paper scattered about the floor;
> I've been waiting years for you.

Irony. This is a form of sarcasm in which the exact opposite of what is meant is said:

> Oh yes, we're having a wonderful time (=we're bored to tears);
> Hm, pretty good, I suppose (=dreadful).

When spoken the words are given in a sneering tone. One of the most famous examples of sustained irony in literature is Antony's speech in 'Julius Caesar' beginning *Friends, Romans, countrymen,* in which he continually refers to Brutus as *an honourable man.* This special form of irony should not be confused with the general term, though the basic involvement of opposites is the same in both. cf. dramatic irony (pp. 234-5).

Climax. This is a list, usually of three statements, of which each is an intensification of the point of the one immediately preceding it, until the last, the climax itself, makes, as it were, the final turn of the screw.
Example:

> . . . and that government of the people, by the people, and for the people shall not perish from the earth;
> . . . to tell the truth, the whole truth, and nothing but the truth.

Connected with climax is *anaphora,* a form of repetition in which the same word or group of words is repeated in successive clauses or sentences for a peculiar effect:

107

Above it stood the seraphims: each one had six wings; *with twain* he covered his face, and *with twain* he covered his feet, and *with twain* he did fly.

('Isaiah' vi. i.)

Anticlimax. This is a similar device, in which, however, the final item in the list is a sudden contrast with all the others, usually of a trifling or even farcical nature. It may have one or two purposes: either to make fun of the preceding items or to enhance their seriousness by the very process of trifling contrast.

Examples:

The celebrated pianist played a popular programme, including Beethoven's 'Pathetic' sonata, several of Chopin's better-known studies, and 'Home Sweet Home';

If the hot iron (=shrapnel) doesn't get you, then the rock-splinters will, and they say the mosquitoes are bad here later on.

Zeugma. Like anticlimax this has to be used carefully if it is to have other than a merely ludicrous effect. It is when two items are placed alongside in the same syntactical position when, in truth, they cannot seriously accompany each other. For instance, one verb may take two objects in this way: *He swallowed the news and a cup of tea.* It can be cleverly used by the witty writer. cf. *He deserted the army and his wife.*

Zeugma is a form of *syllepsis*, a general term for all applications to two words of what can strictly be applied only to one. For instance, it is syllepsis when a verb following *either . . . or* and *neither . . . nor* agrees in number and person with only one of its subjects, e.g. *Neither he nor you is able to do it*: *is* agrees only with *he*, and to make the whole construction grammatically flawless it would have to be rewritten: *Neither he is able to do it nor you are able to do it*, which would be unidiomatic.

Another form of syllepsis is *hendiadys* (Greek=one by means of two), a figure in which a single idea is expressed by two independent constituents joined by a conjunction (usually *and*). 'So try *and* do better,' which really means try *to* do better; 'darkness and the death-hour' (E. B. Browning, 'Sonnets from the Portuguese', 22), which means *the darkness of the death-hour* or *the dark death-hour*.

Prolepsis. This is the use of an adjective as if it were already relevant whereas it only becomes so after the action of the context has occurred.
Examples:

> The negro knocked him *senseless* in the first round;
> The saboteurs shot him *dead*.

Hypallage. This figure, sometimes called *the transferred epithet*, transfers an adjective from the noun which it properly qualifies to another.
Example:

> The *friendly* sun eventually shone down on the huge crowd.

The sun cannot be friendly, it made the crowd feel friendly.
cf. I spent three *weary* hours there.

Antithesis. This is the device of putting two opposed statements, usually short sentences, alongside each other, without joining them by a conjunction or relative pronoun but merely separating them by a comma: thus the contrast of their assertions is heightened.
Examples:

> Animals do, man thinks before he does;
> Man thinks he knows, God knows.

A form of antithesis is the figure known as *chiasmus*, in which two opposing statements are balanced against each

109

other in a special way, the order of words being reversed in the second. A famous example is in St. Matthew's gospel: *He saved others; himself he cannot save.* This reversal of the grammatical order of words in the second statement is known as *anastrophe.* In our example the direct object, *himself,* precedes the verb governing it, *cannot save.*

Antonomasia. This is when the name of a famous personality, either from real life or from fiction, is used to typify a class of people:

A Daniel come to judgment;
He's a proper little Hitler;
He is the Jack Hobbs of our team.

A form of antonomasia is the appellative use by authors of nouns and adjectives as names for characters: i.e. their names betray their social status or personality: e.g. *Sir Benjamin Backbite, Lady Sneerwell* and *Mrs. Candour* in Sheridan's 'School for Scandal'; Addison's *Captain Sentry.* cf. such names in allegory.

Allegory. This is the use of words which gives them a double significance, a superficial one and an underlying and more important one. They mean both what they immediately say and what they ultimately imply. The best-known allegory in English is John Bunyan's 'Pilgrim's Progress', which can be read as an adventure story about Christian, Faithful, Giant Despair and so on, but whose real meaning is the struggle of the true Christian man or woman against the temptations and evils of the world. Fairy-stories and fables are forms of allegory. cf. 'Robinson Crusoe', 'Alice in Wonderland', the novels of T. F. Powys. cf., too, such poems as Spenser's 'The Faerie Queene' and Keats's 'Lamia'.

Allegory, therefore, is less an individual figure of speech

than a way of writing. A whole book can be allegorical. Yet it is possible for isolated words or single characters in a story or play to be used allegorically.

Abstract for Concrete

This is the name given to a way of writing which may be either good or bad according to the context in which it occurs. To say, for instance: Fear is the chief characteristic of *cowardice*, and *self-understanding* its only cure, i.e. using abstract nouns in generalized statement, is to use the abstract for the concrete. The concrete version of the sentence would be: The chief characteristic of *the coward* is fear, which he can cure only *by understanding himself*.

The Bad

Verbosity. Many of the following bad figures of speech are examples of verbosity, which is a generic term for all unnecessary words, whether single words or phrases, clauses or sentences. But the term is also more specifically applied to the use of long and tedious words when shorter ones are available, and to tortuous modes of expression. Verbosity is often ridiculous, and is probably the most serious sin any writer can commit. Thus, if all that need be said is: *He could not answer the accusation satisfactorily*, it would be verbose to write: *He was incapable of rendering a satisfactory rejoinder to the accusation.*

Official and *parliamentary* English is, for some reason, usually as verbose as language can be, not only in its vocabulary but in its constant use of all those little unnecessary phrases which are the very stuff of verbosity:

e.g. as to, in regard to, concerning the matter of, in respect of.

But jargon (q.v.) is the first-born of verbosity.

111

Tautology. It is tautologous to say exactly the same thing more than once:

e.g. The *true facts* of the case are these.

All facts are true, and so the use of the adjective in that sentence is tautologous. cf. The *general* run of events *taken as a whole . . .*

Pleonasm or Redundancy. This is the writing of words which are unnecessary because they add nothing to the sense of the passage. The commonest modern example is the use of *at all*, a phrase which is added to almost every statement: *There was nobody there at all.* Such colloquial adverbs as *awfully* and *really* are also always pleonastic.

cf. *The reason why I am fit is because I don't smoke*, which simply means *I am fit because I don't smoke.*

Solecism. A solecism is *an offence against grammar or idiom, blunder in the manner of speaking or writing* (C.O.D.).

Examples:

Me and my mates done it.
He ran very quick.

Euphemism. It is euphemism to express the unpleasant in a roundabout way instead of candidly:

e.g. *to pass away* for *to die*, *to fall* for *to be killed*, *queer* for *mad*, *to put to sleep* for *to kill.*

But euphemism has deep psychological origins. There are intelligible reasons for the underworld slang term *bracelets* instead of *handcuffs.*

Truism. This means the expression of what is so obvious and familiar that there is no need to say it. Without truism polite conversation would be impossible, but writing should be free from it. No good writer would say that *the sunshine made everything radiant and bright.*

Cliché. This is any *hackneyed literary phrase* (C.O.D.). It is any phrase which has become either completely or almost meaningless through excessive usage, and it would appear to be the easiest of all the bad figures to speak or write. For our language is cluttered with examples:

> e.g. last but not least, a foregone conclusion, grim determination, to make frantic efforts, a fine story finely told, shaking like a leaf.

The bad speaker and writer is quickly identifiable by his use of the cliché; the best by the absence from his words of even a single cliché.

Amphibology. Perhaps this should rank as a bad figure of speech, since good writing ought not to be ambiguous. For it means the expression of a statement in such a way that it may be interpreted in two ways—i.e. it is equivocal. The most common instance is *Feed a cold and starve a fever*, which may either contain two commands or mean that if you feed a cold then you will produce a fever which you will have to starve. It is possible that this particular saying has even more meanings than these two.

Jargon

The best introduction to this subject is the opening sentence of Sir Arthur Quiller-Couch's Cambridge lecture printed in 'The Art of Writing':

> I ask leave this morning to interpose some words upon a kind of writing which, from a superficial likeness, commonly passes for prose in these days, and by lazy folk is commonly written for prose, yet actually is not prose at all; my excuse

113

being the simple practical one that, by first clearing this sham prose out of the way, we shall the better deal with honest prose when we come to it.

According to the Concise Oxford Dictionary jargon is *Unintelligible words, gibberish; barbarous or debased language; mode of speech full of unfamiliar terms . . . twittering of birds.* Any writing, therefore, which is made up of unfamiliar words is made up of debased language and is as meaningful to our intelligence as the twittering of birds, and those who speak and write jargon may be said to twitter. But not all unfamiliar words are necessarily debased, and language is jargon only when the unfamiliar word is used in excess and deliberately; and although those who use jargon may truly be said to twitter, the twittering is not necessarily unintelligible. Every office clerk knows what is meant by such jargon as *Re yours of the 20th inst.* or *Your letter of even date to hand*; every foreign minister knows what is meant by *events of great importance in the international field*; and the rest of us also know what these things mean.

Jargon, therefore, need not be gibberish. The examples show what it is : a form of expression, developed by members of a profession or people with a common interest, a sort of private language which is fully intelligible to its speakers and writers and, because of its public diffusion, usually intelligible to, and often imitated by, the general public as well. And it is frequently meaningless when analysed and is always ugly.

Sometimes convention demands that we all should use it. Members of societies, for instance, must obey *standing orders* and speak their jargon, but such special contexts are excusable so long as the convention does not become a disease. And it is precisely because jargon has become a national disease that all who respect words and wish to express themselves as exactly as possible must be continuously on their guard against it and attacking it whenever opportunity occurs. For today governmental announcements, advertisements and films are filling the minds of millions of men and women with their jargon, their debased language, their twittering. The serious writer has a great duty to perform: to set a better example.

The following examples of jargon of one kind and another are all taken from published writing. Many of them are comic in the reading, but before we laugh we should make a solemn promise never to make such laughing-stocks of ourselves:

(a) The honourable member made a statement in which he came to a certain judgment;

(b) There has been advanced the possibility that the cause of the decay of Roman civilization is to be attributed to the fact that . . .;

(c) I think that picture is a dream: it is a most beautiful blending of form and line and colour, quite technically perfect;

(d) I consider this man to be on essential work which cannot be substituted by rearrangement of the existing staff;

(e) In order that you may be fully conversant with the position in regard to the application for deferment in respect of the above . . .;

(f) Today no birds of peace sit brooding on any charmed wave. War with its horrid convulsions shakes earth and air and sea;

(g) Countless of the young generation will, I am sure, support me if I say, thanks a million for putting the — orchestra on the air. It is nothing short of terrific;

(h) Transitoriness is everywhere plunging into a profound Being. And therefore all the forms of the here and now are not merely to be used in a time-limited way, but, so far as we can, instated within those superior significances in which we share;

(i) She was so beautiful: golden hair falling around her shoulders; big blue eyes, adorable nose, lips made to kiss and a Venus-like figure. Love came to me with a song when I saw her like a vision, enchanting as a dream;

(j) But at these stages art remains overwhelmingly com-

115

munal. The individual accretions are so small and so homogeneous with previous accretions that the enlargement and re-adaptation of the patterns can be treated only as a communal act.

9

The Craft of Composition: The Essay and the Short Story

Foreword

THIS chapter deals with the craft of composition as it applies to the essay and the short story, both of which are still—and perhaps rightly—thought to be good examination tests of one's ability to write originally at some length and in a definite form. The essay and the short story are, nevertheless, considered here as literary forms. The chapter does not deal with the new testing—now common to C.S.E., G.C.E. and Use of English examinations—which requires the translating of data, whether in words, figures or diagrams, into continuous and designed prose. For this objective writing, like the making of notes and the answering of comprehension, is not really analysable and does not need the definition and illustration that are the chief contents of this book.

Though the essay and the short story are literary forms, however, they are, like the letter, forms which everyone can try to use for personal purposes. So the rare creators, the Addisons, Lambs, Bierces and Chekhov, may set the high standard, but they are not to be aped. It is ourselves we have to express.

Here, then, *form* is discussed, those forms which distinguish the essay and the short story from other prose compositions. Examinees who have to write essays, be it for

117

half an hour or for three hours, perhaps cannot write as well as Charles Lamb—certainly no one can repeat his individual style—but they can write *what* he wrote, in the same form as he used, i.e. the essay, if they understand what makes a prose composition an essay. And the would-be author who tries his hand at short-story writing may never be able to write as well as Ambrose Bierce, but he will also not write a short story at all if he does not know what it is that distinguishes the short story from all other forms of prose fiction.

The Essay

> An essay-writer must practise in the chemical method,
> and give the virtue of a full draught in a few drops.
> (ADDISON.)

The Concise Oxford Dictionary defines an essay as 'a literary composition (usu. prose and short) on any subject'. (There have been essays in verse, such as those of Alexander Pope, but they were a very special kind of essay, and in this chapter we are concerned with prose.) This definition tells us two at least of the essay's characteristics: (i) however long it may be, it is always comparatively short, short when compared with a treatise or a book; and (ii) it can be written about any subject.

Essays may be very long—those by Thomas Carlyle often are—but the best are quite short, ranging from two or three to about twelve pages of the average-size book. For it is not in the normal nature of the essay to extend for any great length.

Since everything, from cabbages to kings, can be the subject-matter of the essay, it follows that the nature of the essay is also variable in mood and manner. It may be light-hearted or serious, comic or tragic, factual or fantastic,

118

simply descriptive or intricately analytical, suggestive or belligerent. It is the chameleon of prose.

It is nevertheless a distinct prose-form, and as such has its own personality.

The chief element in this is its method of treatment, for although it is not alone in its adaptability to any subject, it is alone in that it discusses its subject (i.e. its title) not as a whole but in only one of its aspects (i.e. the theme of the essay). From this single aspect, however, a general conclusion about the subject as a whole is evinced. No matter how localized or vague the subject, no matter how large or small in scope and importance, only one of its aspects, manifestations or facets is discussed; but out of this some all-embracing conclusion or main point emerges, not about the aspect itself but about the subject itself. This aspect, therefore, this theme, is a medium towards this conclusion: it is a method of treatment. Every detail, every word in the essay, must serve this single theme, this function and purpose. There may be constant variation played on the theme, meditated or improvised, but the theme is always there, the foundation and well-spring of the whole essay.

Combined with this singularity of theme there is an internal shape or form, an inner orderliness, which gives the essay its artistic character. It falls into three sections:

1 the introduction;
2 the amplification;
3 the conclusion,

which are, however, not three independent sections but three parts of a continuous whole. There may be no breaks between them; there may be a break between the first and second only or the second and third only; or there may be breaks at both points. Probably the best essays are those in which the frontiers are not precisely fixed.

119

These sections correspond to what Aristotle called the beginning, middle and end of a work of art. An essay must make a definite start, impressing upon the reader the assurance that it could not have commenced with any other words or at any earlier or later stage. Its first section must be entirely new and fresh, so that the reader may feel that he is meeting an original conception of the subject; and it must make clear to him what sort of an experience he is about to have, what he may expect to learn, whither he may expect to be taken.

The essay must then proceed to a detailed exposition of its theme in the second section, and move towards an ending no less definite than its beginning, impressing upon the reader the assurance that it could not have ended with any other words or at any earlier or later stage.

The introduction is necessarily a short section in comparison with the length of the whole essay; yet its duration depends on the simplicity or complexity of the theme which is to be introduced. The very first sentences may be a fanfare startling the reader by their magnificence or a quiet announcement simply requesting the reader's attention.

The amplification is the largest section, for it is the main body of the essay, incorporating most of the details which illustrate, prove and vary the theme and lead towards the conclusion. They include arguments, descriptions, personal experiences and reminiscences, anecdotes, quotations and so on. Both the first and the third sections will also require some of these, but there they are subordinated to the main purposes of introduction and conclusion: in the amplification they themselves are the main purpose.

The conclusion is, like the introduction, comparatively short. The reason for the essay's existence, the purpose of the second section, is now made clear. Echoes are heard of the details in the second section, and there is a final reference back to—never a mere repetition of—the introduction to show how the direction there indicated has been followed. The theme, which, though omnipresent in the second section, has retreated into the background as the essay has progressed, now resumes the dominant role it played in the introduction. The final words may ascend to a grand peroration or descend to a quiet and informal dismissal.

The essay is the most personal of all impersonal prose compositions, and the art of writing it lies in the subtle combination of these two contradictory elements, the direct and the indirect. It is at once formal and informal, aloof and intimate, a literary creation and a fireside chat. Its form is at once fixed and fluid. It must have its single theme and its three sections, but it may vary that theme and mingle or separate those sections at will. The plan is certain, but its adaptation is left to the individual whim of the writer. How this is so, how an essay is unmistakably itself while being capriciously variable, is best realized in a reading of the essays of experts like Addison and Lamb. Lamb's essays are the best examples in English of the adaptability of the form to mood and subject, but Addison's are the best examples of the form itself. They are, indeed, models of the art, intimate yet always formal, single-minded yet full of variety, beautifully constructed, fragile yet durable. An analysis of one of them will reveal the blue-print on which they were all planned and show how it is both the master and the servant of the writer.

Its title is 'Ladies' Head-dresses', its single theme their undesirability, especially when they are extravagant, and its conclusion that the human head does not need such artificial adornment. The three sections are skilfully made dependent upon one another, the first two being continuous and the only break coming between the second and the third.

121

LADIES' HEAD-DRESSES

Tanta est quaerendi cura decoris.
(Juv. Sat. vi. 500.)
So studiously their persons they adorn.
(The theme of the essay is already summarized in a prefatory quotation, and the conclusion is already implied.)

There is not so variable a thing in nature as a lady's head-dress. (A memorably definite opening sentence.) Within my own memory, I have known it rise and fall above thirty degrees. About ten years ago it shot up to a very great height, insomuch that the female part of our species were much taller than the men. The women were of such an enormous stature, that 'we appeared as grasshoppers before them'. At present the whole sex is in a manner dwarfed, and shrunk into a race of beauties that seems almost another species. I remember several ladies, who were once very near seven foot high, that at present want some inches of five. How they came to be thus curtailed I cannot learn; whether the whole sex be at present under any penance which we know nothing of; or whether they have cast their head-dresses in order to surprise us with something in that kind which shall be entirely new; or whether some of the tallest of the sex, being too cunning for the rest, have contrived this method to make themselves appear sizeable—is still a secret; though I find most are of opinion, they are at present like trees new lopped and pruned, that will certainly sprout up and flourish with greater heads than before. (The theme of the essay is being built up in this introduction, which is now about to point forward to the conclusion and move into the amplification.) For my own part, as I do not love to be insulted by women who are taller than myself (we cannot have any doubt that this is a light-hearted essay), I admire the sex much more in their present humiliation, which has reduced them to their natural dimensions, than when they had extended their persons and lengthened themselves into formidable and gigantic figures. I am not for adding to the beautiful edifices of nature, nor for raising any whimsical super-structure upon her plans: I must therefore repeat it, that I am highly pleased with the coiffure now in fashion, and think it shows the good sense which at present very much reigns among the valuable part of the sex. (The direction of the essay is now clear: we know exactly to what the reference-back in the conclusion will be: and we now move, within the same paragraph, into the second section.) One may observe that women in all ages have taken more pains than men to adorn the outside of their heads; and indeed I very much admire, that those female architects, who raise such wonderful structures out of ribands, lace, and wire, have not been recorded for their respective inventions. It is certain there have been as many orders in these kinds of buildings, as in those which have been made of marble. Sometimes they rise in the shape of a pyramid (we are getting down to the details now), sometimes like a tower, and sometimes like a steeple. In Juvenal's time the building grew by several orders and stories, as he has very humorously described it:

Tot premit ordinibus, tot adhuc compagibus altum
Aedificat caput; Andromachen a fronte videbis;
Post minor est; aliam credas.

(Juv. Sat. vi. 501.)

With curls on curls they build her head before,
And mount it with a formidable tow'r;
A giantess she seems; but look behind,
And then she dwindles to the pigmy kind.

(DRYDEN.)

But I do not remember in any part of my reading, that the head-dress aspired to so great an extravagance as in the fourteenth century; when it was built up in a couple of cones or spires, which stood so exceedingly high on each side of the head, that a woman, who was but a pigmy without her head-dress, appeared like a colossus upon putting it on. Monsieur Paradin says, 'that these old-fashioned fontanges rose an ell above the head; that they were pointed like steeples, and had long loose pieces of crape fastened to the tops of them, which were curiously fringed, and hung down their backs like streamers.'

(More and more details are being introduced now, and Addison ends his first paragraph here: the new one is to recount an anecdote as further evidence and further variation.)

123

The women might possibly have carried this Gothic building much higher, had not a famous monk, Thomas Conecte by name, attacked it with great zeal and resolution. This holy man travelled from place to place to preach down this monstrous commode; and succeeded so well in it, that, as the magicians sacrificed their books to the flames upon the preaching of an apostle, many of the women threw down their head-dresses in the middle of the sermon and made a bonfire of them within sight of the pulpit. He was so renowned as well for the sanctity of his life as his manner of preaching, that he had often a congregation of twenty thousand people; the men placing themselves on the one side of his pulpit, and the women on the other, that appeared (to use the similitude of an ingenious writer) like a forest of cedars with their heads reaching to the clouds. He so warmed and animated the people against this monstrous ornament, that it lay under a kind of persecution; and whenever it appeared in public, was pelted down by the rabble, who flung stones at the persons that wore it. But notwithstanding this prodigy vanished while the preacher was among them, it began to appear again some months after his departure, or, to tell it in Monsieur Paradin's own words, 'the women that, like snails in a fright, had drawn in their horns, shot them out again as soon as the danger was over'. This extravagance of the women's head-dresses in that age, is taken notice of by Monsieur D'Argentre in his history of Bretagne, and by other historians, as well as the person I have here quoted.

(That is the end of the amplification. The conclusion now begins and the essay moves inevitably to its close. The original theme of the introduction is heard again but with greater emphasis, the point of the essay is driven home, and the last words rise in tone to a final proclamation in which the very first words of the essay are echoed.)

It is usually observed that a good reign is the only proper time for making laws against the exorbitance of power; in the same manner an excessive head-dress may be attacked the most effectually when the fashion is against it. I do therefore recommend this paper to my female readers by way of prevention.

I would desire the fair sex to consider how impossible it is for them to add anything that can be ornamental to what is

THE CRAFT OF COMPOSITION

already the masterpiece of nature. The head has the most beautiful appearance, as well as the highest station, in a human figure. Nature has laid out all her art in beautifying the face; she has touched it with vermilion, planted in it a double row of ivory, made it the seat of smiles and blushes, lighted it up and enlivened it with the brightness of the eyes, hung it on each side with curious organs of sense, given it airs and graces that cannot be described, and surrounded it with such a flowing shade of hair as sets all its beauties in the most agreeable light. In short, she seems to have designed the head as the cupola to the most glorious of her works: and when we load it with such a pile of supernumerary ornaments, we destroy the symmetry of the human figure, and foolishly contrive to call off the eye from great and real beauties, to childish gewgaws, ribands, and bone-lace.

That is about the average length of all Addison's hundreds of essays in 'The Spectator'. It has all the polish and moralizing of the eighteenth century writer, but it is a perfect example of the essay-form. The balance between the personal and the impersonal is kept, the lightheartedness is never allowed to degenerate into farce nor the seriousness allowed to extend into the realm of piety. The intention is serious, but the manner is gentle. The essay is an artistic whole, without a superfluous word and requiring no additions. It does indeed give the virtue of a full draught in a few drops.

Let us now turn to a recent essayist, Robert Lynd, and see how he too followed the plan outlined above. The essay which follows was one of his 'Saturday Essays' in the 'News Chronicle', and is entitled 'The Right to a Workman's Ticket':

It was reported during the week that railway companies were refusing to allow clerks working on Sundays to return home after 4 p.m. on workmen's tickets on the ground that such a privilege could be extended only to the 'bonafide workmen'.

This decision raises once more the old question: 'what is a

125

reasonable definition of the words 'work', 'workman' and "working man"?'

(The introduction ends there: it is very short, but the theme is clearly stated in the second paragraph and the conclusion is implied: that all who work are workmen and so ought to be allowed to travel on workmen's tickets after 4 p.m. on Sundays.)

I remember some years ago (the details are commencing) hearing a famous professional cricketer asking an equally famous professional footballer how he would define 'work'. 'Well,' said the professional footballer, 'work is something you're paid to do.' From this point of view, Jack Hobbs, playing cricket, was a worker, but P. F. Warner was not. Yet from another point of view, Sir Pelham Warner, as he now is, probably had to work even harder than Hobbs, as he bore the additional responsibility of being the captain of his side.

As I listened to this definition of work, it seemed to me that the old distinction between amateur and professional cricketers as Gentlemen and Players ought to be abandoned since the so-called gentlemen are the real Players, whereas the professionals could be more accurately described as Workers.

I should like to see a match between Players and Workers at Lord's, but I doubt whether it would have quite the same appeal as a match in the Gentlemen versus Players tradition, misleading though this name is.

I doubt, however, whether work can be satisfactorily defined as 'something that you are paid to do'. The late Lord Salisbury, when he was Prime Minister, insisted that by any test of industry he and his like belonged to the working classes. He accepted a few thousand pounds a year, no doubt, when he was in office, but I fancy that, rather than not be allowed to do the job at all, he would have done it for nothing.

Mr. Winston Churchill seems to me to be one of the hardest-worked working men who ever lived. Yet when he builds a wall in his garden—to say nothing of his political and literary activities—few people regard this as evidence that he is a representative member of the working classes.

Though born with an antipathy to work, I consider that I myself have been a working man for the greater part of my life. A communist friend maintains that I am only a bourgeois since I have never done any manual labour in my life. But—apart from digging in the garden, which I used to do twenty years or so ago—I contend that I am perpetually engaged in manual labour, pushing a pencil day after day across sheets of paper as a ploughman drives his plough across acre after acre.

(The amplification, while still continuing, now begins to lead into the conclusion, the only break in this essay being between the first and second sections. The opening statement of the essay is echoed at this stage, and echoed once again right at the end when the conclusion is directly pronounced.)

Yet, toil as I may, the railways will not apparently recognize me as a working man to the point of allowing me to travel after 4 p.m. on Sundays on a workman's ticket.

Most of us, of course, are inclined to regard the work that other people do as easy. I used to think that a clergyman's life was easy till I accompanied a clergyman who was ill on his day's round, beginning with a funeral and ending with a prayer-meeting in the evening. At the end of the day, limp as a rag, I congratulated myself on never having become a clergyman.

And you will find that it is the same with almost any kind of work. I would not, for example, be a Member of Parliament, with his committees and his constituents, for £10,000 a year. Even a magistrate, sitting on the Bench from morning to night, trying to discover whether somebody was really drunk and disorderly or not, seems to me to lead a harder life than that of a journalist.

As small boys, most of us have envied policemen, engine-drivers and tram-conductors; but I suspect that, at the end of twenty-four hours in any of these capacities, we should be glad we had chosen an easier career.

All my life I have longed for a soft job, but I have come to the conclusion that there is no such thing as a soft job. The only possible exception I can think of is that of a bathing-box attendant. I think on the whole that I should have been a better bathing-box attendant than Member of Parliament.

Some years ago, Lady Astor asked in Parliament: 'What is a working-class woman?' and Mr. Kirkwood replied: 'The answer is obvious; you are not a working-class woman. It is

127

the class that clothes you and makes your bed.'

But is the answer quite as obvious as that? After all, there are many women who make their own clothes for nothing, and their own beds for nothing. I should certainly call Lady Astor a working woman. The difference between her and other working women lies not in the amount of work done in the course of a year so much as in the greater amount of freedom, economic and other, she enjoys.

As for the clerk, he at least enjoys few of Lady Astor's advantages, and surely deserves the honourable appellation of 'workman' as much as I do. (We have now returned to the clerk of the introduction.)

Like me, he is a trade unionist. Like me, he probably wishes he were a millionaire and could lie in bed in the morning. Like me, unfortunately, he is under the curse of Adam; and it seems to me that anybody who is under the curse of Adam should have the right to go home on the railway after 4 p.m. on Sunday on a workman's ticket.

The sections of this essay are not so well balanced as those of Addison's essay, but it is nonetheless a very good example of the essay-form. The amplification is an admirable succession of illustrations of the theme, which is single and clear, and the conclusion follows inevitably from it. A definite start is made and a definite end is reached. The title itself is limited in scope, yet other themes were possible and Lynd has not allowed them to upset the inherent unity of his essay.

But we must expect experts to write good essays, and it is easy to analyse the best. The following short essay was written by a group of boys in collaboration, working carefully to the essay-plan. They did not set out to write great literature but an interesting little essay, with the emphasis on the last word. It is called 'New Clothes':

The secret behind man's delight in new clothes is the vanity which is in us all. The money which a new suit may cost, and the sacrifices which may be entailed in the finding of that

THE CRAFT OF COMPOSITION

money, may occasion personal hardship, for the buyer, but he thinks it worthwhile to endure them.

Behind the scenes a man may go hungry in order that he may save out of his meagre earnings enough to buy the suit on which he has set his heart. And this is not the only hardship which he may voluntarily suffer. He may work longer hours and come home tired and disagreeable, to a supper cold because he has spent ten instead of eight hours at the conveyor-belt. And then, cold mashed potatoes lying heavily on his stomach, the fire nearly out and his wife and children already in bed, he has neither time nor energy to do more than drag himself up the stairs and collapse into bed to dream fitfully of his new suit swirling past him on the conveyor-belt to destruction. His tiredness, his indigestion and his loneliness gradually increase until that wonderful day—it must be Saturday—when, wellnigh a physical and mental wreck, he goes to the tailor to take possession of his reward.

Still his sacrifices may not be ended. His suit, ready-made and not of the best cloth, may be stiff and uncomfortable, so that the very thought of sitting down appals him. Worst blow of all, his wife may show her disapproval of it by refusing even to walk beside him, and the loneliness which he has endured to obtain it may not only continue but become still more intolerable.

The young man who boasted that he could write a sonnet,

'About your Easter bonnet,'

may find himself, in the pride of his new suit (without even an inside pocket, if it is war-time), eclipsed by what the onlooker considers a very foolish hat indeed. But this is the very problem of vanity. The female wearer seems prepared to transform herself into a not very distant relative of the scarecrow merely because her vanity drives her to wear something different. Even though packs of small, impudent boys chase milady shouting, 'Where did you get that hat?' she must pretend not to hear them. For she may have got that hat, as her young man got his suit, at much personal sacrifice, paying for it a price far in excess of her week's earnings. Yet even had she found the money easily and bought the hat at the most exclusive shop, her pride in it is still too strong to

129

allow her to heed the sly insults of adults let alone the frank scorn of small boys.

For man must have his pride, and although new clothes must one day be bought to replace old ones past respectable wearing, the buyer's joy in them is the joy of pride. And it is not of arrogance that we speak but of natural pride, the pride in a good possession obtained at the expense sometimes of indigestion, sometimes of the naughty cries of urchins.

Let us not scoff, then, at the factory worker in his new suit or milady in her new hat. For we all have our pride. One man is proud of his poems, another of his garden; one woman is proud of her home, another of her knitting. Even the rich woman is too proud to go to more than one cocktail party in the same dress. This world is, however, often dull; it would be a lesser place without new clothes and every man's vanity in the wearing of them.

The writers have not tried to say everything about new clothes, but have selected the single aspect of vanity, and that is the theme of their essay and is never lost sight of. The conclusion to which it leads during the essay is that although new clothes may sometimes be ridiculous and bought only with much self-sacrifice, yet man is proud and his love of new clothes is at least an innocent demonstration of his pride, and the new clothes themselves are an honest source of pleasure.

The introduction is a very short section, ending with the first paragraph. The theme is made clear, however, and the section leads into the amplification, the words *sacrifices* and *hardship* being immediately illustrated by the details of the second paragraph. Perhaps the declaration of the theme in the opening sentence is a little too obvious, but the reader does know the direction which the essay is to take.

The amplification is, as usual, the biggest section, stretching to the end of the fourth paragraph. Two illustrations are given, two variations presented: the factory worker and his new suit, the lady and the new hat. The section is linked to the conclusion by the conjunction *For* and the defence of the factory worker and milady in the first sentence of the conclusion. And now the theme is again clearly heard, the point of this theme is announced, echoes are heard of the details of the amplification, and a final reference-back is made to the opening sentence of the introduction.

The essay made a definite start, almost too definite a start, and it came inevitably to its close. It is not of course a great essay: it is perhaps too self-consciously written to a plan; but it is unmistakably an essay.

How, then, did Addison and Lynd and these boys know what to say about such seemingly uninspiring subjects as ladies' head-dresses, workmen's railway tickets and new clothes? Probably the commonest complaint made by those who write essays—or try to write essays—only because they are compelled to in order to pass examinations, is that although they are told that essays can be written about anything, and although they are ready to believe this (for there is ample proof of it), they themselves never know what to write. One can answer only by repeating that an essay can be written about anything, and that they are unable to write at any length simply because they will not do what is implied in that statement. For if they will only allow their imaginations to play with the subject set, they will be surprised how much there is to say about it; and they will find themselves forced to obey the rules which, however loosely, do govern the form of an essay, in order to select from the mass of material which their imaginations have conjured up that fraction of it which is all they will have time to write about.

The following history of an essay—for which I am indebted to an essay-writing friend—may help them to solve their problem.

The title he chose was 'Afternoons', which on first notice would seem to be as unproductive as any title could be, but

131

is, by reason of its very vagueness, ideal.

To begin with, therefore, the writer had nothing but that word before him: he had no theme and no conclusion. He would have to let his imagination loose upon it according to the psychological law of the association of ideas, jotting down the ideas as they came in the section to which they seemed appropriate. The following is a copy of the 'outline for an essay' which he made in the first quarter of an hour or so of the time allotted to him:

1. INTRODUCTION:	Somehow a different part of the day from morning and evening (night)—a sort of gap between the other two (or a bridge between them?)—the ugly sister of two Cinderellas—seems little purpose in it (in life itself)—but what about the convalescent patient who is allowed to get up in the afternoon?—it's the most important part of the day to him—it is Cinderella, the others are the ugly sisters.
2. AMPLIFICATION:	Consider what writers have said—what have poets had to say about it?—anything?—plenty about morning: Shakespeare's 'Full many . . '—Shelley's 'radiant lines'—plenty about night too: 'How beautiful is night' (by ?)—'sable goddess' (by ?)— Shelley's 'Wrap thy form . . .'—but what about afternoon? —can remember only Shakespeare's 'posteriors of the day'— and Tennyson in 'Lotos-Eaters': 'always afternoon' and 'languid air'—that's the secret—it's the languid part of the day—nature droops—batsmen settle down—relaxation—siesta —after-dinner nap—idleness—but what of games in winter?—only a minority concerned anyway—most people still waiting for this interval (vacuum) to pass away.

3. CONCLUSION: So afternoon a sort of hiatus—they sleep in hot climates—poets too must have been too drowsy to write—even at the thought of it—only convalescent patient, therefore, does appreciate it.

Thus he had a plan to work to and the essay would develop and come to life in the actual writing: improvisation on a theme already decided upon is one of the chief characteristics of the best essays. The theme that he required had soon come to the fore: that the afternoon is a purposeless gap in the day between the morning and the evening; and his conclusion, based on the opening illustration of this, was to be that we have to be convalescent patients before we can appreciate the fact that the afternoon can even be the most purposeful and important part of the day.

It is clear from the notes quoted that the theme, direction and spirit of the essay would be known from the start, and the conclusion implied. The details of the amplification were all relevant and would lead surely into the conclusion, in which they could be echoed and the final return to the original statement of the theme could be made. In fact, the notes are such that one feels that the essay could almost have written itself. The writer would not fold up his imagination and put it away: it would still be actively clothing and adorning the bare framework which was all that he had written so far. And this was the result, not a formless, pointless series of observations but an essay:

AFTERNOONS

The convalescent patient who one winter's afternoon rises from his bed to walk the spacious arena of his room and see the thick snow glistening beneath the sun, may well be glad that he is alive. Elsewhere in the world there may be battle and violent death, wounds and despair, but for him life may yet be full of meaning, and if he is blessed with vision he knows what a multiplicity of tasks is occupying men at that very moment; the great variety of the world gladdens his heart and makes him satisfied to be alive and with eyes to see the snow and the sun. The afternoon is tolerable for him.

And perhaps he may meditate upon this phenomenon of afternoon, which, though being a part of the endless process of time and so sharing in the ever-expanding significance of eternity, is always the ugly sister of those two Cinderellas, Morning and Night. Poor afternoon, he may say, despised and abused. Who has dared to sing your praises?

Well may he ask. For the praises of Morning and Night have been on the lips of all our greatest poets. Shelley tells us of the 'radiant lines' of Morning, and Shakespeare lavishes on her all his Elizabethan genius:

> 'Full many a glorious morning have I seen
> Flatter the mountain-tops with sovereign eye,
> Kissing with golden face the meadows green,
> Gilding pale streams with heavenly alchemy.'

'How beautiful is night!' sang another, and still another spoke of her as a 'sable goddess'. Shelley devoted a whole poem to her, so enamoured of her lethean beauty was he:

> 'Wrap thy form in a mantle gray,
>   Star-inwrought!
> Blind with thine hair the eyes of Day;
> Kiss her until she be wearied-out,
> Then wander o'er city, and sea, and land,
> Touching all with thine opiate wand—
>   Come, long-sought!'

Fortunate, then, have these two sisters been, for they are indeed blessed to whom the poets do homage and pay court. But what of the third member of the family, the ugly-duckling afternoon? She is as loth to die as her sisters and as enamoured of praise, yet all that the prince of poets has deigned to say of her is that she is the name by which 'the rude multitude' call 'the posteriors of the day'. Still, one true poet did not forget her. It was the land of the Lotos-eaters that Tennyson called:

'A land
In which it seemed always afternoon,'

a land around whose coast 'the languid air did swoon'.

The poet has, as usual, found the one perfect word of description. The afternoon is the languid time of day, when the snow melts more gently, man has fed and is indolent, the cricketers settle down to a steady game, the cows droop in the corner of the field, the flowers blink tired eyes and the lizard sleeps. Only the overstrong and the underpaid remain active, yet they too must relax a little when the heat of the sun commands languor. Even along the Siegfried line and in the Burmese jungle guns fired more leisurely and jeeps travelled a mile or so less per hour. It is a time for relaxation and idle conversation, for Menelaus to wax garrulous and sack a hundred Troys, and for his hearers to nod.

It will be argued that that, however, is not the whole story, for is not the afternoon the time for sport? Only in the summer do sportsmen settle down to a steady game, and then only in games of long duration which have known the morning's fury and will know the evening's rush 'to beat the clock'. In the Winter and the Spring there is no afternoon relaxation for the right-wing three-quarter or the centre-half, none for the crowd of partisans who have come to watch, the majority of them standing throughout the whole performance.

But on reflection one sees that such expenditure of energy is, after all, exceptional. The multitudes of men are not massed along the touch-line at three o'clock in cold or heat, sunshine or rain, but confined to the desk, the bench, the lathe, the counter, the driving-seat or the earth or wherever the struggle for existence is waged. And all are glad when three o'clock has passed, and four o'clock with it. The morning may drift slowly by, but it is morning and somehow has a purpose; and evening brings the end of the day's work, the journey home and the night to oneself and one's dreams. But the afternoon is an unreal hiatus, a gap, an abhorred vacuum, like a lingering pause between two realities, a day-dream from which one is glad to awaken. Or so it is in the western hemisphere: in the East they are luckier, for nature commands them to enjoy the full languor of sleep.

135

This, then, must be why the poets have ignored the afternoon: they too were drowsy. And perhaps it is significant that only to the convalescent patient is the truth revealed. For to him the afternoon is not an unreal interlude between two realities, but an interval of reality between two acts in a play. Like the faun, he inhabits another world where reality is 'always afternoon'.

The following titles are offered to students as typical of those set in public examinations:

(a) DESCRIPTIVE:	Life on a farm; Prehistoric Times; Bees; Beggars; The ideal home; The Post Office; Plants; The Fun of the Fair; Christmas; Noise; A boating expedition; My happiest experience; Gypsies; Rivers; Neighbours; My town (or village).
(b) ANALYTICAL:	Militarism; Diaries; National Characteristics; The function of the journalist; Fashions; The Price of Peace; 'Art makes men immortal'; Pride; Ambition; Dreams; The value of a university education; The best books.
(c) CONTROVERSIAL:	'Patriotism is not enough'; School awards and punishments; Conscription; Pacifism; 'Science has revealed nothing but evil'; 'Progress is impossible'.
(d) FANTASTIC:	Castles in the air; Fairies; Through the looking-glass; Visions; On being absurd; 'Ever let the fancy roam'.

The Short Story

The only good definition of the short story yet written is that it is 'a story that is not long'; and yet that leaves out of account the important matter of technique and so needs defining: for what is meant by 'not long'? Tolstoy's 'Family Happiness', which is usually classed as a short story, is 15000 words long; but the average length of stories published today is between 3500 and 5000 words, and the parables of Jesus are much less than 1000 words long. In fact, there is no literary law about the length of the short story, and perhaps all we can say is that if a short story is very, very short, then it is only an anecdote, and if it is very, very long then it is unlikely to be a short story at all.

It is arguable, however, that Tolstoy's story and the so-called 'long-short' stories of writers like Conrad and Stevenson are really short novels, or, as the French call them, 'novelettes'; for to be a short story proper, a work of fiction has to obey certain general principles which necessarily limit its length. These principles may be seen in the earliest forms of the short story: old legends, myths, fables and parables: all the tales of giants and fairies, monsters and heroes the world over: Perseus, Theseus and the Minotaur, the Arthurian legend, Boccaccio's 'Il Decamerone', The Fables of Aesop and La Fontaine.

In English literature the long pre-history of the modern short story includes the verse-tales of Chaucer and Gower, the old ballads, the tales of Froissart and Hakluyt, 'The Travels of Sir John Mandeville', Swift's 'A Tale of a Tub', the journalistic tales-cum-essays by Steele and Addison in 'The Tatler' and 'The Spectator', and Goldsmith's 'The Man in Black' and 'Beau Tibbs'.

But as we now know it, the short story has had a comparatively brief career of barely a hundred years. For the two writers who gave it its modern form, the Russian, Nicolai Gogol, and the American, Edgar Allan Poe, died little more than a century ago.

What, then, is it as we now know it? What, in brief, is the short-story method? H. E. Bates, one of our most successful writers in this form, has well described it: 'The short story, whether short or long, poetical or reported, plotted or sketched, concrete or cobweb, has an insistent and eternal

137

fluidity that slips through the hands.' For its shape is tenuous and its character endlessly changeable. It may be comic like those of the American, Damon Runyon, or tragic like those of the Russian, Chekhov; it may be realistic like those of James Joyce, analytical like those of Katherine Mansfield, horrific like those of M. R. James, fantastic like those of Ambrose Bierce, absurd like those of William Saroyan. And yet it is always itself; because although its shape is tenuous it does have a shape, it is given one by its unique method of economic suggestion, or suggestive economy. For in it there is no room for digression, elaboration and expansive detail. From first word to last it has to be tuned to the highest pitch of concentration, for whereas a novel is an hour, or a day, a week or a century, the short story is a moment. Time stops and the short story grips it tight before it starts up again, and into that moment of timelessness it has to pack its all. A novel may be a panorama, but a short story is a glimpse; a novel may be history, but a short story is an incident. But eternity must be caught in that glimpse and that incident.

The art of the short story is therefore the art of suggestion and impression, telescopic like the art of the camera: its technique is that of the cinematographic close-up. It needs neither plot nor action, neither characterization nor scenic description. In the hands of William Saroyan, for example, it can, as H. E. Bates has said, 'be stripped of every shred of convention, turned inside out and upside down, and yet remain the short story'.

To write a good short story is thus an extremely difficult task, and the gift of accomplishment is bestowed on few of the thousands of its would-be writers. But we cannot know whether or not we have this gift unless we ourselves allow it every chance of revealing itself. One of the ways of doing this, and the only way to understand exactly what the short story is in all its types, is to read the best stories. The following are suggested as being among the finest examples:

'The Signalman' by Charles Dickens;

'A Horseman in the Sky' by Ambrose Bierce;

'The Dead' by James Joyce;

'The Gardener' by Rudyard Kipling;

'The Masque of the Red Death' by Edgar Allan Poe;

'The Mezzotint' by M. R. James;

'The Rocking-Horse Winner' by D. H. Lawrence;

'The Dancers' by Eric Linklater;

'The Withered Arm' by Thomas Hardy;

'The Monkey's Paw' by W. W. Jacobs.

The following are the names of some of the best short-story writers:

ENGLISH AND AMERICAN: H. E. Bates, Ambrose Bierce, Algernon Blackwood, Elizabeth Bowen, G. K. Chesterton, Wilkie Collins, Lord Dunsany, Caradoc Evans, Thomas Hardy, W. W. Jacobs, Henry James, M. R. James, James Joyce, Rudyard Kipling, D. H. Lawrence, Eric Linklater, Katherine Mansfield, Walter de la Mare, H. H. Munro ('Saki'), Frank O'Connor, Edgar Allan Poe, T. F. Powys, Damon Runyon, William Saroyan, H. G. Wells, Oscar Wilde.

FRENCH: H. de Balzac, Anatole France, Guy de Maupassant, E. Zola.

RUSSIAN: Dostoevsky, Gogol, Chekhov, Tolstoy, Turgenev.

The following analysis of a famous short story will show in action the technique only sketched above. It is Ambrose Bierce's 'A Horseman in the Sky', which may be read in the collection of his stories entitled 'In the Midst of Life'.

The very first sentence takes us with laconic suddenness to the scene of the action and introduces us to the chief figure:

> One sunny afternoon in the autumn of the year 1861, a soldier lay in a clump of laurel by the side of a road in Western Virginia.

139

We are told that 'He was asleep at his post of duty'. We are expectant, the atmosphere is heavy with uncertainty: we have been told so much so briefly.

Some panoramic description of the natural setting follows: the soldier was lying on a spur of a cliff: there was a 'large flat rock' jutting out which he could see if awake: the valley was a sheer drop below: 'It might well have made him giddy to look.' The valley seemed shut in, but in it 'lay five regiments of Federal infantry' resting before climbing at night along the only road and surprising the enemy camp on 'the other slope of the ridge'. They were in a 'military rat-trap', and their sentinel was asleep.

It is important to observe the writer's technique so far. The brief, broad description of this setting does not open the story: the sleeping soldier is introduced first, and the dread of something tragic happening as a result of his crime is created from the start. The opening of a short story has to startle the reader in this way, for there is no time, as there is in a novel, to build up a plot gradually. Once the surprise has been sprung, however, some account of the general position can be given.

At this point it is relevant to quote the openings of a few other famous short stories to show how their authors take us at the first moment and without any preliminaries to the incident about to be related:

(i) 'The Sisters' by James Joyce:

There was no hope for him this time: it was the third stroke. Night after night I had passed the house (it was vacation time) and studied the lighted square of window: and night after night I had found it lighted in the same way, faintly and evenly. If he was dead, I thought, I would see the reflection of candles on the darkened blind, for I knew that two candles must be set at the head of a corpse.

(ii) 'The Facts in the Case of M. Valdemar' by Edgar Allan Poe:

Of course I shall not pretend to consider it any matter for wonder, that the extraordinary case of M. Valdemar has excited discussion. It would have been a miracle had it not—especially under the circumstances. Through the desire of all parties concerned, to keep the affair from the public, at least for the present, or until we had further opportunities for investigation—through our endeavours to effect this—a garbled or exaggerated account made its way into society, and became the source of many unpleasant misrepresentations, and, very naturally, of a great deal of disbelief.

(iii) 'The Barber Whose Uncle had his Head Bitten off by a Circus Tiger' by William Saroyan:

Miss Gamma said I needed a haircut, my mother said I needed a haircut, my brother Krikor said I needed a haircut: the whole world wanted me to get a haircut. My head was too big for the world, seven and seven-eighths, maybe eight and seven-eighths. Too much black hair, the world said.

Everybody said, When are you going to get a haircut?

(iv) 'The Lady with the Toy Dog' by Anton Chekhov:

It was reported that a new face had been seen on the quay; a lady with a little dog. Dimitri Dimitrich Gomov, who had been a fortnight at Yalta and had got used to it, had begun to show an interest in new faces. As he sat in the pavilion at Verné's he saw a young lady, blond and fairly tall, and wearing a broad-brimmed hat, pass along the quay. After her ran a white Pomeranian.

Later he saw her in the park and in the square several times a day. She walked by herself, always in the same broad-brimmed hat, and with this white dog. Nobody knew who she was, and she was spoken of as the lady with the toy dog.

After his description of the natural scene, Bierce returns to the soldier:

141

The sleeping sentinel in the clump of laurel was a young Virginian named Carter Druse.

He had decided to join the Northern army in the Civil War and therefore was, as his father said, a traitor. So he left home, but without his mother's knowledge as she was seriously ill.

All this biographical background is packed into two short paragraphs.

Carter soon became a trusted soldier and had been given this important sentry-duty precisely because he was courageous and trustworthy. But

fatigue had been stronger than resolution, and he had fallen asleep.

And so his comrades down in the valley were in danger of being spied upon by the enemy.

Suddenly he awoke and saw on

a colossal pedestal, the cliff, motionless at the extreme edge of the capping rock and sharply outlined against the sky, . . . an equestrian statue of impressive dignity.

This 'statue' is then described briefly. But he could not see more than the outline of the rider's face. At first he thought it was a vision, but then the horse moved slightly. Carter raised his rifle and

covered a vital spot of the horseman's breast. A touch upon the trigger and all would have been well with Carter Druse. At that instant the horseman turned his head and looked in the direction of his concealed foeman—seemed to look into his very face, into his eyes, into his brave, compassionate heart.

This horseman now possessed a vital secret and so had to be killed. But:

Carter Druse grew deathly pale; he shook in every limb, turned faint and saw the statuesque group before him as

142

black figures, rising, falling, moving unsteadily in arcs of circles in a fiery sky. His hand fell away from his weapon, his head slowly dropped until his face rested on the leaves in which he lay. This courageous gentleman and hardy soldier was near swooning from intensity of emotion.

But then the soldier realized his duty: the man had to be

shot dead from ambush—without warning, without a moment's spiritual preparation, with never so much as an unspoken prayer, he must be sent to his account.

Even now, however, Carter hesitated to kill a man in cold blood like this. Perhaps—who knew?—the man had not seen anything after all. Carter looked down, and there were his comrades:

Some foolish commander was permitting the soldiers of his escort to water their beasts in the open, in plain view from a hundred summits.

The story is now rushing forward and yet standing still. Everything is in suspense, an intolerable suspense. We know that there is something more terrible happening than this incident in a war. Suggestion is 'making its masterpiece'.

So Carter looked back at the rider and horse,

and again it was through the sights of his rifle. But this time his aim was at the horse.

And he remembered his father's words: 'Whatever may occur, do what you conceive to be your duty.'

He fired.

With those two dramatic words we immediately leave him. Bierce knew his art too well to leave us with him after the shot had temporarily broken the suspense. We must be taken elsewhere. But Carter will still be in our minds, we are wondering, and we must hurry on, we must be hurried on.

We are taken down into the valley, where an officer had wandered away by himself.

> Lifting his eyes to the dizzy altitude of its summit, the officer saw an astonishing sight—a man on horseback riding down into the valley through the air! . . . Filled with amazement and terror by this apparition of a horseman in the sky—half believing himself the chosen scribe of some new Apocalypse, the officer was overcome by the intensity of his emotions; his legs failed him and he fell. Almost at the same instant he heard a crashing sound in the trees—a sound that died without an echo, and all was still.

Recovering himself, however, he ran to where he expected to see the fallen man and horse:

> it did not occur to him that the line of march of aerial cavalry is directed downward, and that he could find the objects of his search at the very foot of the cliff.

He said nothing when he returned to camp:

> he knew better than to tell an incredible truth.

With a suddenness equal to that with which we left him we now return to Carter:

> After firing his shot Private Carter Druse reloaded his rifle and resumed his watch.

Yet this cannot be all, we know: there is something else, something about this horseman in the sky that has yet to be explained. A sergeant came to Carter and asked if it was he who had fired. Carter said that it was—at a horse, and

> having answered, he turned away his face and said no more.

Impatiently the sergeant questioned him further; and the story ends:

> 'See here, Druse,' he said, after a moment's silence. 'It's no use making a mystery. I order you to report. Was there anybody on the horse?'

'Yes.'

'Who?'

'My father.'

The sergeant rose to his feet and walked away. 'Good God!' he said.

Such an ending, terse, terrible, abrupt, unexpected until we look back over the story, is typical of Bierce's method, and when done as well as this is the ideal ending. For it is in keeping with the whole style and structure of the short story.

This story is an example of only one particular type of short story, but it is a perfect example of the art of short-story writing. It is concentrated and tense almost to breaking-point—and it is this tension, of vocabulary and progress, that gives the story its atmosphere—but it cannot break until its last words, when it must break if it is to succeed. It begins and ends with all the suddenness of the stopping and recommencement of time. We have been present at a moment but have moved far beyond it. The picture is complete, not in spite of but because of the economy of its painting.

It is not the duty of the would be short-story writer merely to imitate the style and manner of the stories of either Ambrose Bierce or any other successful author: but it is also not his duty to ignore them. He has to write his own stories, but that which is original has its origin somewhere, and just as without Shakespeare there might have been no Keats, without Congreve there might have been no Oscar Wilde, and without Fielding there might have been no Dickens, so without Poe and Bierce and the other great pioneers of the short-story form in the nineteenth century there might have been no modern short story.

10

Letter-writing

THE form of a letter is conditioned by its addressee: by whether he or she is a relation, a friend, an acquaintance or someone not personally known to the writer; by the nature of his or her work, position and responsibility.

There are, however, certain components common to most letters:

(i) The writer's own address is written at the top of the first sheet of paper, usually on the right. Many people—and all organizations—have notepaper specially printed for letters, with, of course, their address printed on each sheet.

(ii) Immediately below that comes the date on which the letter is written. There are many ways of writing this. If, for instance, the date were the 20th of September 1970, it could be written in any of the following ways: 20.9.70; 20.9.1970; 20/9/70; 20 September (70, 1970); 20th Sept. (70, 1970); 20.ix.70; The twentieth of September 1970; Sept. (September) 20 (th); etc.

The day of the week can also be added, and some people like to put the apostrophe before the 7 to show the omission of 19.

(iii) The addressee is invoked as *Dear* and then either by his or her name or impersonally as *sir* or *madam*.

(iv) The first word of the body of the letter is written immediately beneath the word following *Dear* and usually starts beneath the first letter of that word.

Example:
>Dear Sir,
>>When I wrote . . .

(v) At the end of the letter the writer calls himself *Your(s)* followed by one of a variety of expressions, the whole going down on to a new line, and then signs his name, also on a new line. Even if all the other parts of a letter are typed, the signature at the end must be written in ink—though on such things as official forms it is usually a facsimile. The written signature may, however, be followed by a typed copy of the name.

There are at least four main types of letter. They differ according to the degree of formality with which they are written.

A. The most informal letter is that written to a close personal relation or friend of about the same age as the writer. It starts by calling the addressee by his or her Christian name or even by some nickname: *Dear Joe, Dear Betty, Dear Stinker* (sometimes the possessive adjective *my* is put before the *dear* to emphasize the closeness of the relationship between the writer and the addressee).

The contents are written in a conversational style, and the writer dismisses himself at the end either simply with *Yours* or with some such expression as *Your loving brother, Your friend, Yours ever, Yours till the cows come home.*

Just how conversational the style is depends on the character of the writer, his purpose, and his relationship with the addressee at the time of writing.

The following short example will illustrate this type:

12, Arthur Rd.,
Walpool.
Nov. 28th.

Dear Harry,

I had your letter this morning, but I don't think I'll be able to get there. It's such a long way from here, isn't it? Still, I'll do my best and let you know soon. There's no great hurry. Well, I must sign off now. I'll write again at some length later.

Yours,
Bill.

B. A less informal letter is that written by children to their parents and vice versa, or by relatives or acquaintances who are not on intimate terms. The style is still conversational but less so than in **A.** The addressee is invoked by his or her style of relationship—*father, daughter, cousin*, etc.—or by name; and the ending is either *Your loving (affectionate, dutiful*, etc.) followed by the style of relationship again (and the name of the writer if he or she is the younger) or by *Yours sincerely* where acquaintances are concerned.
Example:

26, Newport Av.,
Birmingham.
Thursday the 15th.

Dear Mother,

I was glad to know that you are well again. You really must take more care of yourself, you know. Can't you come here for a few weeks and have a good rest? Dad will be all right with Susan—I dare say he has suggested the same thing . . .

Your loving son,
Christopher.

C. The third type of letter is formal in both approach and style. The addressee may be personally known by the writer but not intimately. They may know each other professionally

148

or as members of the same organization. They may be pupil and teacher, for instance.

There are, however, degrees of formality even in this type of letter. If the addressee is fairly well known—and the writer is not too insistent upon formalities—then his or her address will not be written on the notepaper as well as on the envelope. He or she will be simply invoked as *Dear* followed by *Mr.*, *Mrs.* or *Miss* and the surname; and the writer will call himself *Yours sincerely* followed by his usual signature.

The following example was written by a Mr. Walters to a young lady of his acquaintance who had sent him a copy of a book she had written:

> 135, Hebor Rd.,
> London, SW1.
> 3.6.70.

Dear Miss Manly,
    Thank you very much for the copy of your book. I shall read it with interest, knowing as I do your other work, and write to you in detail later.

> Yours sincerely,
> J. N. Walters.

But if addressee and writer are known to each other merely in a formal way, then it is customary for the name and address of the addressee to be put on the letter as well as on the envelope, on the left side of the first page and either above or below—more commonly above—the body of the letter. Sometimes the surname of the addressee is used, preceded of course by *Mr.*, etc., but the opening is more usually *Dear sir*, or *Dear madam*. The ending is either *Yours faithfully* or *Yours truly*—the former being much the commoner today—followed by the usual signature of the writer. Example:

Riverside,
London Rd.,
Richmond.
11/5/70.

The Hon. Secretary,
The Writers' Club.
Witcham.
Dear Sir,
    I regret that I shall be unable to attend the committee meeting on Thursday as I shall be away from the district. Please convey my apologies.

Yours faithfully,
M. E. King.

D. The fourth main type of letter is an extension of the latter. This time the addressee and the writer are not known to each other personally, probably have never met. They communicate only for official reasons. It is the sort of letter a citizen writes to the inspector of taxes for the area in which he lives. The name of the addressee is probably not known, but even if it is known he is addressed in his capacity or position; if the letter is in answer to one received, the reference number—which is usually placed on the left of the page above the address of the addressee—should be quoted. Example:

Your ref. WGB/31.

16, Crossways,
Liverpool, 6.
30.xi.70.

H.M. Inspector of Taxes,
9, Elm Rd.,
Liverpool, 6.
Dear Sir,
    I shall be obliged if you will explain the figures quoted in your letter of the 28th. They do not accord with the return I made on the 15th of last month, and I shall be grateful for some elucidation.

Yours faithfully,
J. C. Edwards.

It will be noticed that the lines of the addressee's name and address on the left side of the paper are set immediately below one another without indentation. This is customary and is done to prevent long addresses from spreading too far across the page.

Some Special Points

(i) There are letters even more formal than **D.** A soldier writing to his Commanding Officer, for example, has (or used to have) to adopt an extremely formal manner, begging whatever it is he is writing about, speaking of himself in the third person and asserting at the end that he is his addressee's *obedient servant*. But one can learn the technique of such letters only from experience.

(ii) Any letter written not to a single individual but, say, to a firm must begin *Dear sirs*: otherwise it is the same as **D.**

(iii) A letter to an editor of a paper or magazine should begin simply *Sir* without a prefatory *Dear* and end *Yours etc.* (followed of course by the writer's signature), the *etc.* standing for the old formula *I am, dear sir, your most humble and obedient servant*.

(iv) The reference number mentioned in **D.** is used by business firms and similar organizations. Each department, often each official, has an individual reference number so that when a letter arrives addressed to the organization as a whole it can immediately be sent to the appropriate place. These references are also necessary for the filing of correspondence. The normal form is a series of letters followed by an oblique stroke and then either further letters or numbers.

Usually in the top left corner of the notepaper, this reference is written either alone or preceded by *Our ref.*, or *Please quote*, or just *Ref.*

(v) If a letter is signed on behalf of its writer by a secretary, or by one person representing an organization, it is

151

customary for the two letters *p.p.* or the fuller *per pro.* to precede the name of the individual or organization and for the signer to write his or her own name underneath. The complete form of the expression is the two Latin words, *per procurationem*, which mean *by way of substitute.*
Example:

> . . . .
> Yours faithfully,
> *per pro.* Mr. J. N. Hardie,
> signature.

Some people prefer the simple English preposition *for*, however:

> . . . .
> Yours faithfully,
> *for* Messrs. W. A. Jones & Co. Ltd.,
> signature.

(vi) Often the official position of the signer is written or typed under the signature:

> . . . .
> Yours faithfully,
> signature.
> *Secretary* to Mr. J. N. Hardie.

(vii) It will be noted that business firms often use the ampersand (&) in their addresses: *J. Hewitt & Sons Ltd.*

As in Chapters 9 and 14, we have here been dealing with technicalities and not with the art of writing; with the correct placing of addresses, for instance, and not with the writing of interesting and valuable letters; for that is another province of study with which this book is not primarily concerned.

It is true that the majority of the millions of letters that are written are private documents and end their careers in waste-paper baskets or fireplaces. But a few have a different destiny, some even become famous as literature. Some men and women have written their letters with one eye on publication; others now long since dead would perhaps be horrified to know that their most private letters are available for us all to read. There is argument for and against such publication, but no student of literature can deny that it would have been wrong not to publish the letters of poets like Byron, Shelley and Keats, for without them our understanding of the three men would be imperfect and some of the most important statements about the art of poetry would have been lost to the world.

But even if our letters eventually reach only a waste-paper basket or a fireplace we ought not to think of them differently from those written for publication. They may, that is, be intensely private, but still they should be written as well as possible. A letter is a special form of writing, with its own conventions and its own pattern. The majority of people never write anything else: for them it is, therefore, supremely important that they should write as interestingly and skilfully as possible. Today we do not, as people in the eighteenth century did, recognize letter-writing as a distinct art-form; but we should have sufficient respect both for ourselves and for our language to think with the eighteenth century that good letters are worth the trouble of writing. Our notes to inspectors of taxes may be as formal as social convention demands, but our letters to relations and friends might be our contributions to the great mass of unpublished literature.

11

Précis

A PRÉCIS is a special kind of summary, a summary within a stated limit, usually one-third or one-quarter of the length of the original passage. There are, therefore, ways and means of doing it efficiently.

(i) The original passage must be carefully read two or three times so that it may be completely understood.

(ii) If there is no title printed above it—and there is not likely to be if it is only an extract—one should be invented: this will be a very brief summary in itself and a guide through original and précis. When the précis is finished this title should fit it as aptly as it fits the original; for it should name the single theme of both the original and the précis.

(iii) The original should then be divided into sections, each dealing with a main point. These should be given sub-titles which state the points briefly, and then be summarized in turn with as little reference back to the original as possible. If the original is divided into paragraphs, these sections already exist—and except for the paragraphs of direct speech, a précis should have the same number of paragraphs as the original. When all the sections have been summarized, they must be joined into a single, continuous whole and not left as notes in watertight compartments.

(iv) A précis has to be no less a passage of continuous prose than the original. It must not read like a series of notes but as far as possible like an original itself. All the rules and conventions of writing must be observed.

154

(v) The exact phrases of the original must not be repeated, for a précis is not an abbreviated copy but a summary of the essence of a passage in one's own words.

(vi) Nor must any new idea or fact be introduced; for the précis writer is engaged on summarizing someone else's words and not on expressing his own mind.

(vii) A précis will seldom be in direct speech but in indirect or reported speech and hence the third person and past tense; and there is little likelihood that inverted commas or quotations will be used. But there cannot be a hard-and-fast rule about this: it depends on the original. In general statements it may be preferable to keep the present tense and the second or first person of the original. For instance, if a speaker were to say: . . . *and I believe that we are* . . . he might be reported as having said that *he believed that we are* . . . : the words *we are*, which refer to people in general with no present significance in the use of the present tense, being retained in the indirect speech.

If it is known who wrote the original passage, his or her name can be introduced at the beginning of the précis; if, on the other hand, the name is not known, the précis can begin with such words as *The writer said that* . . . or *The speaker expressed* . . . These are extra words and are the only ones which do state anything not in the original; but they may be needed to put the précis into indirect speech from the start.

If the original is already in indirect speech there may not be any changes to make.

(viii) Since a précis is so great a condensation of a passage it can be, and is meant to be, only a generalized statement of the theme and essential points of that passage. Few of the original details can be retained, if any. Unless the original is badly written not one of its details will be superfluous, but in the précis there will be small room for more than generalities.

155

This is what is meant by saying that a précis omits everything that is not essential, an unfortunate statement which implies that there are unessential things in the original. Perhaps there are, but, as has been said, it is then a bad original. The aim of précis is merely to reproduce in original form the skeleton without which the flesh and blood of the original could not stand up. Where space allows the skeleton can be given some clothing, but even so that clothing must have a utilitarian and not a beautifying function.

The following analysis of a précis will show these ways and means in operation.

The original is a famous speech by Macaulay:

I find it difficult to express my gratification at seeing such an assembly convened at such a time. All the history of our own country, all the history of other countries, furnishes nothing parallel to it. Look at the great events in our former history, and in every one of them, which, for importance, we can venture to compare with the Reform Bill, we shall find something to disgrace and tarnish the achievement. It was by the assistance of French arms and of Roman bulls that King John was harassed into giving the Great Charter. In the time of Charles I, how much injustice, how much crime, how much bloodshed and misery, did it cost to assert the liberties of England. But in this event, great and important as it is in substance, I confess I think it still more important from the manner in which it has been achieved. Other countries have obtained deliverance equally signal and complete, but in no country has that deliverance been obtained with such perfect peace; so entirely within the bounds of the Constitution; with all the forms of law observed; the government of the country proceeding in its regular course; every man going forth to his labour until the evening. France boasts of her three days of July, when her people rose, when barricades fenced the streets, and the entire population of the capital in arms successfully vindicated their liberties. They boast, and justly, of those three days of July; but I will boast of our ten days of May. We, too, fought a battle, but it was with moral arms. We, too, placed an impassable barrier between ourselves and military tyranny; but we fenced ourselves only with moral barricades. Not one crime committed; not one acre confiscated, not one life lost, not one instance of outrage or attack on the authorities or the laws. Our victory has not left a single family in mourning. Not a tear, not a drop of blood, has sullied the pacific and blameless triumph of a great people.

The précis:

A MORAL VICTORY

Having tried to express his pleasure at so unprecedented a gathering, Macaulay said that of England's past successes comparable with the Reform Bill all were somehow stained, as was seen by the kind of pressure exerted on King John and the violence committed in Charles I's days in the cause of freedom. But the chief significance of this success was the manner of its accomplishment. No other country had won such freedom so peacefully: so constitutionally, so legally, so normally, both for governors and governed. France rightly boasted of her violent assertion of liberty during three July days, but he would boast of this bloodless, law-abiding victory won by moral strength in ten days of May.

Analytical Notes

(i) The précis is one-third approx. of the length of the original: 116 words instead of 342.

(ii) The theme of the original is that the Reform Bill, being a victory won without violence, stands in contrast both with England's own past victories against tyranny and with the French Revolution: this is also the theme of the précis, and the title fits both original and précis equally well.

(iii) The original falls into three sections, each making a single main point, and these were summarized in turn. The first stretches as far as the word *England*, for apart from the special point made in the first two sentences, which serve to introduce the speech, the single point is made that the greatness of England's past history is stained by wickedness and

157

misery. The second section progresses to the word *evening*, the point now being that this event, the Reform Bill, has been achieved in a unique—that is, peaceful—way. And the third section continues to the end, the last point being the contrast between the absence of violence in this victory and the violence of the French Revolution. The following sub-titles were given to these sections:

(*a*) England's past history stained;
(*b*) The Reform Bill was different;
(*c*) Contrast with the French Revolution.

The summaries were first written more or less as notes, with occasional reference back to the original, and then the final précis was made from these notes alone.

In the précis the first section ends at *freedom*, the second at *governed*, and the third continues to the end.

(iv) Since it is known that the original is a speech by Macaulay the words *Macaulay said* are introduced to put the précis into indirect speech.

(v) Since the first two sentences of the original are merely introductory, yet are important in that function, they do figure in the précis but in a grammatically subordinate position as a phrase: *Having tried to express his pleasure at so unprecedented a gathering. Unprecedented* represents the whole of the second sentence of the original, and the adverb *so* qualifying it summarizes *convened at such a time*. Macaulay's difficulty in expressing his gratification is shown in *Having tried*.

All were somehow stained summarizes *we shall find something to disgrace and tarnish the achievement.*

Two sentences then follow in the original containing two detailed illustrations. The illustrations must be retained, but the details are not necessary to the précis; and the two sentences can easily be combined into a single statement and

joined to the previous statement by the subordinating conjunction *as,* which shows that some example is to follow. So
the kind of pressure is a generalization of *French arms and
Roman bulls* and *violence* stands for *how much injustice,
how much crime, how much bloodshed and misery*; and *in
the cause of freedom* is a combined summary of *giving the
Great Charter* and *to assert the liberties of England.*

Thus by the use of an introductory phrase and the subordinate clause beginning with *as* the first section of the
original has been summarized into a single sentence.

(vi) The two sentences of the second section of the original
are complementary: the first and shorter boldly states the
contrast between the new point and the point of the first
section, and the second illustrates it by a series of details. It
is advisable to keep this sentence-division in the précis also,
particularly as there has been only one sentence so far and
the style of the précis would suffer without a balance of long
and short sentences.

The contrasting conjunction *But* of the original is equally
necessary in the précis. The use of the adjective *chief* implies
that there are other aspects of the Bill's significance and so
summarizes by implication *great and important as it is in
substance.* There is no need for any reference to the direct
speech *I confess I think.* It should be noticed that the perfect
tense of the original—*have obtained*—has been put back
into the pluperfect tense—*had won.*

The series of detail which follows in the original bulks too
large to be ignored and is, in any case, important; but as
each detail is adverbial in syntactical function, telling how
the deliverance was obtained, it is possible to substitute for
each a summarizing adverb after *so*: *peacefully* stands for
with such perfect peace; *constitutionally* for *entirely within
the bounds of the Constitution*; *legally* for *with all the forms
of law observed*; and *normally* for the final two details of the

159

section. *Governors* equals *The government* and *governed* equals *every man.*

(vii) There are many details in the third section of the original for which there is no room in the précis, but the colourful contrast of the three days in July and the ten days of May is retained so that the précis may preserve some of the oratorical tone of the original.

The original says twice that France boasted but adds *and justly* the second time: this new point is therefore brought forward in the précis to the single statement: *France rightly boasted.*

Violent assertion of liberty summarizes all from *when her people* to *liberties*; and *bloodless, law-abiding victory* summarizes all from *We, too, placed* to *blood.*

(viii) The précis reads like a short original itself and is not a mere sequence of discontinuous notes. The three sections fit neatly into place to compose a single passage. The rules of précis have been obeyed.

The following is an account of the actual writing of a précis. The original was this letter from Shelley to Joseph Severn:

PISA,
Nov. 29th, 1821.

DEAR SIR,

I send you the elegy on poor Keats—and I wish it were better worth your acceptance. You will see, by the preface, that it was written before I could obtain any particular account of his last moments; all that I still know, was communicated to me by a friend who had derived his information from Colonel Finch; I have ventured to express, as I felt, the respect and admiration which *your* conduct towards him demands.

In spite of his transcendent genius, Keats never was, nor ever will be, a popular poet; and the total neglect and obscurity in which the astonishing remnants of his mind still lie, was hardly to be dissipated by a writer, who, however he may differ from Keats in more important qualities, at least resembles him in that accidental one, a want of popularity.

I have little hope, therefore, that the poem I send you will excite any attention, nor do I feel assured that a critical notice of his writing would find a single reader. But for these considerations, it had been my intention to have collected the remnants of his compositions, and to have published them with a Life and Criticism. Has he left any poems or writings of whatsoever kind, and in whose possession are they? Perhaps you would oblige me by information on this point.

Many thanks for the picture you promise me: I shall consider it among the most sacred relics of the past.

For my part, I little expected, when I last saw Keats at my friend Leigh Hunt's, that I should survive him.

Should you ever pass through Pisa, I hope to have the pleasure of seeing you, and of cultivating an acquaintance into something pleasant, begun under such melancholy auspices.

Accept, my dear sir, the assurance of my sincere esteem, and believe me,

> Your most sincere and faithful servant,
> PERCY B. SHELLEY.

Do you know Leigh Hunt? I expect him and his family *here* every day.

This original was duly read several times and then given the title 'Adonais', the title of Shelley's elegy on Keats: for although it did not touch upon one or two of the minor points in the letter it did summarize the main topic under discussion.

The letter was next divided into four sections: the first being the first paragraph, in which Shelley gave a brief account of the elegy; the second taking in the next two paragraphs, the point now being that Keats was not and could not be popular, yet Shelley wanted to publish his Collected Works; the third containing three separate items, the picture, Shelley's feeling that he would die before Keats, and his hope that Severn would call on him if he came to

161

Pisa; and the fourth being the postscript about Leigh Hunt. The following sub-titles were given to these sections:

(i) 'Adonais': little knowledge but expression of admiration;

(ii) Keats doomed to unpopularity—plan for Collected Works;

(iii) Picture—survive Keats—visit if in Pisa;

(iv) Leigh Hunt.

These sections were then re-read and summarized in turn, and no attention was yet paid to the number of words being used. The précis had to be as close as possible to one-quarter of the length of the original, in which there are 338 words. The first complete draft of the précis was as follows:

> In the letter from Pisa accompanying his elegy on Keats Shelley told Severn that although it was written without detailed knowledge of his death it tried to express the admiration they both felt.
>
> For all his greatness Keats had never been popular, nor could he himself hope to popularize him. Yet he had wanted to publish Keats's Collected Works, and he now asked for Severn's co-operation in this.
>
> He thanked him for the promised picture, said that he himself had not expected to survive Keats, and hoped Severn would call on him if he came to Pisa.
>
> In a postscript he asked if Severn knew Leigh Hunt.

That of course was too long (107 words instead of about 84). Already the summary had been ruthless, but more still of the original would have to go, though the main points would still have to be clear. It was decided, therefore, to omit the detail of the *letter from Pisa*, several shorter expressions were substituted for existing ones, and the final précis of 87 words was written:

> Shelley told Severn that although his elegy on Keats was

written without detailed knowledge of his death it expressed
the admiration they both felt.

Albeit great, Keats could never be popular, nor could he
himself popularize him. Yet he had wanted to publish Keats's
Collected Works, and he now asked for Severn's co-operation
in this.

He thanked him for the promised picture, said that he had
not expected to survive Keats, and hoped Severn might visit
him in Pisa.

Finally, he wondered if Severn knew Leigh Hunt.

Working to exactly the same plan the original was then
summarized to one-third of its length, i.e. to as close as
possible to 112 words. (It is both easier and more satisfactory
to write a précis in one-third than in one-quarter of the
length of the original passage.) It will be seen that the précis
reads more pleasantly and can include some points which
make for a more exact summary:

> Writing from Pisa, Shelley told Severn that he was sending
> his elegy on Keats, which, although written without detailed
> knowledge of his death, did try to express the admiration
> they felt.
>
> Keats, he wrote, could never be popular for all his great-
> ness, nor could he, who shared his obscurity, hope to popu-
> larize him. Nothing about Keats was likely to be read, and
> yet he had planned to publish his Collected Works and
> wondered if Severn knew of any left still unpublished.
>
> He thanked him for the promised picture, said that he
> himself had not expected to survive Keats, and hoped Severn
> would call if he came to Pisa.
>
> Finally, he asked if Severn knew Leigh Hunt.   (116 words.)

Lastly, it may profit students to compare the following
two précis of the same original, one of which was written
by an adult teacher and the other by a group of Certificate
candidates in collaboration. The original was an extract from
a speech by Winston Churchill:

> Turning once again, and this time more generally, to the

163

question of invasion, I would observe that there has never been a period in all these long centuries of which we boast when an absolute guarantee against invasion, still less against serious raids, could have been given to our people. In the days of Napoleon, of which I was speaking just now, the same wind which would have carried his transports across the Channel might have driven away the blockading fleet. There was always the chance, and it is that chance which has excited and befooled the imaginations of many Continental tyrants. Many are the tales that we are told. We are assured that novel methods will be adopted, and when we see the originality of malice, the ingenuity of aggression, which our enemy displays, we may certainly prepare ourselves for every kind of novel stratagem and every kind of brutal and treacherous manœuvre. I think that no idea is so outlandish that it should not be considered and viewed with a searching, but at the same time, I hope, with a steady eye. . . .

I have, myself, full confidence that if all do their duty, if nothing is neglected, and if the best arrangements are made, as they are being made, we shall prove ourselves once again able to defend our island home, to ride out the storm of war, and to outlive the menace of tyranny, if necessary for years, if necessary alone. At any rate, that is what we are going to try to do. . . . Even though large tracts of Europe and many old and famous States have fallen or may fall into the grip of the Gestapo and all the odious apparatus of Nazi rule, we shall not flag or fail, we shall go on to the end, we shall fight in France, we shall fight on the seas and oceans, we shall fight with growing confidence and growing strength in the air, we shall defend our island, whatever the cost may be, we shall fight on the beaches, we shall fight on the landing grounds, we shall fight in fields and in the streets, we shall fight in the hills; we shall never surrender, and even if, which I do not for a moment believe, this island or a large part of it were subjugated or starving, then our Empire beyond the seas, armed and guarded by the British fleet, would carry on the struggle, until, in God's good time, the new world, with all its power and might, steps forth to the rescue and the liberation of the old.   (434 words.)

Both précis were written to one-third of the length of the original.

(a) Mr. Churchill said that it had never been possible fully to ensure the country against invasion or incursions. The wind which would have driven Napoleon's fleet to England might have scattered the defending ships, and other foreign despots had been attracted by this possibility. Now we were promised new methods, and, considering the cleverness of our enemy, had to expect and prepare for anything, however unusual.

But if all precautions were dutifully taken, we should, he was sure, be capable of surviving the onslaught. For in spite of the collapse of much of Europe beneath the foulness of Nazidom, we would maintain the struggle, on land, by sea, and in the air. We would defend England at every point; and even if part of it were overcome, the Empire and the navy would fight on until the great strength of America came to our rescue.   (145 words.)

(b) Mr. Churchill said that in the past England had always been subject to invasion, and the wind which would have driven Napoleon's ships across the Channel might have scattered ours. Other European dictators also had hoped for such luck. This time the enemy would use everything within his power and could not be expected to follow the usual pattern of warfare, and so we had to be vigilant.

But with time, the plans that were being made would be successful if everyone did his duty and even if we had to fight alone. Although great areas of Europe might come under Nazi rule, as some already had, we should continue to fight wherever possible, defending our homes throughout Britain wherever the enemy might come; and if we had to surrender, the Empire would carry on the fight, protected by the Navy, until eventually America came to our aid.   (148 words.)

The Value of Précis

The writing of summaries stretches far beyond the confines of the examination script. The reducing of a passage of prose to one-third or one-quarter of its original length may not now be required of many examinees, but summarizing in

165

one form or another is still regarded as a vital test of understanding and composition. Moreover, anyone who has had anything to do with the production of a periodical, be it a national daily newspaper or a school or parish magazine, knows how important it is to be able to reduce, wisely and speedily, an original manuscript to the number of words that can be allotted to it in the available space. Yet the speed is of less importance than the wisdom, for the former can be achieved by merely crossing out sentences or phrases here, there and everywhere; but the latter commands either that the original be totally reworded or that the deletions be carefully made so that the continuity and style of the original are not destroyed. The limitation to one-third or one-quarter is no more than arbitrary, if obvious; but once one has mastered the technique of summarizing one should have no difficulty in summarizing to any number of words.

But summary operates not only in the editor's office. It has its place in the whole range of the publishing world—think, for instance, of the *blurb* on the dust-jacket; in reviewing of books, plays and films; in politics and government—in the Civil Service; in entertainment; in advertising; in teaching— in a hundred-and-one professions and pursuits.

Further, any student who cannot accurately condense the material of the books he studies, who cannot clearly see the main points and themes of what he reads and phrase them in his own words—and before he can do that he must understand them—will never emerge triumphant from the mass of facts and opinions which surrounds him : he will never be the master of his subject.

For such is the pre-eminent value of précis, that it trains one to become a master of one's subject and hence successful in one's career. If the material one has to deal with is a mixture of the important and the unimportant, then one must be able to separate them; and—more difficult task—if the material is wholly important one still has to be able to put first things first.

In brief, if we can master the technique of précis-writing we shall be able to see the wood however many trees there may be; and even if every tree is beautiful we shall still be able to decide which is the quickest and best way through them.

12

Paraphrase

PARAPHRASE resembles précis in one respect, but differs from it in another: for although it is the restatement in original words of a passage written by someone else, it is not necessarily shorter than that passage and may be even longer.

The passage may be in any form in prose or verse, but the paraphrase is always in prose and usually in indirect speech.

No matter what the style of the original is, it has to be restated in one's own terms and in modern idiom.

Nothing must be omitted that is vital to the restatement, nor must anything new be added to the sense of the original. A paraphrase is not a critical commentary.

Nothing must be merely copied or quoted from the original, and a paraphrase must as far as possible read like an original itself: like a précis, it must not read like notes.

Above all, a paraphrase is not a word-for-word translation: it is, as the dictionary says, a *free rendering of a passage, expression of its sense in other words.*

The method of preparation and writing is similar to that already discussed in the previous chapter on précis. The original should be read and re-read until it is thoroughly understood. If it is very short, there is no need to divide it into sections and paraphrase them in turn, but any long original will need to be split up and paraphrased in that way. In neither case, however, should the original be consulted during the writing of the final version. One is not concerned with number of words, for, if the original is understood as it should be, one may safely trust one's memory.

Verse Original

OZYMANDIAS

I met a traveller from an antique land
Who said: Two vast and trunkless legs of stone
Stand in the desert. . . . Near them, on the sand,
Half-sunk, a shattered visage lies, whose frown,
And wrinkled lip, and sneer of cold command,
Tell that its sculptor well those passions read
Which yet survive, stamped on these lifeless things,
The hand that mocked them, and the heart that fed:
And on the pedestal these words appear:
'My name is Ozymandias, king of kings:
Look on my works, ye Mighty, and despair!'
Nothing beside remains. Round the decay
Of that colossal wreck, boundless and bare
The lone and level sands stretch far away.

PARAPHRASE:
The poet tells how he met a traveller from the East who told him about the ruin of a monument in a desert. Great stone legs stood alone, he said, without a body, and a broken face lay almost buried nearby, its expression, frowning and sneering, showing how well the sculptor had copied into stone the personality of his original. On the pedestal was an inscription which stated that this was a monument to Ozymandias and, in his own words, revealed him as an arrogant and bombastic king. This ruin was all that was left of him, and all around it stretched the infinite desert.

No attempt has been made to do the impossible: to reproduce or rival the artistry of Shelley's poem: merely its general content has been re-expressed in prose. Such expressions as *from an antique land, sneer of cold command* and

The hand that mocked them, and the heart that fed cannot be paraphrased—and need not be; for it is impossible to paraphrase poetic imagery, and all one dare do is say what a poem is *about*: what a poem *is* only itself can say. If, for instance, one were asked to paraphrase the last lines of Walter de la Mare's poem, 'The Listeners':

> And how the silence surged softly backward,
> When the plunging hoofs were gone,

all one could satisfactorily do would be to write what would amount to a prose explanation, making no attempt to preserve the alliteration:

> As the sound of the horse's hoofs died away in the distance, the silence flowed back to fill the space from which it had been driven.

Prose Original

In the lapse of a long series of years, by a progression slow, and for a time almost imperceptible, we have become rich in a variety of acquirements, favoured above measure in the gifts of Providence, unrivalled in commerce, pre-eminent in arts, foremost in the pursuits of philosophy and science, and established in all the blessings of civil society. We are in the possession of peace, of happiness, and of liberty. We are under the guidance of a mild and beneficent religion; and we are protected by impartial laws and the purest administration of justice. We are living under a system of government which our own happy experience leads us to pronounce the best and wisest which has ever been framed; a system which has become the admiration of the world. From all these blessings we must for ever have been shut out had there been any truth in those principles which some gentlemen have not hesitated to lay down as applicable to the case of Africa.

Had those principles been true, we ourselves had languished to this hour in that miserable state of ignorance, brutality and degradation in which history proves our ancestry to have been immersed. Had other nations adopted these principles in their conduct towards us, had other nations applied to Great Britain the reasoning which some of the senators of this very island now apply to Africa, ages might have passed without our emerging from barbarism; and we who are enjoying the blessings of British civilization, of British laws, and British liberty, might at this hour have been little superior, either in morals, in knowledge, or refinement, to the rude inhabitants of the coast of Guinea.

(PITT—1792.)

PARAPHRASE:

Pitt said that very slowly England had advanced under the favour of Providence until she was supreme in such pursuits as trade, the arts, philosophy, science and everything else that made for civilization. She was at peace, she was happy and free. She was safe in her religion, and protected by just laws. Her people considered that English government had proved itself to be the best any country had yet had, and it was admired by the rest of the world. But they would never have attained to this happy state of affairs had they been treated as some Englishmen now wanted to treat Africa.

They would have remained as ignorant and brutish as their ancestors had been. If other countries had treated them as these men now wished to treat Africa, they might have continued indefinitely in their original barbarism, and instead of living in their present state of civilization might have been still no better in any respect than the primitive people of Guinea.

That is shorter than the original, but was not intended as a summary. It makes no attempt to imitate the magnificent oratory of the original, nor is every detail paraphrased. It is a generalized restatement of the content of the speech, in the manner of a *fairly full* report, following the order of the original and, of course, preserving its paragraph-divisions. It might be described as a *paraphrase-summary*.

A special function of paraphrase is to transform bad writing into what it should be: the original may, for instance, be

171

verbose or contain errors of one kind or another. These amusing examples are to be found in Sir Arthur Quiller-Couch's Cambridge lecture on Jargon:

> Original: A singular degree of rarity prevails in the earlier editions of this romance;
> Paraphrase: The earlier editions of this romance are rare.
> Original: I was entirely indifferent as to the results of the game, caring nothing at all whether I had losses or gains;
> Paraphrase: I was careless if I won or lost.
> Original: He was associated with the distinction of the Order of Merit;
> Paraphrase: He was given the Order of Merit.

Finally, there is one further use of paraphrase, in which it will almost always be necessary to amplify the original. This happens when the original is a short statement like a proverb or epigram. For example, the proverb *There's no smoke without fire* would be paraphrased in an explanatory way, perhaps like this:

> A sign is always a sign of something other than itself: if, therefore, you see smoke you know that there must be a fire from which that smoke is emanating, and so you will take warning.

Or if the original were Oscar Wilde's famous epigram, *Vulgarity is the conduct of other people*, the paraphrase might read:

> We do not consider anything that we ourselves do as vulgar, even those very things which we call vulgarity in other people: vulgarity, therefore, is always associable in our minds only with people other than ourselves.

Hundreds of such paraphrases may be read in Dr. Brewer's 'Dictionary of Phrase and Fable'.

An exact paraphrase, whether it is an amplification of an epigram or, say, a transcription of a dramatic soliloquy, is a sure sign of understanding.

172

13

Comprehension

THE noun *comprehension* comes from Latin and means *understanding* (cf. the French verb *comprendre*). Further, we use the adjective *comprehensive* to mean *all-including,* and this gives the clue to what is meant by comprehending or understanding: for to understand anything means to have a comprehensive knowledge of it: you cannot understand a thing unless you know all about it.

An exercise in or test of comprehension is, therefore, aimed both at discovering how much a person has understood of the subject concerned and at increasing his understanding of it: it is not until we begin to ask ourselves searching questions that we realize how much more there is to know about a subject.

Where literature is concerned, the exercise or test takes the form of a series of questions about a given passage of writing, which may be in prose or verse. These questions are about anything and everything: the theme of the passage; its title if any, the writer's mind, opinions and character as revealed in the passage, any historical, literary, scientific or other references, the style, the meanings of phrases and words—and so on.

The following three lists of questions will illustrate the things which those who ask the questions wish to learn from those who answer them.

A. The passage is the speech by Macaulay quoted in the chapter on précis.

Questions:

1. Express the theme of the speech briefly in your own words.
2. Do you think the speech convincing? Does Macaulay sound sincere to you? Support your answers with evidence from the speech itself.
3. Select two groups of words which seem to you aptly to sum up the point of the speech. Why did you select these particular ones?
4. Select three examples of Macaulay's oratorical skill.
5. Do you consider this a good speech, or is it too literary?
6. What is meant by *Roman bulls*?
7. Explain the reference to *bloodshed and misery* in Charles I's time.
8. Name some of the other countries referred to.
9. What are *the bounds of the Constitution*?
10. What is meant by *the forms of law*?
11. What were the *three days of July*?
12. From the phraseology how can you tell that this was a public speech?
13. How can you tell that it is not a modern speech, quite apart from its reference to the Reform Bill?
14. What do you know of the Reform Bill? Was Macaulay justified in making the claims described in this speech?
15. Define the meaning of: gratification, convened, substance, signal, moral, sullied, pacific, great.

B. The passage is an excerpt from Aldous Huxley's essay, 'Popular Music':

The evolution of popular music has run parallel on a lower plane, with the evolution of serious music. The writers of popular tunes are not musicians enough to be able to invent new forms of expression. All they do is to adapt the discoveries of original geniuses to the vulgar taste. Ultimately

174

and indirectly Beethoven is responsible for all the languishing waltz tunes, all the savage jazzings, for all that is maudlin and violent in our popular music. He is responsible because it was he who first devised really effective musical methods for the direct expression of emotion. Beethoven's emotions happen to be noble; moreover, he was too intellectual a musician to neglect the formal, architectural side of music. But unhappily he made it possible for composers of inferior mind and character to express in music their less exalted emotions and vulgarer passions. He made possible the weakest sentimentalities of Schumann, the baroque grandiosities of Wagner, the hysterics of Scriabine; he made possible the waltzes of all the Strausses, from the *Blue Danube* to the waltz from *Salome*. And he made possible, at a still further remove, such masterpieces of popular art as *You made me love you* and *That coal black mammy of mine*.

Questions:

1. Briefly summarize this passage and give it a title.
2. This is a single paragraph. Do you think that it might have been more than one? Defend your opinion.
3. Do you think that Aldous Huxley has made his point clear?
4. What does he mean by *popular music* and *serious music*?
5. How was Beethoven *indirectly* responsible for *popular music*?
6. What do you understand by the *noble* emotions of Beethoven?
7. What is meant by *the formal, architectural side of music*?
8. What do you know of the other composers mentioned?
9. Define the meanings of the following words: evolution, languishing, maudlin, devised, intellectual, formal, grandiosities, masterpieces.
10. Do you think that the comma after *plane* in the first sentence is necessary?

11. Quote some examples of repetition. Are they essential?
12. How can you tell that the passage was written by a modern author?

C. This time the passage is a poem by Walter de la Mare:

THE SLEEPER

As Ann came in one summer day,
    She felt that she must creep,
So silent was the clear cool house,
    It seemed a house of sleep.
And sure, when she pushed open the door,
    Rapt in the stillness there,
Her mother sat, with stooping head,
    Asleep upon a chair;
Fast-fast asleep; her two hands laid
    Loose-folded on her knee,
So that her small unconscious face
    Looked half unreal to be:
So calmly lit with sleep's pale light
    Each feature was; so fair
Her forehead—every trouble was
    Smoothed out beneath her hair.
But though her mind in dream now moved,
    Still seemed her gaze to rest—
From out beneath her fast-sealed lids,
    Above her moving breast—
On Ann; as quite, quite still she stood;
    Yet slumber lay so deep
Even her hands upon her lap
    Seemed saturate with sleep.
And as Ann peeped, a cloudlike dread
    Stole over her, and then,
On stealthy, mouselike feet she trod,
    And tiptoed out again.

Questions:

1. How, apart from its being written in verse, is this poetry and not prose?

2. What are the rhyming and metrical schemes?
3. Do you find the rhymes logical and true or merely artificial?
4. Does the title seem to you the best?
5. Is the metre monotonously obvious, or subtle and rhythmically suited to the theme?
6. Show how the poet creates and maintains the atmosphere of silence.
7. Quote some examples of alliteration and simile and discuss their effectiveness.
8. Discuss the significance of such detail as is found in lines 9 and 10.
9. What do you understand by *sleep's pale light*?
10. Explain the image in lines 15 and 16.
11. How could the mother's mind move in dream?
12. Explain lines 23 and 24.
13. Express in your own words Ann's reaction to the sight of the sleeping figure.
14. What was the *cloudlike dread* which stole over her?
15. Discuss the adjectives which the poet has chosen.

In many language examinations now—and therefore in most textbooks—fewer but bigger questions are asked. These involve less isolation of detail but more consideration of the organic structure of the passage. The whole passage may have to be read again, and notes made, for the answering of a new question. Often the answers amount to small précis of a particular line of argument or series of illustrations. Indeed, numbers of words are given within which the answers must be written or beyond which they must not go.

Short or long, however, specific or general, comprehension questions are all aimed at the same good target.

14

Verse and Poetry

Foreword

'Sir, what is poetry?'
'Why, sir, it is much easier to say what it is not. We
all know what light is; but it is not easy to *tell* what it is.'
(BOSWELL: 'Life of Johnson'.)

IN this chapter, only the technicalities of versification are
discussed, and it should not be thought that poetry necessarily
enters the discussion at any point. There are of course
references to and quotations from unquestionably great poets
and poems, but although it may be true that all poetry is
written in verse—i.e. that there is no such thing as *prose
poetry*—it is not true that all verse is poetry. There is little
difficulty in the composition of verse as distinct from prose,
but as the poet William Cowper said in 'The Task':

> There is a pleasure in poetic pains
> Which only poets know.

Exactly what transforms verse into poetry nobody has yet
been able to define to the satisfaction of everyone else. Even
famous definitions of the word *poetry* by poets themselves
are legion, and many are the works which have been written
in analysis of the art of its composition and the nature of its
composer. We can all say something about the difference
between a friend's limerick and a Shakespearian sonnet, but
178

once we have passed beyond the obvious we are in territory across which progress is impossible without long and patient study.

Here, then, we look at the mechanics of versification: we see, as it were, scaffoldings, blue-prints and plans, but the buildings themselves are elsewhere. The information is an essential part of any study of the art of poetry, but it is only a part.

Some Definitions

Verse:	metrical composition;
Prosody:	the science of versification;
Metre:	the sequence of beats (stresses or accents) and unstressed syllables which creates rhythm;
Foot:	a metrical unit;
Scansion:	analysis into feet, using the symbols ˘ for an unstressed syllable and - or ´ for a stressed syllable; the technical name for an unstressed syllable is *thesis*, for a stressed syllable *arsis*: syllables are thus said to be *in thesis* or *in arsis*;
Stanza:	each separate section of a poem, identical in form with all the others;
Rhyme (or Rime):	common sound or echo.

Prosody. Types of Line. Feet.

A line of verse may be of any length, but there are special names for lines of special length:

a line containing only one foot is a *monometer*;
a line containing two feet is a *dimeter*;

lines containing three, four and five feet are *trimeters*, *tetrameters* and *pentameters* respectively;

lines containing six feet are *hexameters* or *Alexandrines* (*v. Specialities* k *infra*);

lines containing seven feet are *Fourteeners*.

Originally a foot consisted of two syllables, and so the pentameter, for example, had ten syllables and was alternatively called a *decasyllabic* line. Later, when new kinds of feet were realized, composed of only one syllable or more than two syllables, the syllabic names persisted even though there were no longer, say, ten syllables in a pentameter. Thus a monometer was called *dis(s)yllabic*, a dimeter *tetrasyllabic*, a trimeter *sexisyllabic*, and a tetrameter *octosyllabic*. The word *fourteener* shows the original character of the line composed of seven feet. The *hendecasyllabic* line contains eleven syllables.

We can still use the syllabic names as alternatives, but if we do we run the risk of being inaccurate.

The following feet exist:

(*a*) The *iambus* (creating iambic rhythm): this contains two syllables, the first unstressed, the second stressed. It is probably the commonest and the oldest in English poetry. Example:

Aňd whēn ňe ñext dŏth rīde ăbrōad,   (tetrameter)

Măy Ī bĕ thēre to sēe.   (trimeter)

(The starting of a line with an unstressed syllable is called *anacrusis*.)

(*b*) *The trochee* (creating trochaic rhythm): this is the inversion of the iambus, being composed of one stressed syllable followed by one unstressed.

Example:

Týgĕr! Týgĕr! bŭrnĭng brĭght,

Ĭn thĕ fŏrĕsts ŏf thĕ nĭght.　　　　　　(tetrameters)

(The technical word *inversion*—which should not be confused with the figure of speech—is used to describe the effect produced when in an otherwise iambic line a trochee replaces an iambus.)

This foot is alternatively called *choree*.

(*c*) The *spondee* (creating spondaic rhythm): this also has two syllables but both stressed: it is used as a variant of (*a*) and (*b*).

Example:

Mākĭng *swēet mūsĭc*, ăs ēach fōld rĕvōlves.　　(pentameter)

(*d*) The *anapaest* (creating anapaestic rhythm): this is trisyllabic, the first two syllables being unstressed:

Sēats ŏf m̆y yōuth, whĕn ēvĕrў spōrt cŏuld plēase.
　　　　　　　　　　　　　　　　　　　　(pentameter)

(*e*) The *dactyl* (creating dactylic rhythm): this is the inversion of the anapaest, being one stressed syllable followed by two unstressed:

Mērrĭlў, mērrĭlў, shāll Ĭ lĭve nōw.　　　(tetrameter)

Other feet are:

(i) the *tribrach*: three unstressed syllables: e.g. gĕnĕrăl;

(ii) the *amphibrach*: one unstressed syllable followed by one stressed and a third unstressed: e.g. ăvēngĕr;

(iii) the *pyrrhic*: two unstressed syllables: e.g. hŏvĕr;

(iv) the *paeon*: four syllables, only one of which is stressed; if the stress is on the first syllable it is called the First Paeon, and so on: e.g. p̄assĭŏnatel̆y;

(v) the *choriamb*: also four syllables, the first and last of which are stressed: e.g. w̄arrĭŏrlīke;

(vi) the *cretic*: one stressed syllable followed by one unstressed and a third stressed (i.e. opposite of *amphibrach*): e.g. ūndĕrḡo.

Unless it is used for a special effect strict metrical regularity becomes monotonous, and a survey of English poetry shows that every possible variety of metre has been and is being experimented with. Not only can all these different feet be interchanged, but single words of one syllable can stand alone, taking an unaccompanied stress, and constitute feet, as does *bright* in *Tyger! Tyger! burning bright*. Unstressed single words of one syllable, or, more commonly, single syllables in words, can be left out of the metrical plan of a line, particularly when they come at its end, and have what is called a *hypermetric* function. Lines ending in this way are said to have *feminine endings*. Shakespeare made frequent use of them:

> Rumble thy bellyful! Spit, fire! spout, rain!
> Nor rain, wind, thunder, fire, are my daugh*ters*.
> I tax not you, you elements, with unkind*ness*;
> I never gave you kingdom, call'd you child*ren*,
> You owe me no subscription.

> ('King Lear'.)

Still another variation is when a line, which is part of a regular stanzaic pattern, ends when another stress is still awaited. The final stressed syllable of an iambus, for example, may be deliberately omitted for the special effect which the irregularity produces. The metre of such a line is called *catalectic*. If a line has its full complement of foot-syllables it is *acatalectic*.

An example of a catalectic line is *Tyger! Tyger! burning bright*, whose last foot lacks the second, unstressed syllable of a fourth trochee.

The Caesura

In classical, and especially Latin, verse most lines were divided into two sections, and although this division has long ceased to be a rigid convention in English poetry (it was that in Old and Middle English verse) it still occurs, either at some break in the sense of a line or by virtue of a line's punctuation. This break is called the caesura. So in the line *Seats of my youth, when every sport could please*, there is a caesura after *youth*.

The caesura is closely associated with two other technical devices. If the sense of a line ends with its metrical length, the line is said to be *end-stopped*, but if the sense carries on into the next line, the continuation is called *enjambment* (a French word not translated). A poem in which every line, or every couplet (=distich=two lines rhyming), was end-stopped would be rhythmically monotonous, and any poem in which every line's sense continued into the next would also lack that variety of musical effect which is the essence of good verse. So the caesura exists as a pause in a line as distinct from a pause at the end of a line, so that in a passage of verse containing no end-stopped lines the use of the caesura ensures a continuity of rhythmic pauses. The following lines from Browning's 'My Last Duchess' show a most skilful combination of *enjambment*, end-stopped lines and caesura:

> Oh, sir, she smiled, no doubt,
> Whene'er I passed her! but who passed without
> Much the same smile? This grew; I gave commands;
> Then all smiles stopped together. There she stands
> As if alive. Will't please you rise? We'll meet
> The company below, then. I repeat,

183

The Count your Master's known munificence
Is ample warrant that no just pretence
Of mine for dowry will be disallowed;
Though his fair daughter's self, as I avowed
At starting, is my object. Nay, we'll go
Together down, Sir! Notice Neptune, though,
Taming a sea-horse, thought a rarity,
Which Claus of Innsbruck cast in bronze for me.

B. Rhyme

There are several kinds of rhyme:

(i) monosyllabic or masculine: e.g. *go—slow*;

(ii) disyllabic or feminine: e.g. *winding—finding*;

(iii) trisyllabic or triple: e.g. *wearily—eerily*;

(iv) assonance rhymes: i.e. certain letters, either vowels or consonants, sharing a common sound: e.g. s*and*—m*ind*; aba*sh*—bu*sh*; *clouds*—con*cludes*; awo*ke*—wro*te* (assonance rhymes therefore can include consonants—the poetic figure assonance entails vowels only);

(v) eye-rhymes: the words concerned look alike on paper but do not share a common sound: e.g. *cough—through*;

(vi) a variation of the feminine rhyme in which two monosyllabic words are echoed by two others: e.g. in a poem by Gerard Manley Hopkins:

> Leaves, like the things of man, you
> With your fresh thoughts care for, can you?

A similar variation of triple rhyme is also possible;

(vii) imperfect or half rhymes are usually a form of the assonance type: e.g. *love—move*.

In older poetry there appear to be many imperfect rhymes, and in our modern pronunciation they are imperfect; but this is due to the change of pronunciation which the rhymed words have undergone: when the verse was written the

rhymes were perfect. A famous example comes in Pope's
'The Rape of the Lock'.

> Here, thou, great ANNA! whom three realms obey,
> Dost sometimes counsel take—and sometimes Tea.

In the eighteenth century *tea* was pronounced *tay*, as,
indeed, it still is in some parts of the country.

Medial Rhymes

Most rhymes occur at the end of lines, but a poet may
rhyme where he wishes. A favourite with English poets has
been the internal or medial rhyme, that is the rhyming of
a word inside a line either with the word (or syllable) at the
end of its own line or with the word at the end of the preceding line, or with both. So in 'The Ancient Mariner':

> And through the *drifts* the snowy *clifts*
> Did send a dismal sheen:
> Nor shapes of *men* nor beasts we *ken*—
> The ice was all between;

or in 'The Raven' by Edgar Allan Poe:

> Ah, distinctly I *remember* it was in the bleak *December*,
> And each separate dying *ember* wrought its ghost upon the
> floor.
> Eagerly I wish'd the *morrow*—vainly had I sought to *borrow*
> From my books surcease of *sorrow*, sorrow for the lost
> Lenore—
> For the rare and radiant maiden whom the angels name
> Lenore—
> Nameless here for evermore.

The first stanza of 'The Conversation of Prayer' by Dylan
Thomas shows a more elaborate use of this form of rhyming:

> The conversation of *prayers* about to be *said*
> By the child going to *bed* and the man on the *stairs*
> Who climbs to his dying *love* in her high *room*,

185

The one not caring to *whom* in his sleep he will *move*
And the other full of *tears* that she will be *dead*. . . .

There is almost no limit to the variations possible, for any word in a line—including the first—may be rhymed with another or others at any point in its own line or other lines.

C. Forms of Verse—Stanza—Rhyme-Schemes

The commonest stanza in English poetry is the quatrain —most of the old anonymous ballads are written in it. Short though it is, however, numerous variations of line-length, metre and rhyme are possible.

The form which it has in most old ballads is as follows:

line 1 is a tetrameter, line 2 a trimeter, line 3 a tetrameter and line 4 a trimeter; the staple foot is the iambus; and the rhyme-scheme is *abcb* (letters are thus used).

This form is accordingly named *ballad metre*.

Many poets have subsequently used it, William Cowper, for instance, in 'John Gilpin':

> Now let us sing, Long live the king,
>   And Gilpin long live he;
> And when he next doth ride abroad,
>   May I be there to see!

'The Ancient Mariner' is for the most part also written in this form, although Coleridge used other feet in order to create a different rhythm (occasionally he also interpolated a longer stanza):

> He holds him with his glittering eye—
> The Wedding-Guest stood still,
> And listens like a three years' child:
> The Mariner hath his will.

A slight variation of this form is *common metre*. The

lengths of the lines are still 4343 (figures are thus used) but the rhyme-scheme is *abab*. Emily Brontë used this form in 'Song':

> Blow, west-wind, by the lonely mound,
>   And murmur, summer-streams—
> There is no need of other sound
>   To soothe my lady's dreams.

The following other variations of the quatrain have also been used:

(i) Four octosyllabic lines rhyming *abba*; used by Tennyson in 'In Memoriam':

> Forgive what seem'd my sin in me:
>   What seem'd my worth since I began;
>   For merit lives from man to man,
> And not from man, O Lord, to thee.

(ii) Four tetrameters rhyming *aabb*; used by Blake in 'The Tyger':

> Tyger! Tyger! burning bright
> In the forests of the night,
> What immortal hand or eye
> Could frame thy fearful symmetry?

(iii) Four octosyllabic lines rhyming *abab*; used by Tennyson in 'To J.S.':

> God gives us love. Something to love
>   He lends us; but, when love is grown
> To ripeness, that on which it throve
>   Falls off, and love is left alone.

(iv) Four tetrameters rhyming *abcb*; used by Laurence Whistler in 'Fear at the Manor':

> Stay with me, my darling mother,
> Stay with me a little, for I,
> I'm frightened when I think of dying,
> Why were we made if we must die?

187

(v) Four decasyllabic lines rhyming *aaba*; used by Edward Fitzgerald in 'The Rubáiyát of Omar Khayyám':

> Ah, fill the Cup:—what boots is to repeat
> How Time is slipping underneath our feet:
>   Unborn To-morrow and dead Yesterday,
> Why fret about them if To-day be sweet?

(vi) Four pentameters rhyming *abab*; used by Gray in 'Elegy in a Country Churchyard':

> Full many a gem of purest ray serene,
> The dark unfathom'd caves of ocean bear:
> Full many a flower is born to blush unseen,
> And waste its sweetness on the desert air.

This particular stanza is called the *Elegiac stanza.*

(vii) One pentameter, one tetrameter, a second pentameter and a final trimeter, rhyming *abab*; used by Tennyson in 'The Palace of Art':

> I built my soul a lordly pleasure-house,
>   Wherein at ease for aye to dwell.
> I said, 'O Soul, make merry and carouse,
>   Dear soul, for all is well.'

(viii) Three pentameters and one trimeter, rhyming *abab*; used by Tennyson in 'A Dream of Fair Women':

> The dim red morn had died, her journey done,
>   And with dead lips smiled at the twilight plain,
> Half-fall'n across the threshold of the sun,
>   Never to rise again.

By now still other variations have been introduced, such as four pentameters rhyming *abba*; and blank-verse quatrains of tetrameters and/or pentameters have been written. The possibilities are not yet exhausted.

Decasyllabic Blank Verse

The decasyllabic line or pentameter was used in Greek

and Latin elegiac poetry; in English it is the heroic or epic metre.

Most Elizabethan drama is written in it, without rhymes —i.e. in blank verse:

> Signior Antonio, many a time and oft
> In the Rialto you have rated me
> About my moneys and my usances:
> Still have I borne it with a patient shrug,
> (For sufferance is the badge of all our tribe).
> You call me misbeliever, cut-throat dog,
> And spit upon my Jewish gaberdine,
> And all for use of that which is mine own;

or

> But soft, what light through yonder window breaks?
> It is the east, and Juliet is the sun.
> Arise, fair sun, and kill the envious moon,
> Who is already sick and pale with grief,
> That thou, her maid, art far more fair than she.

Milton used it in his epics:

> Of man's first disobedience, and the fruit
> Of that forbidden tree, whose mortal taste
> Brought death into the world, and all our woe,
> With loss of Eden, till one greater Man
> Restore us, and regain the blissful seat,
> Sing, Heavenly Muse. . . .

Browning used it with novel effect in many poems, breaking up the lines according to a conversational idiom: e.g. in 'Bishop Blougram's Apology':

> No more wine? then we'll push back chairs and talk.
> A final glass for me, though: cool, i' faith!
> We ought to have our Abbey back, you see.

Other poets who have used it are Wordsworth in 'Tintern Abbey', Matthew Arnold in 'Sohrab and Rustum', Tennyson

189

in 'Morte D'Arthur', Shelley in 'Alastor' and Keats in 'Hyperion', and it is much used by modern poets.

In any assessment of the rival claims of blank verse and rhymed the points made by Milton in his prefatory note to 'Paradise Lost' must find a place. He had chosen blank verse for his great epic and so championed it, reminding his readers that ancient Greek and Latin poetry had been written in blank verse, that Italian and Spanish poets had rejected rhyme, and that English drama was also rhymeless. Rhyme, he said, was a 'troublesome' thing, a 'bondage' and often only a 'jingling sound of like endings'.

But he had himself used rhyme in his earlier and shorter works, and it was on the undesirability of rhyme in long poems that he was insisting. Many poets have agreed with him, many have disagreed. Some of the greatest poems in English are written in heroic blank verse, such as 'Paradise Lost' itself and Wordsworth's 'The Prelude', but some of the greatest are in rhymed heroic verse, especially the heroic couplet: Chaucer's 'Canterbury Tales' and Pope's 'The Dunciad'; while in other forms Byron's 'Don Juan' alone proves that rhyme is not necessarily a bondage in the longest of poems.

Poets will of course go on using both forms according to their tastes and intentions. More and more poets have used blank verse since Milton's demonstration of its epic power, and by now we have had blank verse lyrics and sonnets. But rhyme is as indispensable an element of poetry as metre, and there is no likelihood of it ever becoming archaic. Modern poets have shown that there is still a great deal of valuable experiment to be carried on with new rhymes, especially with assonance rhymes, and in the same way that they have departed from conventional metrical and stanzaic forms and explored the possibilities of *free verse* (*v. infra*), so they have shown that the poet can turn the 'bondage' of rhyme to

190

his own advantage in many hitherto unsuspected ways.

Decasyllabic or Heroic Couplets

Since the line in use is the same as that in epic blank verse, the term *heroic* was adopted for the decasyllabic couplet in the later seventeenth century, although the subject-matter of the *heroic* poems then in vogue was seldom epic in the Homeric or Virgilian sense.

The first famous example of the form in English literature is Chaucer's 'Canterbury Tales':

> This sely wydwe and eek hir doghtres two
> Herden thise hennes crie and maken wo,
> And out at dores stirten they anon,
> And syen the fox toward the grove gon,
> And bar upon his bak the cok away,
> And cryden, 'Out! harrow! and weylaway!
> Ha! ha! the fox!' and after hym they ran,
> And eek with staves many another man.
> Ran Colle our dogge, and Talbot, and Gerland,
> And Malkyn, with a dystaf in hir hand;
> Ran cow and calf, and eek the verray hogges,
> So fered for the berkyng of the dogges
> And shoutyng of the men and women eeke,
> They renne so hem thoughte hir herte breeke.

So Chaucer proved what a successful form it could be; but it was a long time before it became the dominant fashion. This it became towards the end of the seventeenth and in the eighteenth century. Dryden (1631-1700) and Pope (1688-1744) used it in their satires; and there is no question that it is the ideal form for the verse-satirist:

> Sh— alone of all my Sons is he
> Who stands confirm'd in full stupidity.
> The rest to some faint meaning make pretence,
> But Sh— never deviates into sense.
> Some Beams of Wit on other souls may fall,
> Strike through and make a lucid intervall;

191

> But Sh—'s genuine night admits no ray,
> His rising Fogs prevail upon the Day.
> (DRYDEN: 'MacFlecknoe'.)

Pope also used it in his didactic 'Essays':

> First follow Nature, and your judgment frame
> By her just standard, which is still the same:
> Unerring Nature, still divinely bright,
> One clear, unchanged, and universal light,
> Life, force, and beauty, must to all impart,
> At once the source, and end, and test of Art.
> ('An Essay on Criticism'.)

For some time it was limited to such satirical and moralistic purposes, until poets realized that it might be adaptable to a different purpose. So Goldsmith used it in his 'The Deserted Village':

> Sweet Auburn! loveliest village of the plain,
> Where health and plenty cheer'd the labouring swain,
> Where smiling spring its earliest visits paid,
> And parting summer's ling'ring blooms delay'd:
> Dear lovely bowers of innocence and ease,
> Seats of my youth, when every sport could please.

The transition to Keats's 'Lamia' had been made. The following lines seem hardly to be in the same form as 'MacFlecknoe':

> Before each lucid pannel fuming stood
> A censer fed with myrrh and spiced wood,
> Each by a sacred tripod held aloft,
> Whose slender feet wide-swerv'd upon the soft
> Wool-woof'd carpets: fifty wreaths of smoke
> From fifty censers their light voyage took
> To the high roof, still mimick'd as they rose
> Along the mirror'd walls by twin clouds odorous.

Browning, who made every form sound new, used the couplet in 'My Last Duchess':

That's my last Duchess painted on the wall,
Looking as if she were alive; I call
That piece a wonder, now: Fra Pandolf's hands
Worked busily a day, and there she stands.
Will 't please you sit and look at her? I said
'Fra Pandolf' by design, for never read
Strangers like you that pictured countenance,
The depth and passion of its earnest glance,
But to myself they turned (since none puts by
The curtain I have drawn for you, but I)
And seemed as they would ask me, if they durst,
How such a glance came there; so, not the first
Are you to turn and ask thus.

Other poets to use it were Marlowe in 'Hero and Leander',
Donne in his 'Elegies' and 'Satyres', Dr. Johnson in 'The
Vanity of Human Wishes', and Byron in 'English Bards and
Scotch Reviewers'. It was popular with the Restoration
dramatists until Dryden abandoned it in 'All For Love'. It
is seldom used today outside light, satirical verse.

Octosyllabic Couplets

Chaucer also made this form popular, though here again
it was a long time before any major poet took to it, and it
has never enjoyed the popularity of the decasyllabic couplet.
Chaucer used it in 'The Book of the Duchess', 'The House of
Fame' and 'The Romaunt of the Rose':

> If ye wol you now confesse,
> And leave your synnes, more and lesse,
> Without abod, knele down anon,
> And you shal have absolucion.

Milton used it in 'L'Allegro' and 'Il Penseroso':

> Oft, on a plat of rising ground,
> I hear the far-off curfew sound
> Over some wide-watered shore,
> Swinging slow with sullen roar;
> Or, if the air will not permit,

> Some still removed place will fit,
> Where glowing embers through the room
> Teach light to counterfeit a gloom.

Two other major poets to use it with success were Burns in 'Tam o' Shanter' and Coleridge in 'Christabel'.

The Sonnet

> A sonnet is a moment's monument.
> (D. G. ROSSETTI.)

The sonnet, which traditionally has fourteen lines, was introduced into England in the sixteenth century by poets imitating Italian models. The greatest Italian sonneteer was Francesco Petrarca (1304-74), better known as Petrarch, and it was the form used by him which was first used by English poets. Nicknamed the Petrarch(i)an sonnet, it is a single stanza divided either in or at the end of the eighth line into two parts called the octet and the sestet, the rhyme-scheme of the former being *abbaabba* and of the latter *cdecde*. All the lines are pentameters, as, indeed, are those of most sonnets (Shakespeare's 145th is one of the few written in tetrameters). After Shakespeare had used a variation of this form, the Petrarchan sonnet suffered a decline until Milton revived it and gave it its alternative name of Miltonic. The following sonnet, 'On His Blindness', is a perfect example of the form:

> When I consider how my light is spent,
>   Ere half my days in this dark world and wide,
>   And that one talent, which is death to hide
>   Lodged with me useless, though my soul more bent
> To serve therwith my Maker, and present
>   My true account, lest He returning chide;
>   'Doth God exact day-labour, light denied?'
>   I fondly ask: but Patience, to prevent
> That murmur, soon replies 'God doth not need

Either man's work, or his own gifts. Who best
Bear his mild yoke, they serve him best: his state
Is kingly: thousands at his bidding speed,
And post o'er land and ocean without rest;
They also serve who only stand and wait.'

The variation which Shakespeare used and which became
known as the Shakespearian sonnet usually retained the division into octet and sestet, but had a different rhyme-scheme:
ababcdcdefefgg. It is, in effect, four stanzas, three quatrains
and a final couplet, and sometimes is written down as such.
The following sonnet is his 18th:

Shall I compare thee to a summer's day?
Thou art more lovely and more temperate:
Rough winds do shake the darling buds of May,
And summer's lease hath all too short a date:
Sometimes too hot the eye of heaven shines,
And often is his gold complexion dimm'd,
And every fair from fair sometime declines,
By chance, or nature's changing course untrimm'd:
But thy eternal summer shall not fade,
Nor lose possession of that fair thou ow'st,
Nor shall Death brag thou wander'st in his shade,
When in eternal lines to time thou grow'st:
So long as men can breathe or eyes can see,
So long lives this, and this gives life to thee.

As T. S. Eliot has said, 'The sonnet of Shakespeare is not
merely such and such a pattern, but a precise way of thinking and feeling.'

Almost every poet in our literature has written in the
sonnet-form since the time of its introduction. For a long
time the Petrarchan and Shakespearian patterns were the
only ones to be used, until variations were experimented
with. Shelley, for instance in 'Ozymandias', used the following
rhyme-scheme: *ababacdcedefef*, thus linking the octet to the
sestet by rhyming the seventh and tenth lines.

195

So variation succeeded variation. Rupert Brooke rhymed his famous sonnet, 'The Soldier': *ababcdcdefgefg*, a mixture of the Petrarchan and Shakespearian forms. Modern poets have departed from all the conventional patterns. The octet and sestet are no longer considered essential to the form. Rex Warner, for example, has separated the fourteen lines into four stanzas of 4, 3, 4 and 3 lines respectively so that the sonnet falls into two seven-line halves. Rhyme has also been dispensed with, as by David Gascoyne in 'Spring MCMXL'. A very ingenious innovation was Louis MacNeice's use of two stanzas of ten and four lines rhyming in couplets:

SUNDAY MORNING

Down the road someone is practising scales,
The notes like little fishes vanish with a wink of tails,
Man's heart expands to tinker with the car
For this is Sunday morning, Fate's great bazaar;
Regard these means as ends, concentrate on this Now,
And you may grow to music or drive beyond Hindhead anyhow,
Take corners on two wheels until you go so fast
That you can clutch a fringe or two of the windy past,
That you can abstract this day and make it to the week of time
A small eternity, a sonnet self-contained in rhyme.

But listen, up the road, something gulps, the church spire
Opens its eight bells out, skulls' mouths which will not tire
To tell how there is no music or movement which secures
Escape from the weekday time. Which deadens and endures.

The technical and psychological division was thus placed after the tenth line instead of after the eighth.

Among other experiments with the sonnet we must mention Gerard Manley Hopkins's 'curtal' sonnets, which are divided into sections of 6 and $4\frac{1}{2}$ lines (i.e. the proportions still are 4/3). No doubt there will be even more experiments yet.

But the essential sonnet obviously has fourteen rhymed lines divided into an octet and a sestet, which exist in the thematic relationship of point and counterpoint.

Rhyme-Royal, sometimes called Ballade-Royal. The Ballade.

Rhyme-Royal or Ballade-Royal is a seven-line stanza, all the lines pentameters and rhyming *ababbcc*. Chaucer used it in 'Troilus and Criseyde':

> But ye loveres, that bathen in gladnesse,
> If any drope of pyte in yow be,
> Remembreth yow on passed hevynesse
> That ye han felt, and on the adversite
> Of othere folk, and thynketh how that ye
> Han felt that Love dorste yow displese,
> Or ye han wonne hym with to grete an ese.

Thomas Sackville (1536-1608) used it in 'A Mirour for Magistrates', Milton in the first four stanzas of 'On the Morning of Christ's Nativity', and Wordsworth in 'Resolution and Independence'.

A ballade consists of three stanzas rhyming together, followed by an *Envoy* or final message. Occasionally an eight-line stanza is used, but normally the form is rhyme-royal. The last line of each stanza is a refrain. An amusing example is Chaucer's 'Complaint to his Purse':

> To yow, my purse, and to noon other wight
> Complayne I, for ye be my lady dere!
> I am so sory, now that ye been lyght;
> For certes, but ye make me hevy chere,
> Me were as leef be layd upon my bere;
> For which unto your mercy thus I crye:
> Beth hevy ageyn, or elles mot I dye!
>
> Now voucheth sauf this day, or yt be nyght,
> That I of yow the blisful soun may here,
> Or see your colour lyk the sonne bryght,
> That of yelownesse hadde never pere.

Ye be my lyf, ye be myn hertes stere,
Quene of comfort and of good companye:
Beth hevy ageyn, or ellse moote I dye!

Now purse, that ben to me my lyves lyght
And saveour, as doun in this world here,
Out of this toune helpe me thurgh your myght,
Syn that ye wole nat ben my tresorere;
For I am shave as nye as any frere.
But yet I pray unto your curtesye:
Beth hevy agen, or elles moote I dye!

Lenvoy de Chaucer

O conquerour of Brutes Albyon,
Which that by lyne and free eleccion
Been verray kyng, this song to yow I sende;
And ye, that mowen alle oure harmes amende,
Have mynde upon my supplicacion!

Sometimes a ballade takes the form of more than one set of three stanzas and an envoy.

Three stanzas rhyming together are given the same name as three lines rhyming, i.e. *triplet*, and the technical name for a set of three stanzas is a *tern*.

The Spenserian Stanza

This is the special stanza invented by Edmund Spenser (1552-99) for his long allegory, 'The Faerie Queene'. It has nine lines rhyming *ababbcbcc*, the first eight of which are pentameters and the last is a hexameter or Alexandrine:

A Gentle Knight was pricking on the plaine,
Y cladd in mightie armes and silver shielde,
Wherein old dints of deepe wounds did remaine,
The cruell marker of many a bloudy fielde;
Yet armes till that time did he never wield:
His angry steede did chide his foming bitt,
As much disdayning to the curbe to yield:
Full iolly knight he seemd, and faire did sitt,
As one for knightly giusts and fierce encounters fitt.

Spenser was not the first poet to use a nine-line stanza, but this particular pattern was his invention. Chaucer had used a nine-line stanza in 'The Compleynt of Mars', but all the lines were pentameters and the rhyme-scheme was *aabaabbcc*.

The new pattern attracted other poets. Byron used it in 'Childe Harold', Shelley in 'Adonais', Keats in 'The Eve of St. Agnes' and Tennyson in 'The Lotos-Eaters'.

Ottava Rima

As its name shows, this is an Italian form. It was used by Keats in 'Isabella', but Byron is the only English poet to have used it on a large scale in a single work and with continuous success. In his hands it became the perfect vehicle for his great verse scrap-book, 'Don Juan'. Complex a form though it is, he made it sound and look simple, not only in this poem but also in 'Beppo' and 'The Vision of Judgment', two superbly comic narratives

It is an eight-line stanza, all pentameters, rhyming *abababcc*. The following stanza is from 'The Vision of Judgment':

> The angels were all singing out of tune,
>   And hoarse with having little else to do,
> Excepting to wind up the sun and moon,
>   Or curb a runaway young star or two,
> Or wild colt of a comet, which too soon
>   Broke out of bounds o'er th' eternal blue,
> Splitting some planet with its playful tale,
> As boats are sometimes by a wanton whale.

The Ode and Lyric

Originally odes were poems written to be sung (i.e. Choral Odes). In ancient Greece they were ceremonial in function, and it is their ceremonial and choral origin which is responsible for their complicated forms.

199

There are certain special forms such as the Pindaric ode, so-called because it was invented by the Greek poet Pindar. This is divided into three parts, a strophe, an antistrophe and an epode. An example of it in English is Gray's 'The Progress of Poesy'. It is too long to quote, but the metrical and rhyming plan is as follows:

strophe:	3 stanzas; irregular line-lengths, but most lines either octosyllabic or decasyllabic; 12 lines in each of the first two stanzas, 17 in the third stanza; rhyme-scheme of the first two stanzas: *abbaccddeeff*; of the third stanza: *aabbaccdedefgfghh*.
antistrophe:	3 stanzas ditto;
epode:	also 3 stanzas ditto.

The three parts share the same pattern, therefore. They correspond to three musical movements, the antistrophe being a new theme counterpoised against the theme of the strophe, and the epode serving to resolve the two.

Comparatively few poets have been willing to undertake the writing of so complicated and artificial a form, however, and the ode in English is free from any set plan. In this survey of the ode and lyric we are moving away from special forms and procedures. The poets are free to please themselves about their stanzas, line-lengths and rhyme-schemes. So the ode and the lyric may assume any form, and what constitutes them as distinct from, say, an epic or a satire is what they express. Certain forms, however, such as heroic decasyllabic blank verse, they are obviously unlikely to take.

Two famous Elizabethan odes are Spenser's 'Prothalamion' and 'Epithalamion'. The forms he used were suggested by Italian models, but no more than suggested. The complexity of the rhyme-scheme and the variety of the metre can be seen in a single stanza from 'Prothalamion':

Yet therein now doth lodge a noble Peer,	*a*
Great Englands glory and the Worlds wide wonder,	*b*
Whose dreadfull name, late through all Spaine did thunder,	*b*
And Hercules two pillars standing neere,	*a*
Did make to quake and feare:	*a*
Faire branch of Honor, flower of Chevalrie,	*c*
That fillest England with thy triumphes fame	*d*
Joy have thou of thy noble victorie,	*c*
And endlesse happinesse of thine owne name	*d*
That promiseth the same:	*d*
That through thy prowesse and victorious armes,	*e*
Thy country may be freed from forraine harmes:	*e*
And great Elisaes glorious name may ring	*f*
Through al the world, fil'd with thy wide Alarmes,	*e*
Which some brave muse may sing	*f*
To ages following,	*f*
Upon the Brydale day, which is not long:	*g*
Sweete Thammes runne softly till I end my Song.	*g*

Milton's 'Lycidas' is a continuous elegiac ode. It has 193 lines, most of which are iambic pentameters, but shorter lines occur irregularly, the rhymes come irregularly, and some lines remain unrhymed.

Marvell's 'An Horatian Ode upon Cromwell's Return from Ireland' has a form based on that used by the Roman poet Horace. It has 120 lines, written without stanzaic intervals although in stanzaic paragraphs. The metrical and rhyming pattern is regular, two tetrameters rhyming, followed by two trimeters rhyming:

> So restlesse Cromwell could not cease
> In the inglorious arts of peace,
> But through adventurous warre
> Urged his active starre.

William Collins, a contemporary of Thomas Gray, wrote several odes, the most famous of which is 'An Ode on the

Popular Superstitions of the Highlands of Scotland'. It has 194 lines, divided into stanzas, some of sixteen lines, some of seventeen; the rhyme-scheme is almost regular; and all the lines are pentameters except the last in each stanza, which is an Alexandrine.

Two other famous odes are Wordsworth's 'Ode: Intimations of Immortality from Recollections of Early Childhood' and Tennyson's 'Ode on the Death of the Duke of Wellington'. Both are irregular in metre and rhyme.

The ode has been called 'a rhymed (rarely unrhymed) lyric, often in the form of an address, generally dignified or exalted in subject'.

In Elizabethan and Jacobean days the word *sonnet* was often used as a synonym for lyric, and some of the best lyrics in English are the *sonnets* of Donne, Suckling and other poets of the late sixteenth and early seventeenth centuries.

A poet may use such an established form as ballad metre in a lyric, but that does not make his lyric a ballad in the true sense of the word. Some of Burns's love songs, for instance, and certain poems in 'A Shropshire Lad', are written in ballad metre but are lyrics.

Most lyrics, however, like odes, are not in any of the forms described above. Tennyson's 'The Lady of Shalott' has the unique form of a nine-line stanza, the first four lines of which are tetrameters, the fifth line is a trimeter, the sixth, seventh and eighth lines are tetrameters, and the ninth is another trimeter. The rhyme-scheme is *aaaabcccb*.

Browning's 'A Toccata of Galuppi's' is written in three-line stanzas, i.e. *tercets*, rhyming *aaa*, i.e. in triplets.

Matthew Arnold's 'The Scholar Gipsy' has ten-line stanzas rhyming *abcbcadeed*, all the lines being pentameters except the sixth, which is a trimeter. His 'Thyrsis' has the same form.

Wordsworth's 'Laodamia' has a six-line stanza, all the lines pentameters, rhyming *ababcc*.

Edward Lear's nonsense lyric, 'The Dong with a Luminous Nose', is a good example of free lyrical verse. Its 'stanzas' are of varying length, there is a most diverse metrical plan, and the rhyme-scheme is irregular. The poetry of Thomas Hood and Rudyard Kipling also shows how many variations of form are possible in the lyric. But a glance through Palgrave's 'Golden Treasury' is enough to show the range of forms already used by English poets, and, of course, not all the changes have yet been rung.

Perhaps it will be as well to clarify the difference between an ode and a lyric. They are alike in that they may have an established form—the ode may be Pindaric or Horatian, for instance, the lyric may be written in the Spenserian stanza— but more often they are not in any rigid and labelled form; otherwise they are dissimilar. The difference is not merely or necessarily one of length: Keats's odes are shorter than 'The Lady of Shalott'. Very short odes are uncommon, however, as are very long lyrics. But the essential difference is that the ode is an exalted apostrophe or invocation, an almost impersonal incantation, whereas the lyric is either a descriptive narrative—like 'The Lady of Shalott'—or a direct expression of intimate personal feelings. It is the difference between the 'Ode: Intimations of Immortality' and Burns's 'My luve is like a red, red rose'.

Free Verse. Modern Times

The term *free verse*—a good example of oxymoron—is a literal translation of the French *vers libre*, which was used to specify the technical contrast between the poetry of the Symbolists (Verlaine, Mallarmé, etc.) and the long-established conventions against which that poetry was a reaction. For the Symbolists deliberately released French poetry from the regular metrical, stanzaic and rhyming patterns which had dominated it for over 300 years, so that there was no verse-pattern in the familiar sense in their poetry—their verse was free, both metre and rhyme being subject to a wholly individual and, if necessary, irregular treatment. And both the term *vers libre* and what it named crossed the Channel to exert a pervasive influence on twentieth century English poetry. This does not mean, however, that there was no free verse in England before. Shakespeare had departed from the decasyllabic line wilfully, and so had his Jacobean successors in the drama. The metaphysical poets of the seventeenth century had played tricks with metre which sound sometimes as modern as 'The Waste Land' of T. S. Eliot sounded in 1922. The influence of these poets on our modern poets is widespread and makes a fascinating study. We meet more and more free verse in nineteenth-century poetry, in Tennyson, Browning and Sydney Dobell, for instance:

> Then came the daisies,
> On the first of May,
> Like a bannered show's advance
> While the crowd runs by the way,
> With ten thousand flowers about them they came trooping
> through the fields.
> As a happy people come
> So came they,
> As a happy people come
> When the war has rolled away.
> With dance and tabor, pipe and drum,
> And all make holiday.
>
> ('A Chanted Calendar' by DOBELL.)

In his 'Manual of English Prosody' George Saintsbury spoke of *some modern rhymeless experimenters*, and he was referring to Matthew Arnold and William Henley.

An underrated influence on English poetry in this direction was the poetry of the American Walt Whitman (1819-92), whose 'Leaves of Grass', published in 1855, caused a sensation.

His early poetry had been written in a variety of forms:
ballad metre, lyrics in trimeters and tetrameters, decasyllabic
blank verse and odes. But after a time he began to find a
regular metrical pattern and rhyme intolerable burdens and
experimented with irregular blank verse: it was in this form
that most of the poems in 'Leaves of Grass' were written.

The following poem illustrates this new free verse:

> When I peruse the conquered fame of heroes and the victories
>   of mighty generals, I do not envy the generals,
> Nor the President in his Presidency, nor the rich in his great
>   house;
> But when I hear of the brotherhood of lovers, how it was with
>   them,
> How through life, through dangers, odium, unchanging, long
>   and long,
> Through youth, and through middle and old age, how
>   unfaltering, how affectionate and faithful they were,
> Then I am pensive—I hastily walk away filled with bitterest
>   envy.

The influence of such poetry in England can readily be
seen in the work of D. H. Lawrence, for example, in such a
poem as 'Snake'. As Ezra Pound said of Whitman, he 'broke
the new wood'.

An early love-lyric by Ezra Pound well exemplifies
twentieth-century free verse as it was used to express personal emotions which, earlier, would have seemed to compel
some regularity of both metre and rhyme:

FRANCESCA

> You came in out of the night
> And there were flowers in your hands,
> Now you will come out of a confusion of people
> Out of a turmoil of speech about you.
>
> I who have seen you amid the primal things
> Was angry when they spoke your name
> In ordinary places.

205

I would that the cool waves might flow over my mind,
And that the world should dry as a dead leaf,
Or as a dandelion seed-pod and be swept away,
So that I might find you again,
Alone.

Two further examples of modern free blank verse will suffice to show the new poetry which has been written in our time. The first is from T. S. Eliot's 'The Waste Land', a very important formative influence on subsequent English poetry:

April is the cruelest month, breeding
Lilacs out of the dead land, mixing
Memory and desire, stirring
Dull roots with spring rain.
Winter kept us warm, covering
Earth in forgetful snow, feeding
A little life with dried tubers.
Summer surprised us, coming over the Starnbergersee
With a shower of rain; we stopped in the colonnade,
And went on in sunlight, into the Hofgarten,
And drank coffee, and talked for an hour.

The second is from 'Finale' by the young poet Alun Lewis who died in the Second World War:

To-day he struck a final gesture,
Arms akimbo against the sky,
Crucified on a cross of fire
With all the heroic age magnificent in him.
And now he lies in a pose more rigid
Than any that Life with its gambler's chance
Flung on him at a venture.

But although blank verse has been fashionable during the past few decades, the accumulated store of metrical and rhyming patterns has still been drawn upon by young poets as well as old. Sometimes a compromise has been reached between free metre and rhyme, as in C. Day Lewis's 'Ode to Fear':

Now Fear has come again	*a*
To live with us	*b*
In poisoned intimacy like pus,	*b*
Hourly extending the area of our pain,	*a*
It seems I must make the most	*c*
Of fever's pulsing dreams and thus	*b*
Live to allay this evil or dying lay its ghost.	*c*

Certain other technical innovations have been made in our time and for varying reasons. Thus only those lines which start new sentences begin with capital letters:

> Against the window pane
> against the temple of my brain
> beat the muffled taps of pain.
>
> Upon the scorched and mottled leaves
> upon the blenched and pented sheaves
> the land receives
>
> the liquid flood:
> water like a blush of blood
> returns to the parched rood.
> (From 'Summer Rain' by HERBERT READ.)

Sometimes all punctuation has been dispensed with, as it is felt that in verse at any rate the arrangement of the words in lines makes punctuation superfluous:

> No seed they have no seed
> their tendrils are of wire and grip
> the buttonhole the lip
> and never fade
>
> And will not fade though life
> and lustre go in genuine flowers
> and men like flowers are cut
> and withered on a stem
> (From 'A Short Poem for Armistice
> Day' by HERBERT READ.)

Finally, it is not surprising that in this century there have been poets whose work cannot be classified, so individualistic is it. There have been as many pseudo-poets and freaks as in

207

previous ages, of course; but among the true poets themselves there have been those who have taken verse far from
anything Shakespeare or Keats, Tennyson or Bridges would
have recognized. Edith Sitwell, for example, has written verse
of a wholly new type, complex of form and planned along
musical lines, in 'Façade': e.g.

> When
> Sir
> Beelzebub called for his syllabub in the hotel in Hell
>   Where Proserpine first fell,
> Blue as the gendarmerie were the waves of the sea,
>   (Rocking and shocking the bar-maid).

But modern poetry is much more than all this, and it
must not be judged from a merely technical sketch, which is
all that is intended in this chapter. Not all living poets are
modern, in any case. For *modernity* is a new style both of
thinking and of writing: it is, in T. S. Eliot's words, 'a
subjective difference of method'.

The Poetic Figures of Speech

Alliteration

This is the repetition of the same consonant(s) in neighbouring words:

> Music that brings sweet sleep down from the blissful skies;

> And his horse in the silence champed the grasses
>   Of the forest's ferny floor.

Assonance

This is the repetition of the same vowel-sounds in neighbouring words:

> The man that hath no music in himself,
> Nor is not moved with concord of sweet sounds,
> Is fit for . . .;

('Merchant of Venice' v. 1.)

It seemed that out of battle I escaped
Down some profound dull tunnel, long since scooped
Through granites which titanic wars had groined.
                    (WILFRED OWEN: 'Strange Meeting'.)

Onomatopoeia

This means the use of words to simulate sounds. Many
single words are onomatopoeic or echoic, but onomatopoeia
as a figure of speech means the use of two or more words
close to one another, which, not necessarily echoic in separation, create a sound-effect in their deliberate juxtaposition.
Both alliteration and assonance are, of course, onomatopoeic.
The following lines contain a brilliant modern example of
this figure:

> After the first powerful plain manifesto
> The black statement of pistons, without more fuss
> But gliding like a queen, she leaves the station.
>   (From 'The Express' by STEPHEN SPENDER.)

Apostrophe or Invocation

This is the name given to a direct address by the poet to the
subject of his poem; it is most appropriate in epics and odes.
So Milton apostrophizes the Muse in the opening lines of
'Paradise Lost':

> Of man's first disobedience, and the fruit
> Of that forbidden tree, whose mortal taste
> Brought death into the world, and all our woe,
> With loss of Eden, till one greater Man
> Restore us, and regain the blissful seat,
> Sing, Heavenly Muse . . .

Perhaps the most famous apostrophe in English poetry is
the first line of Shelley's 'To a Skylark':

> Hail to thee, blithe Spirit!

209

Inversion

This means the inverting of the normal, prose order of words in order to give them a verse cadence. Coleridge used it throughout 'The Ancient Mariner':

> The bride had paced into the hall
> Red as a rose is she;
> Nodding their heads before her goes
> The merry minstrelsy.

Metaphor

This has already been explained in an earlier chapter, for it is as frequent in prose as in verse. A famous poetic example occurs in Shelley's 'Song to the Men of England':

> Wherefore, Bees of England, forge
> Many a weapon, chain and scourge,
> That these stingless drones may spoil
> The forced produce of your toil?

Simile

This too has already been explained. A fine poetic example comes in Keats's sonnet, 'On First Looking into Chapman's Homer':

> Then felt I like some watcher of the skies
> When a new planet swims into his ken;
> Or like stout Cortez, when with eagle eyes
> He stared at the Pacific . . .

There is also the 'epic simile', as used by Milton, in which the comparison is sustained in detail for several lines of verse.

Parallelism

This means the restatement of the same thought in one or

more different ways. It is, in fact, a form of repetition.
Numerous instances occur in the Bible and 'Paradise Lost':

> To whom the great Creator thus reply'd,
> O Son, in whom my Soul hath chief delight,
> Son of my bosom, Son who art alone
> My word, my wisdom, and effectual might . . .;
>
> He ask'd, but all the Heavenly Quire stood mute,
> And silence was in Heav'n . . .

Personification (or Prosopopoeia)

This is the attribution to non-human things of human
qualities and abilities:

> The Rainbow comes and goes,
> And lovely is the Rose,
> The Moon doth with delight
> Look round her when the heavens are bare.
>
> (WORDSWORTH.)

Imagery

All figures of speech are images, but there is a special style
of poetic expression in which a comprehensive metaphor is
used to make a whole poem an image. The best poetry of this
kind was written by the metaphysical writers of the seventeenth century, Donne in particular. The following stanza
from his 'A Valediction of Weeping' illustrates the process:

> On a round ball
> A workman that hath copies by, can lay
> An Europe, Afrique, and an Asia,
> And quickly make that, which was nothing, All,
> So doth each teare,
> Which thee doth weare,
> A globe, yea world by that impression grow,
> Till thy teares mixt with mine doe overflow
> This world, by waters sent from thee, my heaven dissolved so.

211

During the 1914-18 war there arose a group of poets who called themselves *Imagists*; among them were D. H. Lawrence, Richard Aldington, F. S. Flint and 'H.D.' Their manifesto, championing among other things the use of free verse and common speech, proclaimed that their poetry was written in concentrated imagery, each thought or experience being given the image which would most clearly express it. Imagism, therefore, refers to this special branch of twentieth-century poetry and is not synonymous with the general term imagery, though it is an example of poetry conceived in and composed as a single image. The following short poem by T. E. Hulme (1883-1917), one of the leaders of the Imagists, is an especially good example of their poetry:

ABOVE THE DOCK

Above the quiet dock in midnight,
Tangled in the tall mast's corded height,
Hangs the moon. What seemed so far away
Is but a child's balloon, forgotten after play.

Some Specialities

The Technical Innovations of Gerard Manley Hopkins (1844-89)

Gerard Manley Hopkins, most of whose poems were not published until 1918, made several technical experiments.

For example:

(i) he rhymed a part of a word only and completed the word on the next line:

Example:

. . . on an age-old anvil wince and sing—
Then lull, then leave off. Fury had shrieked 'No lingering! Let me . . .';

(ii) he used *run-over* rhymes: the first letter or letters of the first word on the second line were, for the purpose of

rhyme, counted as though they were still on the first line:
Example:

> But what black Boreas *wrecked her*? *he*
> *C*ame equipped, deadly *electric*;

wrecked her he C is rhymed with *electric*;

(iii) he concentrated his metre into a combination of trochees and dactyls, called *logaoedic rhythm*, which was by no means traditional in English verse: e.g. from 'Felix Randal', one of his best-known poems:

> Felix Randal the farrier, O he is dead then? my duty all ended
> Who have watched his mould of man, big-boned and hardy-
> handsome;

(iv) he also used what he called *sprung rhythm*, which is measured in feet of any number of syllables, the stress, as in the trochee and dactyl, always falling on the first syllable. So either one stress could immediately follow another or be separated from the next by a number of so-called *slack* syllables—there is no question of unstressed syllables. This, like Hopkins's *counterpoint rhythm*, often meant that a new rhythm was artificially imposed on the natural rhythm of the words, and so a new cadence was heard in English poetry which has frequently been heard since. Take for example the opening of 'Spring and Fall: to a young child':

> Margaret, are you grieving
> Over Goldengrove unleaving?

That first line seems to be composed of one dactyl— *Márgărĕt*—and two trochees—*āre yŏu grīevĭng*. But it is not. Hopkins himself marked where the stresses of the rhythm come:

> Márgarét, are you griéving.

He did other things too of a new, even revolutionary, kind

213

with words and imagery; and he has had much influence on some of the poetry of our time, most noticeably on that of Dylan Thomas.

The Limerick

This is a single stanza rhyming *aabba*, lines 1, 2 and 5 being trimeters and lines 3 and 4 dimeters. It is an established popular favourite and can almost be classed among English folk-verse. The most famous examples were written by the Victorian nonsense poet, Edward Lear. The following one, however, is by the novelist, Arnold Bennett:

> There was a young man of Montrose
> Who had pockets in none of his clothes.
> When asked by his lass
> Where he carried his brass,
> He said, 'Darling, I pay through the nose.'

The Clerihew

This also is a single stanza, but of 4 lines rhyming *aabb* and with no set metre. It takes its name from Edmund Clerihew Bentley (1875-1956), two of whose best-known pieces are:

> What I like about Clive
> Is that he is no longer alive.
> There is a great deal to be said
> For being dead.
>
> Edward the Confessor
> Slept under the dresser.
> When that began to pall
> He slept in the hall.

The Sestina

This is a poem of six stanzas, each containing six lines, usually pentameters, rhymed or unrhymed. The last words of

214

the lines are the same in each stanza, but their position varies each time. Thus if the last word of the first line of the first stanza is *dream*, it will be the last word of the second line in another stanza (not necessarily the second stanza), the last word of the third line in another and so on. Any example would be too long to quote here, but an interesting modern example may be read in W. H. Auden's 'The Sea and the Mirror'.

The Rondeau

This form is characterized by having only two rhymes throughout and its opening words (often the first three) repeated as a refrain. One of the most famous English examples—for it is a French form originally, as its name shows—is John McCrae's 'In Flanders Fields':

> In Flanders fields the poppies blow
> Between the crosses, row on row,
>   That mark our place; and in the sky
>   The larks, still bravely singing, fly
> Scarce heard amid the guns below.
>
> We are the Dead. Short days ago
> We lived, felt dawn, saw sunset glow,
>   Loved and were loved, and now we lie
>   In Flanders fields.
>
> Take up our quarrel with the foe:
> To you from failing hands we throw
>   The torch; be yours to hold it high.
>   If ye break faith with us who die
> We shall not sleep, though poppies grow
>   In Flanders fields.

The Triolet

This is an eight-line stanza (only the one), rhyming *abaaabab*, the first line recurring as the fourth and seventh, and the second line recurring as the eighth.

215

Examples:

> Rose kissed me to-day.
> Will she kiss me to-morrow?
> Let it be as it may,
> Rose kissed me to-day,
> But the pleasure gives way
> To a savour of sorrow;—
> Rose kissed me to-day,—
> *Will* she kiss me to-morrow?
>
> (HENRY AUSTIN DOBSON.)

> When first we met we did not guess
> That Love would prove so hard a master;
> Of more than common friendliness
> When first we met we did not guess.
> Who could foretell this sore distress,
> This irretrievable disaster
> When first we met?—We did not guess
> That Love would prove so hard a master.
>
> (ROBERT BRIDGES.)

Burns Metre

This is the name given to a special six-line stanza used frequently and effectively by Robert Burns. It rhymes *aaabab* and is metrically arranged as follows: lines 1, 2 and 3 are tetrameters, line 4 is a dimeter, line 5 is another tetrameter, and line 6 is a second dimeter.

Example:

> Let other poets raise a fracas
>   'Bout vines, and wines, an' drucken Bacchus,
> An' crabbet names an' stories wrack us,
>   An' grate our lug:
> I sing the juice Scotch bere can mak us,
>   In glass or jug.

Poulter's Measure

This was the nickname given to the particular metrical

pattern which the poet Surrey (1517?-47), one of the introducers of the sonnet into England, made popular for a time among Elizabethan poets. The name is thought to derive from the number of eggs that might make up a dozen, sometimes twelve and sometimes fourteen; for the lines alternate between Alexandrines and fourteeners.

Example:

> Good ladies, ye that have your pleasures in exile,
> Step in your foot, come take a place and mourn with me a
> while;
> And such as by their lords do set but little price,
> Let them sit still, it skills them not what chance come on the
> dice.
> But ye whom love hath bound by order or desire
> To love your lords, whose good deserts none other could
> require,
> Come ye yet once again and set your foot by mine,
> Whose woful plight and sorrows great no tongue can even
> define.

Terza Rima

This is a pattern (originally Italian) in which each stanza has three lines, i.e. is a tercet, of which the first and third rhyme and the second rhymes with the first and third lines of the following stanza: i.e. the rhyme-scheme is *aba bcb cdc ded* and so on. The lines are usually pentameters. Shelley wrote 'Prince Athanase' in this form:

> There was a youth, who, as with toil and travel,
> Had grown quite weak and gray before his time;
> Nor any could the restless griefs unravel
>
> Which burned within him, withering up his prime
> And goading him, like fiends, from land to land.
> Not his the load of any secret crime,
>
> For nought of ill his heart could understand,
> But pity and wild sorrow for the same:—

217

> Not his the thirst for glory or command . . .

cf. also his 'The Triumph of Life'.

The Villanelle

This form consists of five three-line stanzas and a final quatrain, there being only two rhymes throughout. The first and third lines of the first stanza are repeated alternately as a refrain in the succeeding stanzas and form a final couplet in the quatrain. The following example is taken from W. H. Auden's 'The Sea and the Mirror', a verse-commentary on 'The Tempest' (Miranda is speaking):

My Dear One is mine as mirrors are lonely,	*a*	*R1*
As the poor and sad are real to the good king,	*b*	
And the high green hill sits always by the sea.	*a*	*R2*
Up jumped the Black Man behind the elder tree,	*a*	
Turned a somersault and ran away waving:	*b*	
My Dear One is mine as mirrors are lonely.	*a*	*R1*
The Witch gave a squawk; her venomous body	*a*	
Melted into light as water leaves a spring	*b*	
And the high green hill sits always by the sea.	*a*	*R2*
At his crossroads, too, the Ancient prayed for me;	*a*	
Down his wasted cheeks tears of joy were running:	*b*	
My Dear One is mine as mirrors are lonely.	*a*	*R1*
He kissed me awake, and no one was sorry;	*a*	
The sun shone on sails, eyes, pebbles, anything,	*b*	
And the high green hill sits always by the sea.	*a*	*R2*
So, to remember our changing garden, we	*a*	
Are linked as children in a circle dancing:	*b*	
My Dear One is mine as mirrors are lonely,	*a*	*R1*
And the high green hill sits always by the sea.	*a*	*R2*

The Hexameter

The hexameter was the staple line of Greek and Latin heroic verse:

218

Ārmă vĭr | ūmqŭe căn | ō, Trōi | ae quī | prīmŭs ăb | ōrīs
Ītălī | am fat | ō prof | ūgŭs Lăv | ĭnăquĕ | venĭt
Litora . . .

(VIRGIL: 'Aeneid' Bk. I opening lines.)

Not many English poems have been written wholly in hexameters. Longfellow's long narrative, 'Evangeline', is one of the few:

> In the Acadian land, on the shores of the Basin of Minas,
> Distant, secluded, still, the little village of Grand-Pré
> Lay in the fruitful valley. Vast meadows stretched to the eastward,
> Giving the village its name, and pasture to flocks without number.

cf. Coleridge's 'Hymn to the Earth'.

Special use of Triplets

As we have seen, three lines rhyming are called a triplet. Poets writing in the heroic couplet find it desirable to introduce a triplet from time to time: on one occasion the difficulty of the rhyme-scheme itself may be the determining factor; on another the poet may be seeking the special effect of the variety which the triplet will create; on another the sense may make a triplet preferable.

Example:

> Of these the false Achitophel was first,
> A Name to all succeeding Ages curst.
> For close Designs and crooked Counsels fit,
> Sagacious, Bold, and Turbulent of wit,
> Restless, unfixt in Principles and Place,
> In Pow'r unpleased, impatient of Disgrace;
> A fiery Soul, which working out its *way*,
> Fretted the Pigmy Body to de*cay*:
> And o'r informed the Tenement of *Clay*.
>
> (DRYDEN: 'Absalom and Achitophel'.)

219

Serpentine Verse

This is the name given to a line which begins and ends with the same word or words—i.e. it has its tail in its mouth. Example:

> *Put out* the lamps! *Put out*
> The lamps (silent the answer)
> The shroud descending
> Over . . .
>> (From 'The Broken Sea' by
>> VERNON WATKINS.)

Weak Ending

Lines of verse which end with a proclitic, i.e. some small word lacking syntactical independence (the articles, auxiliary verbs, etc.), are said to have weak endings. Example:

> Friends, be gone: you *shall*
> Have letters from me to some friends that *will*
> Sweep your way for you.
>> ('Antony and Cleopatra', III. xi.)

Some Definitions and Illustrations

In this chapter a number of further technical terms, linguistic and literary, are defined and illustrated.

Aesthetic Movement

This is the literary label affixed to a number of writers, most prominent among whom were Walter Pater (1839-1894) and Oscar Wilde (1856-1900), who held the theory commonly known as *art for art's sake*. Pater was its most serious and intellectual champion, but Wilde was the 'evil genius' who expressed it in the most popular manner, especially in 'The Picture of Dorian Gray'. In the preface to that novel are written some of the most memorable epigrams expounding the theory:

e.g. There is no such thing as a moral or an immoral book; Books are well written, or badly written. That is all; Vice and virtue are to the artist materials for an art; All art is quite useless.

There were painters too in the movement—Whistler for example—and it became one of the furious controversies of *The Nineties*, that unique decade of the Yellow Book, of Max Beerbohm, Aubrey Beardsley—and, still, Queen Victoria.

Anachronism

'Error in computing time; thing out of harmony with the

221

present' (Concise Oxford Dictionary).

The term is used in literature to mark the inclusion, say in a play or novel, of an incident or statement which could not have occurred at the time of the plot or story. The most famous example of it in Shakespeare's plays—in which it occurs several times—comes in 'Julius Caesar':

> TREBONIUS. There is no fear in him; let him not die;
> For he will live, and laugh at this hereafter.
> (Clock strikes.)
> BRUTUS. Peace! count the clock.
> CASSIUS. The clock hath stricken three.

There were, of course, no clocks to strike in ancient Rome. cf. the reference to theatres in 'Richard the Second'.

Anagram

This is the name given to a word which is composed by a rearrangement of the letters of another word. So *dear* is an anagram of *read* or *dare*. One word may also be an anagram of two or more: *bathing—bang, hit*.

Some writers use anagrams as pen-names. Swift's poem, 'Cadenus and Vanessa', tells of his own love-affair with Vanessa: i.e. 'Cadenus' is an anagram of *Decanus* (=Dean). And perhaps Lamb chose 'Elia' not merely because it was the name of an Italian clerk at the South-Sea House—for is it not an anagram of *a lie*?

Apocrypha

This is the collective name of those books which are included in the Septuagint (i.e. Greek) and Vulgate (i.e. Latin) versions of the Old Testament, but were not originally written in Hebrew. At the Reformation they were not included in what we now know as 'The Bible': thus they were collected into a sort of appendix, to which the name *Apocrypha* was given. The word literally means *hidden things* (Latin from Greek).

The corresponding adjective *aprocryphal* was coined to mean *suspect, unlikely to be authentic*.

Among the books are 'Tobit', 'Judith', 'The Wisdom of Solomon' and 'Ecclesiasticus'.

Apologue

This is the technical name for a fable or parable with a moral, but since there are few fables which do not have a moral it is, to all intents and purposes, synonymous with the word *fable*. So an apologue is either a short anecdote, in prose or verse, or a longer story, again in prose or verse, told so that one may learn from it a certain moral lesson. Chaucer's 'The Nun's Priest's Tale' is a famous example of the latter. Among examples of the former are the fables of Aesop and La Fontaine. La Fontaine's are in verse. The following is a prose paraphrase of 'La Poule aux Oeufs d'Or':

> The greedy man loses everything by wishing to gain everything. For instance, there is the case of a man who had a hen which laid a golden egg every day. Thinking that it must have gold in its body, he killed it and opened it up, but found that it was no different from any ordinary hen: so he had deprived himself of his best treasure. It's a good lesson for the rich. How many people become poor simply because they do everything to get rich quickly?

Aposiopesis

This is the name given to a device used by public speakers —or to a habit associable with them—in which they break off suddenly in the middle of a sentence, leaving it grammatically incomplete.

Example:

But I do not for one moment believe that the British people will fail now any more than they have failed in the past; *because the British people* . . . But there is no need for me to weary you with what you already know as well as I do.

It is syntactically similar to *anacoluthon*, which means the commencement of a new construction in a sentence before the existing one is completed.
Example:

If that is true—but since it is obviously not true, then there is no point in publicizing it and causing unpleasantness.

The subordinate adverbial clause of condition, *if that is true*, is left without any main clause, and the new construction of a subordinate adverbial clause of reason followed by its main clause is introduced.

Augustan Age

Since during the reign of Augustus in ancient Rome many famous writers lived—Virgil and Horace, for instance—this term is applied to a similar period in English history to distinguish it as the period in which the literature reached a pinnacle of sustained excellence. One might have expected Elizabeth's reign to bear the label, but it is given to the last years of the seventeenth century and the first few decades of the eighteenth, i.e. to the period of Dryden, Addison, Pope and Swift. For although that period cannot compare in greatness with either the Elizabethan or the fifty years or so of the *Romantic Revival* (*v. infra*), it was the great period of classicism (*v. infra*), in which the eminent writers were mentally and stylistically nearer to those of Greece and Rome than other English writers had been or were to be.

Baconian Theory

This is the theory that Francis Bacon (1561-1626), the

essayist, scientist and philosopher who became Lord Chancellor in 1618, wrote the plays we assign to Shakespeare: i.e. 'Shakespeare' was his pen-name. The Bacon Society spreads its gospel tirelessly by means of pamphlets, books, meetings and so on. The evidence offered to support it is lengthy, being both internal (i.e. from within the plays themselves) and external (i.e. from Bacon's life and career). The comparative paucity of reliable fact about Shakespeare's own life is a powerful weapon in the hands of the *Baconians*, who nevertheless have other pretenders to the throne to deal with besides Shakespeare himself, among them Christopher Marlowe. No doubt every student of Shakespeare should know the theory.

Bathos

It was Pope who called this 'the art of sinking in Poetry' and used it as a form of anticlimax for a satirical purpose, as in the couplet quoted in the previous chapter:

> Here, thou, great ANNA! whom three realms obey,
> Dost sometimes counsel take—*and sometimes Tea.*

But more often than not the term is used to mark a descent from the serious to the comic which the poet—for bathos occurs more frequently in verse than in prose—did not intend. Examples abound, even in the poetry of the greatest. Keats's poem, 'Isabella', for example, which is written with intense seriousness and has a profound allegorical significance, so often sinks suddenly into lines of most amusing bathos that the whole poem is in danger of collapse. Examples:

> Why were they proud? Because their marble founts
> Gush'd with more pride than do a wretch's tears?—
> Why were they proud? Because fair orange-mounts
> Were of more soft ascent than lazar stairs?—

225

> Why were they proud? Because red-lin'd accounts
>   Were richer than the songs of Grecian years?—
> Why were they proud? Again we ask aloud,
>   *Why in the name of Glory were they proud?*

or

> 'Love, Isabel!' said he, 'I was in pain
>   Lest I should miss to bid thee a good morrow;
> Ah what if I should lose thee, when so fain
>   I am to stifle all the heavy sorrow
> Of a poor three hours' absence? but we'll gain
>   Out of the amorous dark what day doth borrow.
> *Good-bye! I'll soon be back.*'—'Good-bye!' said she:—
> And as she went she chanted merrily.

Bestiaries

These were the allegorical poems of the Middle Ages in which human conduct and thinking were satirized or moralistically discussed, though all the characters in the stories were animals. They were thus akin to the apologues, fables, etc. and no doubt had the same ancient origin.

The unfinished poem of the whale, panther and partridge is one of the earliest survivals of Old English verse; and the Middle English 'Owl and the Nightingale' was a literary development of this rather crude form of didactic poetry. Swift's fourth book of 'Gulliver's Travels' was a prose elaboration of the same primitive form—and perhaps we should also include among the developments of the old bestiaries Chaucer's 'Parliament of Fowls' and 'Nun's Priest's Tale'.

Blue-Stocking

This was the name, or nickname, given, originally in the eighteenth century, to any woman who took a creative interest in literature and 'the things of the mind'. For in that century, as earlier (and, too often, as today), woman's place was in the home and her role was man's plaything; so that any women who aspired to the sort of life only men were supposed to lead were looked at askance by all except the truly intelligent.

It was Mrs. Elizabeth Vesey (1715-91) who first used the expression to Benjamin Stillingfleet, when she told him to come to one of her literary *soirées* 'in your blue stockings', i.e. in everyday attire without bothering to put on any formal 'dress'. So *blue-stocking* gatherings became notorious, and the nickname stuck like a burr to all the Mistresses Vesey who lived then and later—even in our own enlightened day it is still occasionally heard.

The most famous of the blue-stockings was Hannah More (1745-1833), whose poem, 'Bas Bleu, or Conversation', contains much information about the whole phenomenon.

Naturally some women made a ridiculous fetish of learning, and it is to them that any disrepute into which their better comrades fell must be attributed. (Jane Austen brilliantly satirized the wrong kind of blue-stocking in her character, Mary, in 'Pride and Prejudice'.) But without the courage of Mrs. Vesey, Mrs. Elizabeth Montagu, Elizabeth Carter and the other leaders of the eighteenth-century blue-stockings it is doubtful whether we should have had Fanny Burney, Jane Austen and the three Brontë sisters (who, as it was, found it necessary to publish their works under the male pseudonyms of 'Currer, Ellis and Acton Bell')—or, at any rate, we should have had to wait a good deal longer for them.

Taken as a single-word adjective, *blue-stocking* has come to mean something like 'absurdly pedantic, pretentiously intellectual', and the word has also been miscellaneously applied as a term of abuse to both sexes. Macaulay, for example, called Frederick the Great 'this haughty, vigilant, resolute, sagacious blue-stocking'.

Burden

The original meaning of this word is the continuous bass-note or *drone* of a bagpipe (=*bourdon*, the bass-stop of an organ or harmonium). It therefore signifies in literature words which keep recurring, i.e. a chorus in a poem. A famous comic example is the chorus of Edward Lear's 'Pelican Chorus':

> Ploffskin, Pluffskin, Pelican Jee,—
> We think no Birds so happy as we!
> Plumpskin, Ploshkin, Pelican Jill,—
> We think so then, and we thought so still.

Tennyson uses the burden or chorus to great effect in 'The Lady of Shalott' by slightly varying the fifth and ninth lines of each stanza while continuously repeating *Shalott*.

In the Prologue to 'The Canterbury Tales' the Pardoner is said to have sung while the Summoner 'bar to hym a stif burdoun', i.e. accompanied him with a 'ground melody'.

Catachresis

This means the use of words in senses which they do not originally have. As may be seen in the chapter on the English language, words do both assume different meanings and degenerate in meaning, and although catachresis is thus pardonable as a phenomenon in the living development of words, it is wrong for men to take the law into their own hands and deliberately hasten any degenerating process which may ultimately be inevitable.

The commonest example of catachresis is the use of *nice* meaning *pleasant*. Another modern example is the use of *terrific* meaning nothing more than *exciting, sensational*. Most schoolboys of today also seem to think that *smashing* means *good*.

Catachresis has probably never 'had it so good' as now.

Everyone is having a *fabulous* time with it. The English language will survive, however, much changed but never *redundant*.

Chapbooks

These were the cheap booklets of the eighteenth century sold by *chapmen* or pedlars, containing, anonymously, old romances and ballads: they were forerunners of the modern *comic*, for, though they had a general appeal, children must have been especially fascinated by them. Tom Thumb, John Gilpin, the heroes and heroines of nursery rhymes and fairy stories—these were their people; and another world than that of the England of the eighteenth century was where these people lived and loved, fought and died.

Classical and Romantic

Classical is defined by the C.O.D. as 'first-class . . . of ancient Greek or Latin standard authors or art . . . in, following the restrained style of classical antiquity'; and romantic as 'characterized by or suggestive of or given to romance, imaginative, remote from experience, visionary . . . subordinating form to theme . . . preferring grandeur or picturesqueness or passion or irregular beauty to finish and proportion'.

But there does not exist a satisfactory short definition of either term, and—probably because of this—both words are vaguely applied to writers and periods. So the eighteenth century is called classical and Pope was a classical poet, and the nineteenth century was romantic and Shelley was a romantic poet. On the whole this is true. For the most part the eighteenth century was classical and so was Pope; for the most part the nineteenth century and Shelley were romantic. But we have no right to say so unless we have a clear notion of what we mean by the two words. Keats wrote under the influence of classical Greek thought and literature yet was a romantic poet.

The words are literary antonyms, and the difference is twofold, technical and psychological. That is classical whose form is regular, *restrained* and *finished*—say, the decasyllabic couplet of Pope or the blank verse of Milton—and he is classical who wishes to and does express himself completely in such a form. Classicism means seeing the world, including oneself, in terms of external reality, that is, seeing life objectively.

That is romantic whose form is, as the dictionary puts it, 'subordinated to theme': what is said is infinitely more important than how it is expressed in a formal pattern, and if the five beats of the pentameter cannot contain the expression then they must be ignored. Free verse is the most romantic of literary media. And he is romantic whose personality is the master of whatever form he may use. Keats's use of the decasyllabic couplet is a romantic's use: Dryden's is a classicist's. Romanticism means seeing the world in terms of internal reality, subjectively. In the poetry of writers like Milton and Dryden we are seldom primarily concerned with Milton and Dryden themselves; in the poetry of writers like Shelley and Coleridge it is of Shelley and Coleridge that we are primarily aware: in classical poetry—in all classical art —we are concerned with the subject-matter in itself—the philosophy, the history, the politics, etc.; but in romantic art we are concerned with how the particular poet, painter, composer, etc., interpreted life.

The so-called *Romantic Revival* in English literature names the last decade or two of the eighteenth century and the first thirty years of the nineteenth, say a period of fifty years, the period in which poetry gradually shifted away from the classical to the romantic. There had been romantics in the days of Addison and Pope but they were unheeded and unwanted; there were classical thinkers and writers in the fifty years of the romantic revival, but then it was their turn to be out of fashion.

English literature is, by its very nature, throughout fundamentally romantic, and there have been few genuinely 'classical' English writers. Nevertheless, comparatively speaking, there was this gradual romantic revival, and whereas in 1700 it was Pope who was twelve years old, in 1800 it was Byron; whereas in 1700 England was to have the essays of Addison and the satires of Pope, in 1800 she was about to have De Quincey's 'Confessions', and 'Don Juan'.

The Cockney School

In William Blackwood's 'Edinburgh Review', a Tory periodical first published in 1817, appeared a series of articles, attributable to its two editor-critics, John Wilson and J. G. Lockhart (the biographer of Burns and Scott) attacking 'The Cockney School of Poetry'. Leigh Hunt was the chief object of the attack, but Hazlitt, Keats and others were abused with almost as much venom. The 'extreme moral depravity' of the writers was singled out for special condemnation: of Hunt, for instance, it was said: 'He talks indelicately like a tea-sipping milliner girl.' The poets were considered not to be poets at all but merely self-centred and vicious little poetasters, and it was no sign of their poetic importance that they sat 'among themselves, with mild or with sulky faces, eating their mutton steaks, and drinking their porter at Highgate, Hampstead, or Lisson Green'.

The articles caused a great stir, and the nickname stuck. In a letter to his publisher, Murray, on April 26, 1821, Byron wrote: 'Is it true, what Shelley writes me, that poor John Keats died at Rome of the Quarterly Review? I am very sorry for it, though I think he took the wrong line as a poet, and was spoilt by Cockneyfying . . .' (The reference is to

231

the famous attack on Keats in the 'Quarterly Review', another widely read Tory journal.)

Exactly what *Cockneyism* implied so far as the technicalities of versification are concerned can be understood only by reading some of Leigh Hunt's poetry and those works of Keats (and others) which were written under its influence. But we may sum up the general implication as a dislike of the politics of the poets, of the rather sentimental urbanity and colloquial language of their poetry, and of what was regarded as the presumption of men who lived in London in writing about nature. Who, for instance, was Keats to write when all he knew about life was what Leigh Hunt had told him or he had learnt in and about London and in books? He was just a silly boy writing silly verses. We think differently today about him at least.

Comedy and Tragedy

These are, of course, the two main types of drama. As with 'classical' and 'romantic', there are no concise definitions of the words. Obviously 'The Comedy of Errors' is a comedy and 'Macbeth' is a tragedy, but what is the essential difference between them? There have been many answers. Since Aristotle in 'On the Art of Poetry' stated his opinions about the nature of tragedy, writers have added their agreement or disagreement.

Briefly, the difference is that in comedy human beings are seen enjoying and celebrating life and finding it good, while in tragedy they are seen tormented by life and paying their tribute to death. Charles Lamb defined 'the regions of pure comedy' as those 'where no cold moral reigns'; in comedy, said Aristotle, 'the bitterest enemies in the piece walk off good friends at the end'. In comedy, as in fairy tale and pantomime, all ends 'happily', in tragedy all ends 'unhappily': on the one hand, Benedick and Beatrice are married; on the other, Macbeth and his wife are dead.

Attempts have been made to combine the two in *tragi-comedy*. Dryden, for example, wrote several tragi-comedies, and they were fashionable in his day. The main plot was tragic but a comic underplot was combined with it, the former being usually written in verse, the latter in prose. Such a mixture of verse and prose was not new, of course, as any reader of Shakespeare knows, and there had been occasional comic contrasts in tragedy before (though these were never just funny—e.g. The Porter in 'Macbeth') and tragic contrasts in comedy, though these had never been truly tragic (e.g. the Hero plot in 'Much Ado About Nothing'). But blood and champagne will not mix, and it was soon realized that tragi-comedy was a monster whose offspring could only be new monsters themselves, and whose breed should not, therefore, be encouraged.

Diacritic

This is the general term for the signs used either over or under letters to mark their special pronunciation: e.g. accents in French, the cedilla, the diaeresis.

The *diaeresis* is the name of the two dots placed over the second of two adjacent vowels to prevent these from being sounded together as a diphthong:

e.g. *Noël*.

Its antonym is *synaeresis*, which means the sounding as a diphthong of two adjacent vowels, as in *subpoena*.

Dialogue

A dialogue is of course a conversation (not necessarily between two people), but in literature it is also the name given to a composition in which the subject matter is expressed in the form of conversation. The most famous writings of Plato were dialogues, and it is from the conversations of

Socrates and his disciples that we learn Plato's philosophy. Similarly, Lucian, the Greek writer of the second century A.D., wrote his 'Dialogues of the Dead' and 'Dialogues of the Gods' as a means of satirizing philosophers and society.

In English the philosopher George Berkeley (1685-1753) followed the Platonic method in, for instance, 'Alciphron, or The Minute Philosopher', in which four men question one another in the way the disciples of Socrates question their master: out of the discussion, the argument, 'the cut-and-thrust of debate', come Berkeley's own philosophical theories.

Other dialogues in English are Hume's 'Dialogues Concerning Natural Religion' and Prior's 'Four Dialogues of the Dead', the latter of which are imaginary conversations analogous to the more famous ones of Walter Savage Landor (1775-1864).

Modern examples of this literary form have been written by Eric Linklater.

Doggerel

This is the name for any verse which is merely verse and crude verse at that. Sometimes it may be written deliberately in the form of parody (q.v.), but very often it is intended seriously. Today we are surrounded by it in one form or another, in mottoes and on advertisement-hordings. E.g. in a certain bathroom:

> The use of this well-watered spot
> Is short, extension can't be got:
> Haste then, for in ten minutes more
> The next will thunder on the door.

Dramatic Irony

Since this occurs in tragedy far more significantly than in comedy it is also known as tragic irony (that is, in a tragedy only). It is the name given to words spoken innocently which

234

a later event proves either to have been mistaken or to have prophesied that event. A famous instance is when Lady Macbeth looks at her own and her husband's blood-stained hands and says, 'A little water clears us of this deed.' Water cannot wash away guilt and torment, however; and later in the play, when she is walking in her sleep, she cries: 'What, will these hands ne'er be clean? . . . Here's the smell of the blood still; all the perfumes of Arabia will not sweeten this little hand.'

Elegy

An elegy (sometimes known as a *monody* or *threnody*) is a poem in honour of the dead. Either it is occasioned by the death of an individual, as Shelley's 'Adonais' was by the death of Keats, or it is about the dead generally, as was Gray's 'Elegy in a Country Churchyard'. Some of the best poems in English were written to lament the deaths of poets: 'Adonais', Thomas Carew's 'An Elegie Upon the Death of the Deane of Pauls, Dr. John Donne', William Collins's 'Ode on the Death of Thomson'. It may take any verse-form. The following was W. H. Davies's elegy on the death of his friend, the poet Edward Thomas, in the 1914-1918 war:

KILLED IN ACTION
(EDWARD THOMAS)

Happy the man whose home is still
　　In Nature's green and peaceful ways;
To wake and hear the birds so loud,
　　That scream for joy to see the sun
Is shouldering past a sullen cloud.

And we have known those days, when we
　　Would wait to hear the cuckoo first;
When you and I, with thoughtful mind,
　　Would help a bird to hide her nest,
For fear of other hands less kind.

235

But thou, my friend, art lying dead:
  War, with its hell-born childishness,
Has claimed thy life, with many more:
  The man that loved this England well,
And never left it once before.

The Elizabethan Theatre

(i) The stage jutted out into the auditorium, the front portion being known as the *apron*. Thus the audience was on three sides of the actors and there were no *wings* like those of the later and modern theatres. The performances were enacted in an atmosphere of intimacy with the spectators, and the soliloquy was realistic because the solo actor could come forward and be at quite a distance from the other actors at the back of the stage. The *aside* was equally convincing, for an actor would literally speak aside to the section of the audience on one side of the apron.

(ii) At the back of the stage were the *inner stage* and, on either side of that, two doors by which the characters entered and left. These doors were also used to symbolize opposing sides, say in battle: in the last act of 'Macbeth', for instance, Macbeth and his few followers would always enter through one door and Malcolm and the besieging army through the other, with the result that at one moment the stage represented the interior of Macbeth's castle and at another it stood for the countryside around.

The inner stage, which was separated from the rest by a curtain, was used for tombs (e.g. in 'Romeo and Juliet'), cells (e.g. in 'The Tempest'), the players' scene in 'Hamlet', the witches' cave in 'Macbeth', and so on. Since there was no curtain in front of and around the sides of the main stage, it was only in this inner stage that actors could be ready in their positions before any action started and could remain in a position (say, of death) when the action ended.

(iii) As there was no main curtain the actors had to come

on before any play could commence and had to walk or be carried off at the end. This explains why there is so much carrying-off of corpses at the end of Elizabethan tragedies.

All performances were continuous—normally lasting about two hours—and so the couplet which often comes with apparent suddenness into the blank verse was used as 'a kind of emotional curtain', to quote M. R. Ridley's phrase.

This absence of curtain and this continuity of action made numerous short scenes possible: e.g. in 'Antony and Cleopatra'.

(iv) Above the inner stage a balcony ran for the width of the building. The middle of this was used in many ways: as the balcony from which Juliet spoke to Romeo, as the window from which Jessica threw down to Lorenzo her father's jewels, and, most frequently of all, as the battlements of castles (e.g. in 'Henry V').

On either side of this were two boxes in which distinguished members of the audience sometimes sat to watch performances.

Sometimes the small orchestra which provided musical interludes and accompaniment to songs sat in this balcony.

Sometimes too a ladder was used by which actors mounted to or descended from the balcony to the stage.

(v) There was at least one trap-door in the stage, through which ghosts and witches could make their appearances and disappearances—the witches' cauldron in 'Macbeth' would sink through it.

(vi) Behind the inner stage and the balcony were the tiring-houses or dressing-rooms.

(vii) The auditorium consisted of a promenade where the *groundlings* stood to watch—this was known as the *cockpit* because the same area was used for cock-fighting when no play was in production; and there were three tiers of seats, the lowest, on the ground level, being the cheapest. The poor groundlings could, however, hire seats and even cushions if they had enough money.

Sometimes rich and important personages sat on the stage itself to watch the proceedings.

(viii) The theatre was usually circular or hexagonal and open to the sky. It was small, yet as many as 1200 people could be packed into the famous Globe Theatre (which was, incidentally, octagonal).

The stage itself was protected against rain by a canopy, sometimes made of thatch, sometimes tiled. This was known as *the shadow* or *the heavens*, and from it tapestries were hung to show the type of play to be presented—they were always black for a tragedy.

(ix) *Noises off* usually came from the tiring-house. The Globe was burnt down as a result of the faulty firing of a cannon in Act I of 'Henry the Eighth'.

Many 'props' were used, though there were no painted canvases or flats. These props were used symbolically: a branch or two of a tree would signify that the scene was set in a wood or forest.

The performances took place in the afternoon in daylight, and so the dramatist had to tell his audience in the words of his characters what the weather and time of day were:

Light thickens, and the crow makes wing to the rooky wood;

But look, the morn in russet mantle clad,
Walks o'er the dew of yon high eastern hill.

To this limitation must be attributed some of Shakespeare's best poetry: indeed, the limitation was his opportunity.

Artificial lights were occasionally used, e.g. in the inner stage, but only to give some special effect.

There were no programmes, but boards or notices were either held or stuck up (e.g. over the two doors) to announce titles, names of places, etc.

238

Three flourishes on a trumpet announced that the play was about to commence, the trumpeter standing in the balcony.

(x) To make up for the lack of scenery the Elizabethans made lavish use of costume and disguise. According to Sir Henry Wotton (1568-1639), ' "Henry the Eighth" was set forth (in 1613) with many extraordinary circumstances of Pomp and Majesty, even to the matting of the Stage; the Knights of the Order, with their Georges and Garters, the guards with their embroidered Coats, and the like: sufficient in truth within a while to make greatness very familiar, if not ridiculous.'

(xi) There were no women or girls among the actors, and all female parts, young and old, were played by boys or youths whose voices had not yet broken. 'If,' Rosalind says in the Epilogue to 'As You Like it', 'I were a woman I would kiss as many of you as had beards . . .' Sometimes masks were worn by these youths.

No doubt the absence of truly aged women or very mas-culine women from Elizabethan plays is due to the youth-fulness of those who were called upon to play the female parts.

To this all-male convention must also be attributed—at least in part—the device whereby young women dress up as young men: e.g. Rosalind, Jessica, Viola and Portia. For thus boys would merely have to be themselves.

The first actress did not appear on the English stage until 1660.

(xii) The first permanent playhouse in London was not built until 1576. All earlier dramatic performances took place either in private halls, royal palaces, the Inns of Court, inn-yards or public squares—or within the precincts of chuches. The inn-yard was the model on which all the public, open-air theatres were built—the *cockpit*, the *apron*, the

239

galleries, etc.

Private theatres were of course roofed, their stages were artificially illuminated, and their productions were altogether more elaborate than those of the public theatres.

The opening Chorus of 'Henry V' reveals Shakespeare's consciousness of the limitations of his theatre:

> . . . can this cockpit hold
> The vasty fields of France? or may we cram
> Within this wooded O the very casques
> That did affright the air at Agincourt?

Emblem-Books

It was an Italian, Alciati, who in the early sixteenth century first published a book containing pictorial designs whose meanings were expressed in accompanying words. The best example of such a book in English was 'Emblemes' (1635) by Francis Quarles (1592-1644). Other seventeenth-century poets, and notably Crashaw and Vaughan, also combined drawings with verse in this way.

In our time the process has been reversed by painters whose designs are, apparently, necessary to explain the deep and mysterious meaning of the poetry they accompany.

Epic

Epic poetry—or *epopee*—celebrates in narrative some great theme of human life, of legend or of tradition. An epic is necessarily long, and its diction and form, however imaginative, are in 'the high style'. Its meaning is essentially allegorical.

Among the most famous epics are Homer's 'Iliad' and 'Odyssey', Dante's 'Divine Comedy', Ariosto's 'Orlando Furioso', Milton's 'Paradise Lost' and 'Paradise Regained', William Morris's 'Sigurd the Volsung' and Robert Bridges's 'The Testament of Beauty'.

The unrhymed pentameter has generally been chosen by English epic poets. If, therefore, any single definition of the English conception of the word can be given, an epic poem is one which is written in unrhymed pentameters and treats of some universal, philosophical theme, such as that of 'Paradise Lost', in a narrative form. Thus Spencer's 'Faerie Queene' is not an epic, nor is Chaucer's 'Troilus and Criseyde'.

Euphuism

This is an example of a new word given to our language by a fictitious proper name. For John Lyly (1554-1606), the dramatist and poet, wrote two famous prose books, 'Euphues, the Anatomy of Wit' (1578) and 'Euphues and his England' (1580), the sequel to the first book, both written in a new style. It became very fashionable afterwards and was imitated by many lesser Elizabethan writers, and it is they who are responsible for the term Euphuism being one of disfavour. Lyly's books were written in a strangely elaborate style, the sentences being intricately planned and varied, the vocabulary learned and figurative, the allusions to historical and legendary characters numerous. It is at once a learned and a fanciful way of writing. But its imitators took to extremes, and so the word Euphuism was coined to mean any prose exaggeratedly ornate and formal. Not until the aesthetic movement (*v. supra*), and especially Walter Pater, did any serious writer deliberately revert to the style.

Folio, Quarto, etc.

Students of Shakespeare are always meeting the expression *First Folio*, which refers to the collected edition of his plays published in 1623, and the expressions *First Quarto, Second Quarto* and so on, which refer to the editions of his plays published in quarto at various dates. 'Hamlet', for example, was published in two quartos and in the first folio; and all three texts vary a great deal in content.

The names are technical terms used by printers. A folio is a sheet of paper which is folded only once, and so a folio edition of a book is a book made of sheets folded once. One folio sheet thus gives four sides for printing, and a folio edition is a fairly large book.

A quarto edition means one in which each sheet of paper is folded twice, thus giving eight sides of printing, each side a quarter of the size of the unfolded sheet.

An octavo size is one in which each sheet is folded three times, thus giving sixteen sides for printing, each side an eighth of the size of the unfolded sheet.

The expression *demy 8vo* (=*octavo*), frequently seen in estimates from printers for school magazines, pamphlets, etc., means that the sheet of paper to be folded three times is $17\frac{1}{2}$ inches by $22\frac{1}{2}$.

Foolscap paper is folio size, the common typing size being 13 inches by 8.

Duodecimo size is one in which each sheet is so folded that each side is one-twelfth of the whole. A 12mo book is thus very small.

The Four Humours

Medieval physiologists considered that men's personalities originated from the four humours or moistures of the body: blood, choler, black bile and phlegm. Either one of these predominated or they were mixed in some way or other, but usually one did predominate, and a man showed both physically and mentally which it was. Thus if blood predominated he had a ruddy complexion and was a cheerful, hearty fellow; if black bile predominated he was sallow and saturnine.

So a man belonged to one or other of the humours. He was a type. The *comedy of humours* was an extension into drama of this old theory.

For old it is, and not yet dead. We still speak of *sanguine temperament*, *choleric* and *phlegmatic* people, and *melancholia*, and even if we do not accept the medieval idea as such we still—scientifically—divide human beings into types so that one man is introspective and another extraverted, or one man is an *endopath* and another an *ectomorph*; and there are *complexes* and *strains*, high and low blood-pressures and so on.

A famous example of one of the humours, or types of men, is Chaucer's gay and pleasure-loving Franklin: 'Of his complexioun he was sangwyn'; and it is the hen, Pertelote, in 'The Nun's Priest's Tale', who analyses Chauntecleer's dream by telling him that he has too much red bile or blood,

> Right as the humour of malencolie
> Causeth ful many a man in sleep to crie
> For feere of blake beers, or boles blake,
> Or elles blake develes wole hem take.
>   (*blake*=black;   *beres*=bears;   *boles*=bulls.)

Georgian Poetry

This was the title of an anthology compiled by Edward Marsh and published in 1912. Taking its name from the reigning monarch the poetry was composed by a group of writers whose work reappeared in further editions until 1922. Among the poets were W. H. Davies, Walter de la Mare, John Drinkwater, W. W. Gibson, H. Munro, Lascelles Abercrombie, W. J. Turner, Robert Nichols, Robert Graves, Siegfried Sassoon and Edmund Blunden.

It was a simple poetry, small, quiet, often sentimental, much concerned with form, a reaction against the 'decadence' that had gone before and a retreat from the turmoil of its own time. The famous Methuen *Anthology of Modern Verse*

243

(1920) collected together many of its best examples.

Grimm's Law

Jacob Ludwig Carl Grimm (1785-1863), who with his brother, Wilhelm, wrote the famous fairy-tales, formulated in a work on grammar a law showing the consonant-shift which occurred as one language of the Aryan group grew out of another. For instance, the *p* of Latin became *f* or *v*: *pater* became English *father* and German *vater* (cf. French *père* which preserved the original letter); the *t* of Latin became *th*—so *three* from *tres*; and *k* (or hard *c*) became *h*: *cornu—horn*.

Hudibrastic

This adjective was coined to describe any poem written in the burlesque-heroic metre and style of the satire by Samuel Butler (1612-80) called 'Hudibras'. The metre is the tetrameter rhyming in couplets.

Example:

> He knew the seat of Paradise,
> Could tell in what degree it lies:
> And as he was dispos'd, could prove it,
> Below the moon, or else above it.
> What Adam dreamt of when his bride
> Came from her closet in his side.
>
> (From 'Hudibras'.)

Hilaire Belloc was one of the most successful writers of Hudibrastic verse in modern times.

Hypocorisma

This is the technical term for any word used as a pet-name, diminutive, or affectionate nickname: e.g. *Betty* (=*Elizabeth*), *hanky* for *handkerchief*. It also includes such euphemisms as *story* for *lie*.

SOME DEFINITIONS AND ILLUSTRATIONS

Swift's 'Journal to Stella' contains the most famous literary examples of hypocorisma.

The Lake Poets

This was the nickname given to Wordsworth, Coleridge and Southey because all three lived—or had lived—in the Lake District.

Malapropism

Mrs. Malaprop is a character in Sheridan's comedy, 'The Rivals'. It is her misfortune to be uncertain of words: when she means an alligator she speaks of an allegory, when she means epitaph she says epithet. And so she has added a word to our language, a malapropism being the use of a word with a different meaning from the word intended but which has some letters in common with it. Yet there were malapropisms before she existed: Shakespeare made Bottom in 'A Midsummer Night's Dream' say that 'comparisons are odorous', while Dogberry in 'Much Ado About Nothing' manages to get most of his big words wrong. To Mrs. Malaprop, however, goes the credit of uttering more malapropisms than most people, and of giving her name to the unfortunate but always amusing weakness from which she suffered. As H. W. Fowler said, 'She is now the matron saint of all those who go word-fowling with a blunderbuss.'

The following is a selection of Mrs. Malaprop's own malapropisms, of the 'hard words she don't understand', of the 'select words so ingeniously misapplied without being mispronounced':

illiterate	for	obliterate
extirpate	,,	exculpate
progeny	,,	prodigy
contagious	,,	contiguous
superstitious	,,	superfluous

superfluous	,,	superficial
illegible	,,	eligible
locality	,,	loquacity
punctuation	,,	compunction
conjunction	,,	injunction
hydrostatics	,,	hysterics
derangement	,,	arrangement
insurance	,,	assurance
affluence	,,	influence
perpendiculars	,,	particulars

Masque

Throughout the long life of the Elizabethan and Jacobean drama the specific theatrical form called *masque* remained popular, especially at court and in private production at great households. Most of the leading playwrights were commissioned to provide the words. But the words were only a part, and often only a minor part, of the whole performance, for the masque was a mixture of spoken drama, opera and ballet, and on it was lavished all the Elizabethan love of costume, colour and tableau. Inigo Jones (1573-1652), the architect, was responsible for many of the sets and Ben Jonson for many of the libretti.

The characters were nearer to those of the Moralities, old legends and allegory than to those of drama proper, and often had abstract names like Melancholy.

Shakespeare occasionally introduced masques into his plays: e.g. in Act IV of 'The Tempest'; and 'A Midsummer Night's Dream' may almost be classed as a long masque.

The *anti-masque* was introduced during the early years of the seventeenth century (e.g. in Jonson's 'The Masque of Queens'). This was similar to the antistrophe of the ode and the sestet of the sonnet, in that it took the form of a variation of, an answer to, even a contradiction of, the theme of the masque. For instance, evil characters would be shown to contrast with the good ones of the masque.

But except in secret performances the masque barely survived the Puritan attack on the stage, and it is by now a period-piece. Perhaps it will be revived one day—indeed, a modern attempt to revive it was Ronald Duncan's 'This Way to the Tomb', which included an anti-masque.

Melodrama

In the early nineteenth century this was a species of drama in which songs (Greek *melos*=song) were included, but these eventually dropped out and all that was left was the violence, the sensation and the absurd happy ending. It is a drama of extremes and types: the good are incredibly good, the evil are incredibly evil, and the former always triumph. Some of the most famous melodramas—'Maria Marten' and 'Sweeney Todd' for obvious examples—were originally written as serious contributions to the theatre, but by now audiences have taken things into their own hands and joined in the fun, cheering the sweet young heroine whenever she appears and hissing the villain whenever he comes on. To describe an incident or a statement as *melodramatic* means that it passes beyond the border of credibility, is artificial, and makes suffering ridiculous.

Melodrama is probably a bathetic form of comedy: if it is, then farce is a bathetic form of tragedy; the difference between them is that farce is deliberately silly.

Metathesis

This is the name for that curious transposition of letters which has occurred in the development of our language. So the old b*ri*d has become b*ir*d, c*ru*l has become c*ur*l, th*ur*gh has become thr*ou*gh and th*ir*led has become thr*il*led.

The Muses

According to early writers these were the goddesses of

song, but later they were considered to be the inspirers of all the arts and sciences.

In mythology they were the nine daughters of Zeus and Mnemosyne (i.e. Memory):

Clio, the Muse of history;
Euterpe, the Muse of lyric poetry;
Thalia, the Muse of Comedy;
Melpomene, the Muse of Tragedy;
Terpsichore, the Muse of choral dance;
Polymnia or Polyhymnia, the Muse of sacred poetry;
Erato, the Muse of love poetry;
Urania, the Muse of astronomy;
Calliope, the Muse of epic poetry.

The two mountains, Helicon and Parnassus, were sacred to them.

Nonce-Words

A nonce-word is one which is *coined*, i.e. invented, to serve a special purpose for which no known word exists. Slang includes many nonce-words: e.g. *scram*. Some authors have created them, though not all have survived. Milton's 'Pandemonium', the name he invented for the devils' parliament in Hell, is an example of those which have joined the language proper. James Joyce's 'Finnegans Wake' is full of nonce-words, but how many of them will live outside his book only time will show. Certainly *muckinslushes* (*mackintosh—muck—slush*) deserves to continue.

The general name *coinings* (or *neologisms*) is given to all words invented by individual people. Lewis Carroll's 'Jabberwocky' poem in 'Alice Through the Looking-Glass' contains many nonsense-coinings—*brillig*, *toves*, *frumious*, *vorpal*—one of which, *chortled*, has since become what we might call an ordinary word. Other nonsense-coinings may be seen in Edward Lear's poems—*runcible*, *Gromboolian*, *Pobble*.

Commercial organizations have coined *trade-names*: *Kodak*, *Decca*, *Ronuk*, etc.; and the entertainers of the earth, led by the Americans among them, have allowed their imaginations to run riot in this matter: *fundrome*, *novachord*, *lunatickling*, *oomph*.

There are good and bad coinings, but all give testimony of the living quality of language and of man's continuous struggle for self-expression.

Palindrome

This is the name of any word or group of words which reads the same backwards as normally. The proper noun *Anna* is an obvious example.

Parody

A parody is a deliberately comic imitation of a serious original, in which the subject-matter of the original is mocked at, either merely for a literary joke or because in the opinion of the parodist it does not deserve the serious attention it has won in some quarters. The form of the original is used, and it is upon the successful combination of this with the new subject-matter that the good parody depends. Among the best parodists of this century was G. K. Chesterton, whose sense of fun extended easily to the literary joke. In 'Answers to the Poets' he wrote some very clever parodies of famous poems, one of the best of which is the following:

LUCASTA REPLIES TO LOVELACE

Tell me not, friend, you are unkind,
  If ink and books laid by,
You turn up in a uniform
  Looking all smart and spry.

249

> I thought your ink one horrid smudge,
>   Your books one pile of trash,
> And with less fear of smear embrace
>   A sword, a belt, a sash.
>
> Yet this inconstancy forgive,
>   Though gold lace I adore,
> I could not love the lace so much
>   Loved I not Lovelace more.

The following is the famous original which he was parodying:

TO LUCASTA, GOING TO THE WARRES

> Tell me not, Sweet, I am unkinde
>   That from the Nunnerie
> Of thy chaste breast, and quiet minde,
>   To Warre and Armes I flie.
>
> True; a new Mistresse now I chase,
>   The first Foe in the Field;
> And with a stronger Faith imbrace
>   A Sword, a Horse, a Shield.
>
> Yet this Inconstancy is such,
>   As you too shall adore;
> I could not love thee, Deare, so much,
>   Lov'd I not Honour more.
>
>   (RICHARD LOVELACE, 1618-58.)

Connected with this word—and with satire (*q.v. infra*)—are several other terms:

lampoon: any published attack which is savage and full of hatred;

pasquinade: any anonymous published attack, especially those stuck up in public places;

skit: any playful imitation, almost synonymous with parody;

burlesque: also a playful, mocking imitation, but usually of action—e.g. on the stage;

caricature: an imitation which deliberately distorts certain features of the original—analogous to the pictorial cartoon;

travesty: an unintentional parody: i.e. it is meant to be as serious and as good as its original.

Paronomasia

This is the general term for all *play upon words*, including puns. Perhaps the most famous example is that in the Bible: 'Thou art *Peter*, and upon this *rock* I will build my church.' *Peter* and *rock* were originally the same word in Greek (cf. *Pierre* in French).

An amusing allusion and illustration come in 'The Cock and the Bull' by Charles Stuart Calverley (1831-1884):

> You see this pebble-stone? It's a thing I bought
> Of a bit of a chit of a boy i' the mid o' the day—
> I like to dock the smaller parts-o'-speech,
> As we curtail the already curtail'd cur
> (You catch the paronomasia, play 'po' words?)

Pastoral

Pastoral literature came to England from Greece and Rome. Theocritus was the most famous of the Greek pastoral poets, and it was from him that Roman poets received the idea—e.g. Virgil in his 'Eclogues'. As the name implies, it is literature about the country. Pastoral novels like Sidney's 'Arcadia' have a rustic setting, pastoral poems like Spenser's 'Shepheard's Calender' are about the simple civilization of country people.

But the word has a specific technical connotation, and any work about the country as distinct from the town is not necessarily pastoral. For during the sixteenth century a special type of composition, both in verse and in prose, became popular, in which country people and country doings were described with a sentimental lavishness which removed them far from this rough-and-tumble world, so that they took on a fairy-like, *Arcadian*, quality, idyllic, beautiful but

251

ideal. Pastoral literature of the Elizabethan period is an early example of art for art's sake; for it tells of an existence in which the faithful, pipe-playing shepherd is the hero and Chlorinda, lovely and limp, is the heroine.

Pastoral poems are sometimes called *bucolics*.

Pathetic Fallacy

This again is a term of disfavour, although not all critics agree with Ruskin that what it names should be looked upon disapprovingly. For it names that use of personification by poets which makes nature itself think and talk like a human being. It is particularly applied to Wordsworth, to whom nature was almost a kind of superhuman being whose thoughts and words he recorded in his verse. It does not include the personifying of inanimate objects like windmills but refers only to the personification of nature, life, death, etc.

Example:

> Three years she grew in sun and shower,
> Then Nature said, 'A lovelier flower
> On earth was never sown;
> This child I to myself will take;
> She shall be mine, and I will make
> A lady of my own . . .'
>
> (WORDSWORTH, 1799.)

Peripeteia

This means any reversal of fortune—usually sudden or unexpected—which befalls a person in a play or story. So in Shakespeare's 'Macbeth' when Macduff tells Macbeth:

> Despair thy charm,
> And let the angel whom thou still hast served
> Tell thee, Macduff was from his mother's womb
> Untimely ripp'd,

one of the last hopes of survival which Macbeth had was suddenly dashed. Earlier, another of these hopes: 'Fear not, till Birnam wood Do come to Dunsinane', was similarly dashed.

Compare the sudden change of Shylock's fortune in 'The Merchant of Venice' during the trial of Antonio. All had apparently gone in his favour, and then Portia turned the wheel:

> Tarry a little, there is something else,

and a few minutes later he left the court, crushed, to disappear from the play.

It should be noted that in these two instances the peripeteia contains echoes of earlier words. Macduff's words echo the prophecy of the second apparition:

> . . . laugh to scorn
> The power of man, for none of woman born
> Shall harm Macbeth;

and Gratiano mockingly echoes Shylock's praise of the disguised Portia:

> O upright Judge, mark Jew, O learned Judge.

Poet Laureate

This is the title given to one poet who is chosen on his reputation to be, as it were, the royal or national poet. He receives a small, nominal salary as an officer of the Royal Household. It is not clear who was the first poet so to be employed. Ben Jonson is considered by some people to have first had the honour, but probably Dryden was the first to have the title officially. He was succeeded by Shadwell, whom he had attacked in his satires, and since then the order has been: Nahum Tate (1652-1715) in 1690, one of the poets satirized by Pope in 'The Dunciad'; Nicholas Rowe (1674-

253

1718) in 1715; Laurence Eusden (1688-1730), also satirized in 'The Dunciad', in 1718; Colley Cibber (1671-1757), the hero of 'The Dunciad', in 1730; William Whitehead (1715-85) in 1757; Thomas Warton (1728-90) in 1785; Henry James Pye (1745-1813) in 1790; Robert Southey (1774-1843) in 1813; Wordsworth in 1843; Tennyson in 1850; Alfred Austin (1835-1913) in 1892; Robert Bridges (1844-1930) in 1913; and John Masefield, who died in 1968, was succeeded by the present holder of the title, C. Day Lewis.

It is clear that the poet laureate is not necessarily the best poet of his day: indeed, several poets laureate were objects of ridicule in their own day and have enjoyed no praise since; and the attitude of many true poets to the honour is seen in the fact that Thomas Gray declined it when it was offered to him.

The Pre-Raphaelites

The pre-Raphaelite movement or brotherhood consisted of a group of painters and writers, formed about 1850, who set out to paint and write in a manner totally different from that of any of their contemporaries. They believed that there had been no great European art since the time of the Italian painter Raphael (1483-1520), and, since they intended to create great art, they decided to go back to the subjects and methods of his day. The leader of the movement was Dante Gabriel Rossetti (1828-1882), who gave it its name and expounded its doctrine in a journal which he founded—'The Germ'. Both in painting and literature the emphasis was on the past, on religious and legendary subject, and the method was that of meticulous accuracy of detail. Art itself was extolled to the status of a religion before which men should feel a sense of awe. The movement was thus the forerunner of the aesthetic movement.

The painters included Holman Hunt, Millais, Watts and

254

Burne-Jones, the writers included Rossetti, Swinburne and William Morris, who also extended the idea to the decorative arts of book-illustration and production, furniture and so on.

The movement died with its champions. Rossetti's passionate and lavish verse was nicknamed *the fleshly school of poetry*, and the whole idea of pre-Raphaelitism became as much an object of scorn as aestheticism and the aspidistra; yet this does not mean that there was nothing of value in either the painting or the poetry. Rossetti, his sister, Christina, Swinburne and Morris are not inglorious names in our literature.

Prologue and Epilogue. Chorus

A prologue is to a play what a foreword or preface is to a book. Sometimes there may be a prologue to a poem in the way that Chaucer wrote a 'General Prologue' (as it is usually called) to his 'Canterbury Tales' and a series of prologues for the tales themselves. In the 'General Prologue' he introduces us to the pilgrims and their host and outlines the plan of the whole work.

But it is especially with plays that the prologue is associated, though it has not been fashionable even in this context for a long time. It was common in ancient Greek drama and frequent in Elizabethan. Shakespeare's 'The Second Part of King Henry the Fourth' opens with what is there termed an 'Induction' spoken by Rumour. There is a prologue to 'King Henry the Fifth', another to 'Troilus and Cressida'.

Dryden wrote verse-prologues not only for his own plays but also for other dramatists', and it became common for one playwright to compose this form of introduction to another's work.

The prologue sets the scene and time, prepares the audience

for what is to come, and appeals for its sympathy (or, if it is Shaw's prologue to 'Caesar and Cleopatra', tells the audience not to presume to clap). As an example the following is the prologue to 'Troilus and Cressida':

> In Troy, there lies the scene. From isles of Greece
> The princes orgulous, their high blood chafed,
> Have to the port of Athens sent their ships,
> Fraught with the ministers and instruments
> Of cruel war: sixty and nine, that wore
> Their crownets regal, from th' Athenian bay
> Put forth toward Phrygia: and their vow is made
> To ransack Troy; within whose strong immures
> Th' ravished Helen, Menelaus' queen,
> With wanton Paris sleeps; and that's the quarrel.
> To Tenedos they come;
> And the deep-drawing barks do there disgorge
> Their warlike fraughtage: now on Dardan plains
> The fresh and yet unbruised Greeks do pitch
> Their brave pavilions: Priam's six-gated city,
> Dardan, and Tymbria, Ilias, Chetas, Trojan,
> And Antenonidus, with massy staples,
> And corresponsive and fulfilling bolts,
> Stir up the sons of Troy.
> Now expectation, tickling skittish spirits,
> On one and other side, Trojan and Greek,
> Sets all on hazard: and hither am I come
> A prologue arm'd,—but not in confidence
> Of author's pen or actor's voice; but suited
> In like conditions as our argument,—
> To tell you, fair beholders, that our play
> Leaps o'er the vaunt and firstlings of those broils,
> Beginning in the middle; starting thence away
> To what may be digested in a play.
> Like, or find fault; do as your pleasures are;
> Now good or bad, 'tis but the chance of war.

An epilogue is a similar direct address to the audience at the conclusion of a play. Not every play with a prologue has an epilogue—there is no epilogue to 'Troilus and Cressida'—

and some plays have epilogues which do not have prologues —'As You Like It', for instance.

In his epilogue the dramatist bids adieu to his audience and hopes they have enjoyed his play. He has done his best that they should, and, as Dryden ends his epilogue to 'All For Love',

'Tis more than one Man's work to please you all.

Whether or not either a prologue or an epilogue is necessary to a play or to anything else, is a matter of opinion. Shakespeare makes Rosalind express his opinion in the epilogue to 'As You Like It':

If it be true that good wine needs no bush, 'tis true that a good play needs no epilogue: yet to good wine they do use good bushes; and good plays prove the better by the help of good epilogues.

It will be seen from that quotation that an epilogue—and it is true for a prologue too—may be in prose no less than in verse.

Shaw's Prefaces to his plays are not to be considered as prologues. They exist separately from their plays, being discussions of the controversial, political, philosophical, religious, sociological and moral themes which underlie the actions of those plays. Similarly, the prose prefaces written by poets like Shelley and Byron to their poems are prefaces and not prologues.

The Chorus was an integral part of ancient Greek drama and early liturgical ceremonies. It danced and it sang. It was both actor and, since it was not a character in the plot, spectator, able to comment on the characters and the plot. Sometimes it consisted of only one person in the earliest drama.

In Elizabethan drama it retained only the function of being

257

a kind of commentator on and interpreter of the plot. So the Chorus in 'Henry the Fifth'—a single person—speaks the prologue to the whole play, comes on again to speak a prologue before each of the acts after the first, and finally speaks the epilogue.

But even by Elizabethan times it was an archaism, and it soon dropped out of English drama. In modern times certain verse-playwrights have reintroduced it—T. S. Eliot, for example, in 'Murder in the Cathedral', whose chorus is a group of 'Women of Canterbury' speaking chorally. In a verse play it can be appropriate and effective, but an instance of the artificiality of a chorus in a modern prose play—moreover, a chorus (of two chroniclers) speaking verse, i.e. the only verse in the whole work—can be seen in John Drinkwater's 'Abraham Lincoln'.

Pun

Everyone knows what a pun is, and everyone fancies himself at punning. It is therefore introduced here only for two special reasons. One is to observe that it was very popular with the Elizabethan dramatists, and that not only in comedy. Today it has only a comic function, as a vehicle for wit, but in the sixteenth century it was used seriously as well, especially in sarcastic or ironic contexts. In the first scene of 'Julius Caesar' the cobbler taunts the officious tribune:

> Truly, sir, all that I live by is with the awl.

But later Cassius taunts Brutus:

> Now is it Rome indeed, and room enough,
> When there is in it but one only man.
> > (*Rome* and *room* were then pronounced alike.)

The second reason for speaking of puns here is to remind

readers of the excellent advice given by Charles Lamb, who was, like Thomas Hood, a prince of punsters—in his essay, 'Distant Correspondents':

> A pun hath a hearty kind of present ear-kissing smack with it; you can no more transmit it in its pristine flavour, than you can send a kiss.

In inferior words, a pun dies on utterance and cannot be repeated.

The Reformation

This is the name of the religious movement whose aim was the reform of the teachings and observances of the Roman Catholic Church. It culminated, in the sixteenth century, in the establishment of the differing branches of Protestantism, the Church of England having the sovereign, and not the Pope, as its head. Such men as Luther, Calvin and John Knox were its leaders.

So far as literature is concerned, we owe to the Reformation not only the English Bible and the Book of Common Prayer but, among other great works, the sermons of Donne and 'Paradise Lost'.

The Renaissance

This was the revival of art and literature in Italy during the fourteenth century, under the influence of classical models. Gradually the Middle Ages (a general term for the period fifth century A.D. to fourteenth century) came to an end. There was great learning and much artistic creation during the Middle Ages, but they were largely confined to the precincts of the Church: the Renaissance (i.e. the re-birth) was to bring a dawn of unfamiliar brilliance to scatter for good the mere twilight of the past. The light spread over the Alps to the rest of Europe, and eventually to England.

English literature blazed into Spenser, the sonnet and the drama, into 'Hamlet' and 'The Tempest'. The Renaissance in England has, indeed, been summed up in one word: Shakespeare.

Rhetorical Question

Originally this names the trick used by public speakers of asking a question to which no answer is expected (though a heckler may provide one, of course).
Example:

> But Germany has received her punishment. *Who would live in Germany to-day?* I have been there, ladies and gentlemen, and seen the shattered towns, the hungry people . . .

Similarly, when we say such things as *Why bother?* we do not expect any answer from our listener; because we are not really asking a question, but are saying *there's no point in bothering* in the form of a question merely as a conventional expression.

Roots and Derivatives

The root or stem of a word is that part of it which cannot be analysed and which remains unchanged when the word inflects or when any affix is joined to it in the creation of a new word. So the word *boy* is a root in itself, for it remains constant in all words: *boys, boy's, boyhood, boylike*. In the words *macrocosm, microcosm, cosmic, cosmopolitan*, etc., the root is *cosm* (from Greek).

Such roots are also known as *primitives* to distinguish them from derivatives, i.e. words which are composed of roots and affixes. So *boyhood* is composed of *boy* and the suffix *hood*, and *microcosm* is composed of *cosm* and the prefix *micro*.

Satire

This differs from parody in that it is never merely a literary joke played by a friend, nor does it mock the style of the original for fun. Instead, it is the work of an enemy, an enemy either of a general human vice or weakness or of some individual or group of people. So Swift's 'Gulliver's Travels' is a satire on the human race, Pope's 'The Dunciad' is a satire on the would-be poets and the sciolists of his day, and Byron's 'The Vision of Judgment' is a satire on Southey's absurd poem of the same title. The object of the satire is held up to ridicule, which may be subtle or abusive, in order that men may learn to be better: as Dryden said in the preface to 'Absalom and Achitophel', 'The true end of satyre is the amendment of vices by correction.' 'Absalom and Achitophel' has been called 'the greatest political satire in our literature'. The chief objects of its tremendous attack are Lord Shaftesbury (Achitophel) and the Duke of Monmouth (Absalom): the following lines, taken from the first part, are among the most vituperative of the onslaughts against the former:

> Of these the false Achitopel was first,
> A Name to all succeeding Ages curst.
> For close Designs and crooked Counsels fit,
> Sagacious, Bold, and Turbulent of wit,
> Restless, unfixt in Principles and Place,
> In Pow'r unpleased, impatient of Disgrace;
> A fiery Soul, which working out its way,
> Fretted the Pigmy Body to decay:
> And o'r informed the Tenement of Clay.
> A daring Pilot in extremity;
> Pleas'd with the Danger, when the Waves went high
> He sought the Storms; but, for a Calm unfit,
> Would steer too nigh the Sands to boast his Wit.

Sock and Buskin

In ancient Greek, and later Roman, drama the characters

in comedy wore the *soccus*, a low shoe which prevented anyone from appearing very tall, while the characters in tragedy wore the *cothurnus*, a buskin or high shoe which increased their natural height. So *sock* in English has come to mean *comedy* and *buskin* has come to mean *tragedy*. 'In sock or buskin,' wrote Charles Lamb in his essay 'On Some Of The Old Actors', 'there was an air of swaggering gentility about Jack Palmer.'

The fact that in ancient drama human beings were supposed to look smaller in comedy than they did in tragedy is a clue to the original difference between the two forms: only in tragedy were men heroic and did they rise beyond their normality; in comedy they were not called upon even to think of so rising.

Soliloquy

The word is from Latin and literally means *speaking alone*. It is a technical term in drama, and names any passage spoken by a character, not to some other character but apparently to himself. He (or she) may or may not be alone on the stage, but if others are with him they are supposed not to hear what he says. For he is only speaking aloud so that the audience may hear what is going on in his mind unknown to the other characters in the play.

It is not an exaggeration to say that the most important lines in many Elizabethan tragedies occur in soliloquies, for in them men like Macbeth and Hamlet reveal their secrets, their fears and hopes, and in them Shakespeare wrote some of his finest poetry.

The soliloquy has long disappeared from most theatrical drama but has taken on a new role in the film and on television.

SOME DEFINITIONS AND ILLUSTRATIONS

Spoonerism

The Rev. W. A. Spooner, Warden of New College, Oxford, suffered from the weakness of transposing letters in words, with the result that what should have sounded and been received seriously sounded ridiculous and produced laughter. But unlike Mrs. Malaprop he actually existed (1844-1930). The most famous spoonerism, though one whose authenticity is in doubt, is his announcement of the first line of the famous hymn as 'Kinquering Congs their titles take'. A favourite one among schoolboys—for we can invent our own at will— is to speak of the poets Sheats and Kelly.

Such a transposition of letters is a form of metathesis (v. supra).

Stichomyth

This is the technical name for dramatic dialogue in which each character speaks only a few words—never more than one line of verse—with the resulting impression of excitement and speed.

Example:

LADY MACBETH. Did not you speak?
MACBETH. When?
LADY MACBETH. Now.
MACBETH. As I descended?
LADY MACBETH. Ay.
MACBETH. Hark! Who lies i' the second chamber?
LADY MACBETH. Donalbain.
MACBETH. This is a sorry sight.
LADY MACBETH. A foolish thought to say a sorry sight.

Trilogy

This means any literary work which is written in three parts. Many Greek dramas were thus written, and it is from the Greek theatre that the word has come into English. Shakespeare's 'Henry VI' is a trilogy.

Any work in four parts is a tetralogy. There is no special name for a work in two parts—such as 'Henry IV'—or in five parts—such as Shaw's 'Back to Methuselah'. (A *duologue* is a dramatic composition for only two actors—e.g. early Greek plays.)

The Three Unities, of Time, Plot and Place

In his 'On the Art of Poetry' Aristotle said that tragedy 'endeavours to keep as far as possible within a single circuit of the sun, or something near that'; that it 'is the imitation of an action that is . . . complete in itself'; and that in it 'one is limited to the part on the stage and connected with the actors'. These three statements were assumed by Renaissance critics in Italy and later by French dramatists to be rules; and any play (comedy or tragedy) which did not obey them, whose action (*a*) took longer than its two or three hours of performance, or, at most, twenty-four hours, (*b*) was not single and self-contained, or (*c*) departed from the scene set on the stage, was denounced as not a play in the true sense of the word.

The student of drama continually meets the challenge of those who believe in the validity of these three unities: he sees that many plays have been written in accordance with them; but he also sees that great dramatists have often ignored them.

APPENDIX A

A Short History of English Literature

Foreword

IN his 'Life of Nathaniel Hawthorne' Henry James, the American novelist, said that 'it takes a great deal of history to produce a little literature'. There has been a great deal of English history, but it has produced a great deal of literature: so large, indeed, is the amount and for so long a time has it endured that he would be a rash man who presumed to define its beginning and its origins—as rash as he who dared to prophesy its end.

Most popular histories of our literature start with Chaucer and give their readers the impression that it did suddenly begin with him. But, as Professor B. Ifor Evans has pointed out, 'this would give England six centuries of literature. Actually there were more than six centuries of literature before Chaucer was born.' He might have been bolder and said that it is impossible to state how old our literature is. For literature, like language, cannot have started suddenly at any one time or in any one place that we can determine: rather must it have grown imperceptibly from unknowable origins until either extant manuscripts or references allow us to make a start somewhere with our recording of it.

The reason why Chaucer's works are so often chosen to mark the beginning is, however, obvious and twofold. For although he was not the first English writer, he was the first Englishman to write on a large scale and with lasting artistry works which can still be read without undue difficulty by the educated modern reader. John Gower, his contemporary, also wrote a poem which the educated modern reader can understand, 'Confessio Amantis', whose 30000 lines constitute the first large collection of tales in

265

English verse or prose; but compared with Chaucer's 'Canterbury Tales' it is likely to interest only the specializing student.

Old English, or Anglo-Saxon, literature is written in a language which has to be learnt as though it were foreign, and must remain unknown, except in translation, to the general reader. Middle English literature is more accessible, but it is not until Chaucer's time that the language, for all its difference from ours today, can be read without much trouble (though it too commands study, and notes and a glossary will always be needed). Chaucer's language is, in the main, ours, for, as has often been said, he created it.

It is still his individual pre-eminence which preserves him for us all, however, for many of the poets who lived after him in the fifteenth and sixteenth centuries, are only of historical importance. So far as the general reader is concerned, therefore, there is a gap between 1400, the year in which Chaucer died, and the Elizabethan period, which is only partially filled by one or two poets and prose writers.

The books and poems whose titles are about to be quoted, therefore, from pre-Chaucerian and pre-Elizabethan literature, may remain only titles for the general reader, and the names of the writers may remain only names; but in the cause of continuity and a comprehensive picture of our literature they must be recorded here.

The Earliest Known Literature

VERSE

The most famous of the Old English writings still preserved is 'Beowulf', a long narrative poem in two parts. It remains in a single manuscript, now in the British Museum, dating from about A.D. 1000, and tells the story of the battle fought by Beowulf against a monster named Grendel, Grendel's mother and a dragon. He is mortally wounded by the dragon and his body is burnt on a pyre.

The rest of the surviving Old English poetry is contained in three books, the Exeter Book, the Vercelli Book and the Junian manuscript, and in a manuscript found as late as 1860 in Copenhagen. Among the poems are 'Widsith' (143 lines), which describes the wanderings of a minstrel, 'The Complaint of

Deor' (who is also a minstrel), 'The Wanderer', 'The Seafarer', 'The Ruin' and 'Waldere'.

The device of alliteration was used by all the poets and is a marked characteristic of Anglo-Saxon verse. It occurs in a regular pattern in each line, as is seen in these lines from Ezra Pound's translation of 'The Seafarer', in which he retained the original pattern:

> Bitter breast-cares have I abided,
> Known on my keel many a care's hold,
> And dire sea-surge, and there I oft spent
> Narrow nightwatch nigh the ship's head
> While she tossed close to cliffs, Coldly afflicted,
> My feet were by frost benumbed.
> Chill its chains are; chafing sighs
> Hew my heart round and hunger begot
> Mere-weary mood.

All these Old English poems are anonymous, and the first poet known to us by name is Caedmon, who was alive about 670. Only his 'Hymn' survives, however, and that only in a quotation by Bede, but it used to be thought that the religious poems in the Junian manuscript were his work.

The next poet whose name is known is Cynewulf (c. 760), to whom some of the religious poems in the Exeter and Vercelli books have been ascribed: for instance, 'Elene', which tells the story of the finding of the cross by the Empress Helena, the mother of Constantine.

Of the other poems in these old manuscripts not yet mentioned, two at least deserve reference: 'Genesis' and 'Judith'. 'Genesis' is divided into its main part, known as 'Genesis A', and an interpolation known as 'Genesis B', which tells the story later told by Milton in 'Paradise Lost'. That Milton knew and used this interpolation cannot be proved but is likely.

'Judith' recounts the Apocryphal story of how Judith slew the tyrant Holofernes.

PROSE

The earliest prose written by Englishmen of which we can be certain was written in Latin by Aldhelm, Bishop of Sherborne (d. 709), Bede (672-735), author of the famous 'Ecclesiastical

267

History of the English Race', and Alcuin (735-804); and England had to wait until the reign of King Alfred (849-901) before translations into the vernacular were made available.

Alfred himself was a great scholar, and a shortened translation of Bede's 'History' is attributed to him by some, but not all, historians. He did translate other Latin works, including Boethius's 'De Consolatione Philosophiae', a treatise which influenced medieval thinking and was to be retranslated by Chaucer and Queen Elizabeth, and it was under his guidance that the 'Old English Chronicle', the first systematic record of West Saxon history, was compiled. This was the first important book of English prose; it continued after Alfred's death until 1154.

During the tenth century much religious prose was written by ecclesiastics, best known of whom are Aelfric (955?-1022?) and Wulfstan (d. 1023). Three English versions of the gospels were also made.

Between the time of the conquest and the birth of Chaucer (c. 1340) very little important prose was written in English, for most of the scholars and ecclesiastics preferred to write in Latin. The best known work in English was the 'Ancren Riwle' (c. 1200), which gives advice to three anchoresses and makes delightful reading for anyone who understands the language.

Thirteenth-Century Verse

Much more interesting verse was written during the thirteenth century than prose. The important poems are long, most of them being metrical romances written under the influence of French originals and the European cult of courtly love.

The biggest was the legendary history of Britain written by Layamon, beginning with the arrival of Brutus (?) and going as far as Cadwallader (A.D. 689). It gives the first English accounts of the Arthurian story and the reigns of the two kings whose lives Shakespeare was to dramatize—Lear and Cymbeline. It is known as 'Brut'.

To the early part of the century also belongs the light-hearted but devout poem, 'The Owl and the Nightingale'. Its author is not certainly known. Written in the octosyllabic couplet, nearly 2000 lines long, it is a debate between a nightingale, which represents the world and love, and an owl, which represents the monastery and religion.

The Fourteenth Century

It is not until the fourteenth century, however, that the history of English literature begins, for most people, to have an enduring importance. For now we come to works of interest outside the Chaucerian canon. There is the single manuscript containing the four poems, 'Pearl', 'Patience', 'Purity', and 'Sir Gawayne and the Grene Knight', all written on the old alliterative pattern.

'Pearl' is an allegorical account of the sorrow of a father for his dead daughter, of the vision he has of her in paradise, and of his final resignation.

'Patience' tells the story of Jonah, 'Purity' deals with the Flood, Sodom and Gomorrah and Belshazzar. Possibly all three poems were by the same writer.

'Sir Gawayne' is the best and the longest of the four. It forms part of the medieval literature concerned with the Arthurian legend, and tells the story of Gawayne's temptation at the hands both of a knight whom he has beheaded and of his wife.

Contemporary with Chaucer were several important writers: William Langland (or Langley), born about 1330, the author of 'The Vision Concerning Piers the Plowman', about whose three versions and text (as well as his authorship) there exists much scholastic dispute; John Wyclif (1320-84), who, with Nicholas Hereford, John Purvey and others, made two translations of the Bible, and who wrote a large amount of theological literature in English; John of Trevisa (1326-1412), translator; the unknown author of 'The Travels of Sir John Mandeville', a translation from French and one of the most popular books in the fifteenth century, adventurous, fantastic, entertaining, introducing to England the Great Cham and Prester John and setting a new style of English prose; and John Gower (1325-1408), author of French and Latin works and the long poem, 'Confessio Amantis', already referred to.

CHAUCER

All critics agree that Chaucer is the first of the major English poets, and poets of all subsequent periods and styles have held him in deep affection and esteem: indeed, of all English poets he is unique in being both the most widely loved and the most admired. Spenser wrote in 'The Faerie Queene':

Dan Chaucer, well of English undefiled,

On Fame's eternal beadroll worthy to be filed.

Dryden called him 'a perpetual fountain of good sense' and said that ' 'Tis sufficient to say, according to the proverb, that here is God's plenty.' Perhaps only Byron of the great poets has found him—to use his own word—'contemptible'.

His world-wide reputation rests on 'The Canterbury Tales', a series of stories told by a band of pilgrims on their way to the shrine of Thomas à Becket in Canterbury. The age and English Christendom parade before us. Now we are listening to a crusading knight, now to a sham pardoner; now a miller is telling a bawdy tale, now a nun's priest is recounting the famous incident of the cock and the fox down on the farm, now a prioress relates the sad story of a little saint and a mother's grief. All is variety, piety and shame, comedy and pathos, the individuality, honourable and dishonourable, of the living English scene. 'The Canterbury Tales' is one of the monumental poems like 'The Faerie Queene', 'The Prelude' and 'The Testament of Beauty', but it is also what they cannot always claim to be, the best of entertainment.

Chaucer's other writing was still large in quantity and high in quality. In verse he wrote, besides numerous short pieces, 'Troilus and Criseyde', which tells the story later to be dramatized by Shakespeare; 'The Romaunt of the Rose'; 'The Book of the Duchess'; 'The Parliament of Fowls'; and 'The Legend of Good Women'; and in prose he made a translation of 'De Consolatione Philosophiae' and wrote a 'Treatise on the Astrolabe'.

Chaucer dominates pre-Elizabethan literature as Shakespeare dominates Elizabethan: it is no wonder that after him for some time no new poet arose able to challenge his supremacy and divert men's attention from him.

The Fifteenth Century

VERSE

Disciples by the score followed him and, obviously enough, imitators as many. During the fifteenth century they were so many that they have been labelled 'The English Chaucerians' and 'The Scottish Chaucerians' (for poetry was written north of the border no less than south of it). Among the former were John Lydgate (1370?-1450?), a voluminous versifier whose 'Troy Book' extends to 30000 lines; Thomas Occleve or Hoccleve (c. 1368-c.1450), author of 'Regiment of Princes'; and, later, Stephen Hawes (1474-1523), whose best poem is 'The Pastime of Pleasure'.

Among the Scottish Chaucerians the best were the king, James I, who wrote 'The Kingis Quair' (i.e. the king's book) in honour of his queen; Robert Henryson (c. 1425-c.1500), who continued the story of Chaucer's 'Troilus' in 'The Testament of Cresseid'; William Dunbar (c. 1460-c. 1520), author of 'The Golden Targe' and satirical poems like 'The Flyting of Dunbar and Kennedie'; and Gavin Douglas (1475?-1522), whose 'Eneados' was the first metrical translation into English of Virgil's 'Aeneid'.

The Scottish poets, particularly Dunbar, were more poetically original than their English contemporaries despite their affirmed allegiance to Chaucer. It must be admitted, however, that neither they nor the English Chaucerians can expect much attention from readers who have at their disposal the great English poets. Even in their own context and time it is questionable whether they have much claim on us, for if we devote any time to fifteenth and early sixteenth-century poetry we are more likely to spend it enjoying the work of one known poet, John Skelton, and many unknown poets, the writers of the ballads.

SKELTON

John Skelton (1460?-1529) was unique in his time. Writing in a variety of metrical forms but best in short, staccato lines since called *Skeltonics*, he is different and original, admiring Chaucer but not imitating him.

Two quotations will illustrate his two moods in the same short line. The first shows him in elegiac mood ('Jane Scroop's Lament for Philip Sparrow'):

> When I remember again
> How my Philip was slain,
> Never half the pain
> Was between you twain,
> Pyramus and Thisbe,
> As then befell to me:
> I wept and I wailed,
> The teares down hailed;
> But nothing it availed
> To call Philip again,
> Whom Gib, our cat, hath slain. . . .

It had a velvet cap
And would sit upon my lap
And seek after small wormes
And sometimes white bread crumbes;
And many times and oft
Between my breastes soft
It woulde lie and rest;
It was proper and prest . . . (=handsome and neat)

The second ('The Tunning of Elinour Rumming') shows his skill in realistic description:

. . . Her visage
It would assuage
A man's courage,
Comely crinkled
Wondrously wrinkled
Like a roast pig's ear
Bristled with hair . . .
She is ugly fair.
Her nose some deal hooked
And camously crooked, (=turned up at the end)
Never stopping
But ever dropping;
Her skin loose and slack
Grained like a sack,
With a crooked back . . .

THE BALLAD

The fifteenth century was a century of continuous war, and perhaps literature was not given a chance to flourish, perhaps the times were too out of joint. It was nevertheless a century of abundant literary activity. Not only were the Chaucerians hard at work, not only was English prose being developed and then printed, not only was the drama beginning to emerge: this was also the century of the anonymous ballad and carol, the folk-songs of England.

Ballads and carols had been written down before, including the famous:

I sing of a maiden
That is makeless,

> King of all kinges
> To her sone sche ches. . . .
>
> He cam also stille
> To his moderes bour,
> As dew in Aprille
> That falleth on the flour. . . .
>
> Moder and maiden
> Was never non but sche;
> Well may swich a lady
> Godes moder be.

But it was during the fifteenth century that many of our old ballads, English and Scotch, were passed around by itinerant minstrels and eventually written down by someone. They differ from conscious individual poetry in their economy of form and diction, their realism and their communal meaning; they have that quality of suddenness and narrative brevity which characterizes all popular art. Their subjects cover a wide range of legend, folk-lore and national and local history, and their heroes and heroines include Robin Hood, the Nut Brown Maid, the Babes in the Wood, Child Waters, Sir Patrick Spens, the Wandering Jew and that Jewish moneylender whom we all know by the name which Shakespeare gave him, Shylock. The refrain, including the nonsense line, is common in them and gives proof of their communal origin and function.

Yet they remain a mystery. It is impossible to give them any precise date and difficult to believe that he who wrote them down was not aware that he was recording literature. Only a few of them survive in manuscripts older than the seventeenth century, and the source of most of them is the folio volume found by Bishop Percy from which he compiled his 'Reliques of Ancient English Poetry', published in 1765. The folio itself has since been published, and other scholars and poets have discovered other ballads: Sir Walter Scott, for instance, whose 'Minstrelsy of the Scottish Border' (1812) revealed still further the wealth of folk-poetry in Scotland.

PROSE

There is little of the fifteenth century prose written before 1476, large in volume though it is, that need detain us. Among the writers were Reginald Pecock (1395?-1460?), theologian, Sir John Fortescue (1394?-1476?), and Margery Kempe, whose autobiographical account of religious conviction and pilgrimage was not discovered and printed until 1936; and among the works were collections of legends and chronicles, and the famous 'Paston Letters', which tell the story of three generations of a rich Norfolk family and are a valuable source of information about the social life of the second half of the century.

PRINTING

The most important event in the century was the coming of printing to England from the Continent. Hitherto all manuscripts were hand-written and so no author could be known to more than a few people. Printers were working in at least eight European countries before Caxton set up his press in London in 1476. He himself had seen a press in Germany and had printed the first English book in Bruges in 1475.

Once he had set up his own press books began to pour from it, including Chaucer's works, 'The Canterbury Tales' in 1478. Gower's 'Confessio Amantis' was printed in 1483 and Sir Thomas Malory's 'Morte D'Arthur' (written c. 1470) in 1485. William Caxton (1422?-1491) was a writer as well as a printer, and it is his revision of Malory's book which we have.

Printing-presses were set up in other towns before the end of the century, and although less English than foreign were printed for more than half a century to come, England's booktrade had begun with all that that implied for writers and readers alike.

Apart from Malory's 'Morte D'Arthur', a fairy-tale of medieval chivalry adapted from various uncertain French and English tales, only Caxton's own translation from French, 'The Golden Legend' (1483), stands out as important and entertaining from the English prose of the last years of the fifteenth century.

THE DRAMA

The beginnings of English drama are not known. The Romans had had their theatrical performances, but these cannot be considered in any history of English drama. Drama is of course inherent in all folk-literature, but the earliest acting of which we can be certain was that of individual performers like jesters and minstrels.

It was in the medieval church, however, that the drama as a separate and corporate ceremony was developed. Tableaux, impersonations, even burlesques, were common, and by the thirteenth century the whole church building was being used, processions also extending out into the market-place on special occasions. Easter services were characterized by short interpolated scenes, and, in a word, the drama was a popular adjunct of the normal church ritual. The religious plays of the twelfth and thirteenth centuries were known as *Miracles* and *Mysteries*, later to be renamed, as they were transformed, *Moralities*.

All the early drama, therefore, of which we have record was on sacred themes and acted in liturgical contexts. Gradually, however, it left the church precincts. The feast of Corpus Christi with its processions and tableaux made by guilds of local craftsmen at last gave rise to the lay drama, whose themes were still biblical but whose actors and environment were no longer clerical. Whereas the strictly ecclesiastical drama had been spoken in Latin, the vernacular was now used, and the stage was no longer in the Church but on mobile platforms like carts. Corpus Christi plays are recorded in Beverley, Yorkshire, in 1377 and at York in 1378.

This co-operative drama was clearly widespread, for although the majority of the plays are now lost, four main cycles have been preserved: those of York, Chester, Wakefield or *Towneley,* and Coventry. All the Bible characters are in them— Noah, Herod, the Magi, Eve, the Shepherds; the plays are crude but genuine, and often very funny.

After these came the Moralities like 'Mankynde' (*c.* 1473) and 'Everyman', in which the characters are not flesh-and-blood creatures but allegorical figures called Nought, New-gyse, Nowadays, Fellowship, Good Deeds, Beauty and so on. And then came the *Interludes,* short plays, partly allegorical, partly farce, acted not in the market-place but in the private home of the aristocrat. The transition from the old plebeian drama to the conventional drama of the theatre was thus made, and now for the first time we know the names of the playwrights. For one Henry Medwall (*c.* 1486) wrote an Interlude called 'Nature', and Skelton wrote in verse 'Magnyfycence, a goodly interlude and a mery, Devysed and made by Mayster Skelton, Poet

Laureate' (he is not today classed as one of the poets laureate proper), which was printed *c.* 1530. The Interludes continued into Elizabeth's reign, but by then the Miracles, Mysteries and Moralities were part of history.

We have now reached the sixteenth century, by the end of which Shakespeare had written some of his greatest plays. But a century is a long stretch of time and there is much poetry, prose and drama to be briefly reviewed before we reach the lavish days of Elizabeth's England.

Sixteenth-Century Verse

Apart from Skelton the only notable poets of the first half of the sixteenth century were Alexander Barclay (1475-1552) and Sir David Lyndsay (1490-1555). Barclay's most famous poem was 'The Shyp of Folys of the Worlde', commonly known as 'The Ship of Fools', which was published in 1509. A free translation of a German original, over 14000 lines long, its aim was to 'redres the errours and vyces of this our royalme of Englande'. Sir David Lindsay, a Scotch poet, wrote the long didactic poem, 'The Dreme' (1528), in which John the Commoun Weill told of Scotland's need for 'ane gude and prudent Kyng': like 'The Ship of Fools' it is written in rhyme royal. Lyndsay also wrote a satirical play called 'Ane Satyre of the Thre Estaitis in commendation of Vertew and Vituperation of Vyce'.

Interesting though both poets are, however, neither can rank with the great English poets who were soon to be born. Both stand on a bridge, as it were, which links the old world with the new. In the old world one great poet, Chaucer, and one or two lesser writers like Skelton, alone stand out from the mass of signed literature as having an appeal to the modern reader. There are many giants in the new world.

'TOTTEL'S MISCELLANY'

An important literary event in 1557 was to initiate what has been called *the new way in English poetry*. The Wars of the Roses had faded from men's minds and England had become a proud country, self-ruled in religion and nationalistic, governed by powerful and colourful monarchs, its aristocrats the lords of the earth. And the lords of the earth have time for art. Cultured men all, these romantics were voracious readers of foreign and especially Italian literature. They did not wish to allegorize in the medieval manner nor teach and satirize with the old Chaucerians and Barclay and Lyndsay: instead, they wished to sing. In 1557 'Tottel's Miscellany' was published and Elizabethan poetry had begun, one year before the accession of Elizabeth. In this book, named after its publisher, Sir Thomas Wyatt (1503-42) and Henry Howard, Earl of Surrey (1517?-47), introduced the sonnet into England. Elsewhere Surrey also used the strange *poulter's measure* and translated the second and fourth books of Virgil's 'Aeneid' into blank verse, thus being the first poet to use on such a scale the form later to be used by the great Elizabethan dramatists and Milton.

Other poets contributed to the anthology but none of them was of the order of Wyatt and Surrey. A new type of poetry had come into English letters, a short, stylized, lyrical, personal poetry, and it had come to stay. After the thousands of lines of fifteenth and early sixteenth-century allegory, didacticism and satire, stanzas like these of Wyatt, conventional though they may later have become, were a freshness badly needed, pointing to a new life for English verse:

FORGET NOT YET

The Lover Beseecheth his Mistress not to Forget his Steadfast Faith and True Intent

> Forget not yet the tried intent
> Of such a truth as I have meant;
> My great travail so gladly spent,
> Forget not yet!
>
> Forget not yet when first began
> The weary life ye know, since whan
> The suit, the service, none tell can;
> Forget not yet!
>
> Forget not yet the great assays,
> The cruel wrong, the scornful ways,
> The painful patience in delays,
> Forget not yet!
>
> Forget not! O, forget not this—
> How long ago hath been, and is,

277

The mind that never meant amiss—
Forget not yet!

Forget not then thine own approved,
The which so long hath thee so loved,
Whose steadfast faith yet never moved:
Forget not this!

Among subsequent poets were Thomas Tusser (1524-80), Barnabe Googe (1540-94), George Turberville (1540?-1610), Thomas Sackville (1536-1608) and George Gascoigne (1542?-77). More collections like 'Tottel's Miscellany' were published, such as 'The Paradyse of Daynty Devises' (1576), while the famous anthology called 'A Myrroure for Magistrates', which came out in numerous editions after 1559, included the two fine poems by Sackville, the 'Induction' and 'The Complaint of Henry Duke of Buckingham', written in rhyme royal.

SPENSER

But the first great non-dramatic poet of the Elizabethan age was none of these: it was Edmund Spenser (1552-99). Sonneteer; author of 'The Shepheards Calender, Conteyning twelve Aeglogues proportionable to the twelve monethes' (1579), a pastoral poem written in the archaic English of Chaucer; lyrical poet of 'Prothalamion', 'Epithalamion' and 'Astrophell, a Pastorall Elegie upon the Death of the Most Noble and Valorous Knight, Sir Philip Sidney'—it is yet for his 'The Faerie Queene' that he is one of England's most celebrated poets.

'Disposed into twelve bookes' according to the title-page, it reached only the second stanza of the eighth canto of the seventh book; yet it is one of the longest poems ever written. A complicated allegory, a collection of legends, classical, continental, medieval, a glorification of Queen Elizabeth to whom its author dedicated 'these his labours to live with the Eternitie of Her Fame', it is like a huge mural tapestry, far too big to be looked at as a whole, and to be enjoyed a part at a time. Its characters are legion, its incidents are legion.

Though it has never been, and by reason of its length and manner probably never could be, a popular poem, it has always been admired by poets themselves and has influenced many. In 'The Prelude' Wordsworth wrote:

> Sweet Spenser, moving through his clouded heaven
> With the moon's beauty and the moon's soft pace.

Few of those who have read 'The Faerie Queene' can fail to understand what Wordsworth meant: few of those who have read it can quote Landor's answer to him as their own:

> Thee gentle Spenser fondly led;
> But me he mostly sent to bed.

THE SONNET

Spenser's first appearance as a poet was with twenty-six sonnets in 1569, and later he wrote the sequence called 'Amoretti' (1595): he was perhaps the true founder of the form in England, since he was a finer poet than either Wyatt or Surrey. Other sonneteers soon joined him, the first and best being Sir Philip Sidney (1554-86) with his sequence, 'Astrophel and Stella' (1580-84). Then came Henry Constable's 'Diana' (1592), Samuel Daniel's 'Delia' (1592), Michael Drayton's 'Ideas Mirrour' (1594) and the sonnets in Fulke Greville's 'Caelica'. But these are only four collections selected from many. The sonnet was the exciting poetic fashion of the day: every poet wrote it, Shakespeare not least among them with his wonderful and tantalizing examples, until over-indulgence led to disgust and the 'sugared sonnet' became an object of ridicule. England had to wait for Milton to restore the form to favour.

Other poets of the period include, of course, the dramatists who wrote lyrical poetry outside their plays: Christopher Marlowe, for instance, who wrote 'Hero and Leander' and 'Come, live with me and be my love', and Ben Jonson.

We must leave sixteenth-century poetry there for the moment, for Shakespeare and the other famous poets contemporary with him who have not yet been named lived on into the next century. Our survey so far cannot have done justice to the poetry of the last thirty years or so of this remarkable century. England was riding the crest of the wave. The incalculable queen sat on the glittering throne of a country whose rulers led its armies and navies to victory, whose adventurers were founding her imperialism, and whose way of life was that of a proud performer blest with, and suffering from, too much energy and too much wit. A book like Lytton Strachey's 'Elizabeth and

Essex' makes this clear. It was a radiant England, a radiant London, and its literature both reflected and enhanced the radiance. The poetry was not full of self-pity except where lovely maidens were concerned, it was not moralistic or heavy-footed. It was gay, flowery and light on its feet, and even when it was sad it was not morbid. The uncertainty was there, death was always obvious; but death, constantly reminding men of its inevitability, urged them to make the most of life. Death was the great leveller—why fret then?

> Golden lads and girls all must,
> As chimney-sweepers, come to dust.

Much of the imagery and language of Elizabethan lyrical verse was conventionalized, for versification had become a hobby as well as a personal necessity. There are many weaknesses, indeed, in it, in this unique mixture of ebullience, idyllic love of nature, idealization of woman, literary artifice; but they do not spoil the over-all effect it produces. Without doubt the rich Elizabethans loved life and loved literature.

We shall be coming back to the poets, but now we must retrace our steps and look at the prose and drama of the century. Both had been developed out of all resemblance to their forbears, and the latter part of the century is memorable in that it produced the beginnings of the novel and some of the best drama in our literature.

Sixteenth-Century Prose

After Caxton and Malory the first interesting writer of prose was Sir John Bourchier, Lord Berners (1467-1533), whose free translation of the 'Chronicles' of Froissart introduced into England Oberon, a new kind of history-writing and a new style. This is his account of the intervention by the queen which saved the lives of the Burghers of Calais:

Than the quene beynge great with chylde, kneled downe and sore wepyng sayd: A, gentyll sir, syth I passed the see in great perill I have desyred nothyng of you, therefore nowe I humbly requyre you in the honour of the son of the virgyn Mary and for the love of me, that ye will take mercy of these sixe burgesses. The kyng behelde the quene and stode styll in a study a space, and than sayd, A, dame, I wold ye had ben as nowe in some other place, ye make suche request to me that I can nat deny you; wherfore I gyve them to you that do your pleasure with theym. Than the quene caused them to be brought into her chambre, and made the halters to be taken fro their neckes and caused them to be newe clothed, and gave them their dyner at their leser. And than she gave ech of them six nobles, and made them to be brought out of thoost in save guard and set at their lyberte.

The best work of Sir Thomas More (1478-1535), his 'Utopia', was written in Latin and not translated into English until 1551, but it has remained one of the most famous and admired works of the century. He wrote many other works, however, in English, and helped to establish that classical style which was to become fashionable in this and the following century.

Meantime several writers were championing the classical learning of the Renaissance. Men like Sir Thomas Elyot (1490?-1546), Sir Thomas Wilson (1525?-81), John Colet (c. 1467-1519) and Thomas Linacre (c. 1460-1524), for example, were advocating this as the basis of all true education, and their advice was not ignored. Latin and Greek did become the unexceptionable subjects of the English Grammar School curriculum.

One name in particular cannot be omitted from a survey of English prose during the first half of the century—Erasmus. A Dutchman, he became Lady Margaret Reader at Cambridge in 1511, and it was he who inspired the ecclesiastical scholars of the period, men like Tyndale, Coverdale and Cranmer, and the Reformation which they led. 'The Book of Common Prayer' resulted from the movement which he and Cranmer led at Cambridge, and so did the best known book in English, the Bible, which was now to be translated anew. Wyclif's fourteenth-century prose was too archaic to be read with pleasure: a new version was needed, and William Tyndale (1490-1536) and Miles Coverdale (1488-1568) made it.

Being unable to work in England, Tyndale crossed to Germany and by 1525-6 had translated the New Testament and sent it here. In 1534 he published a revised edition. Two years later he paid for his heretical views with his life, being burnt at the stake at Vilvorde.

Coverdale followed him abroad and published his complete

translation of the Bible at Zurich in 1535. Published as a second edition in England in 1537, his was the first complete Bible to be printed here. In 1539 he brought out a still newer edition known as the Great Bible, which, appearing in a second printing the following year with a preface written by Cranmer, was ordained for use in all churches.

The Geneva Bible, dedicated to Queen Elizabeth, was published in Geneva in 1560, and in 1611 the Authorized Version was published in England. A new and powerful influence had come to exert itself on English literature: never before had men been able to read (and hear) words like these:

'Then the same day at evening, being the first day of the week, when the doors were shut where the disciples were assembled for fear of the Jews, came Jesus and stood in the midst, and saith unto them, Peace be unto you.

And when he had so said, he showed unto them his hands and his side. Then were the disciples glad, when they saw the Lord.

Then said Jesus to them again, Peace be unto you; as my Father hath sent me, even so send I you.

And when he had said this, he breathed on them, and saith unto them, Receive ye the Holy Ghost.

Whose soever sins ye remit, they are remitted unto them; and whose soever sins ye retain, they are retained.

But Thomas, one of the twelve, called Didymus, was not with them when Jesus came.

The other disciples therefore said unto him, We have seen the Lord. But he said unto them, Except I shall see in his hands the print of the nails, and put my finger into the print of the nails, and thrust my hand into his side, I will not believe.

And after eight days again his disciples were within, and Thomas with them; then came Jesus, the doors being shut, and stood in the midst, and said, Peace be unto you.

Then saith he to Thomas, Reach hither thy finger, and behold my hands; and reach hither thy hand, and thrust it into my side; and be not faithless, but believing.

And Thomas answered and said unto him, My Lord and my God.

Jesus saith unto him, Thomas, because thou hast seen me,

thou hast believed; blessed are they that have not seen, and yet have believed.'

(St. John, c. 20, vv. 19-29)

The Reformation found its spokesman in Scotland also. John Knox (1505-72), its leader there, fled for safety to the Continent as Tyndale and Coverdale had fled, and in 1558 he published in his exile the work which was inspired by his hatred of the Catholic queens of England and Scotland, 'The First Blast of the Trumpet against the Monstrous Regiment of Women'. In the following year the reformers won the day and he returned to Scotland to write his 'Historie of the Reformatioun within the Realm of Scotland'.

To the middle of the century belong many works of literary and linguistic criticism—those of Roger Ascham, Sir John Cheke and Thomas Wilson, for instance—and to later years Stephen Gosson's 'School of Abuse' (1579), Sir Philip Sidney's answer to it, 'Apologie for (or Defence of) Poesie' (1595), William Webbe's 'Discourse of English Poetrie' (1586), and the duel about the importance of rhyme between Thomas Campion in his 'Observations in the Art of English Poesie' (1602) and Samuel Daniel in his 'A Defence of Ryme' (1603). There had been little literary criticism before 1550: from now on it was to develop into a separate existence destined to attract many fine, original minds.

Common among the prose writings of Tudor times were chronicles. Not histories in the modern sense, they approximate to collections of anecdotes like Lord Berners's version of Froissart. Among their compilers were Edward Hall (d. 1547); Raphael Holinshed, whose 'Chronicles of England, Scotland, and Ireland', first published in 1577 and again in an enlarged edition in 1586, provided poets and dramatists, including Shakespeare, with historical material for their works; John Stow (1525-1603); John Speed (1552-1629) and William Camden (1551-1623).

A different kind of chronicle was collected by John Foxe (1516-1587): the 'Actes and Monuments of these latter and perilous days . . . wherein are comprehended and described the great persecutions that have been wrought and practised by the Romish Prelates', which became, with the more popular title of 'Foxe's Book of Martyrs', the great book of English Protestantism.

283

Among other works occasioned by the religious controversy were all those associated with the attack on the bishops by 'Martin Marprelate', the pen-name of an unknown satirist who issued pamphlets from a secret printing press in 1588-9; and the defence of the new Church of England by Richard Hooker (1554?-1600) in 'Of the Laws of Ecclesiastical Politie' (1594-7).

FICTION

Still other kinds of prose were being written, including fiction, translation and travel-books. Though no one Elizabethan book can be said to be the first English novel, it is to this period that we can trace the formal origin of prose fiction as a separate literary creation. For then books were written which, whatever their purpose, did resemble what we today understand as novels. Translations from Italian had for some time been making fiction popular in England, and story-telling was much in vogue before George Gascoigne published his 'The Pleasant Fable of Ferdinando Jeronimi and Leonora di Velasco', which has been called 'our first modern short story in prose'. The stories were about courtly love and written in a stylized convention which needed only a masterpiece to end it and give a new and more original method a chance to flourish. It was John Lyly (1554-1606), the poet and dramatist, who supplied this masterpiece in his two books about Euphues.

The next 'novels' were the 'Arcadia' of Sir Philip Sidney, posthumously published in 1590, a story of pastoral love still far removed from the modern novel; the romances of Robert Greene (1560?-92), whose 'Pandosto' provided Shakespeare with the plot of 'The Winter's Tale'; 'Rosalynde' by Thomas Lodge (1558?-1625); Thomas Deloney's 'The Gentle Craft', which Dekker dramatized as 'The Shoemaker's Holiday'; and 'The Unfortunate Traveller, or the Life of Jacke Wilton' by Thomas Nashe (1567-1601).

Yet these tales failed to establish a tradition, and we have to wait a long time before prose fiction became popular and esteemed. For the time being the drama absorbed the public imagination and the private ambition, and compared with the best plays of the Elizabethan age the best novels are literary trifles.

TRANSLATION

The most famous translation of the period was Sir Thomas North's version of Plutarch's 'Lives of the Noble Grecians and Romanes' (1579), the source-book of several of Shakespeare's plots. The translation of Pliny's 'Natural Historie of the Worlde' by Philemon Holland (1552-1637), and John Florio's translation of Montaigne's works, were also widely read and used by writers. Florio's work (1603) introduced the essays of Montaigne to England: they were re-translated by Charles Cotton in 1685, but we may say that ever since 1603 Montaigne and his essays have been present in English literature. His intellectual scepticism can be seen in English works, including in Florio's own day the essays of Bacon and the plays of Shakespeare, and the essay has since become a specialized literary form.

George Chapman (1559?-1634?) published his version of Homer, which Keats extolled in a celebrated sonnet, in 1598: it is a translation of seven books of the 'Iliad'. Among other verse translations were Edward Fairfax's of Tasso's 'Gerusalemme Liberata', and Sir John Harrington's of Ariosto's 'Orlando Furioso'. Tasso and Ariosto were both among the most famous of the Italian epic poets.

So scores of foreign writers were made available to English readers and writers: besides those already mentioned, Seneca, the Roman dramatist whose work influenced early Elizabethan drama, Livy, Sallust, Aristotle, Boccaccio, Machiavelli, Cervantes.

TRAVEL

Many accounts of sea-voyages and discoveries were published, for these were the days of ocean-going pioneers. Best known of the writings today are Richard Hakluyt's 'The Principall Navigations, Voiages and Discoveries of the English Nation, made by Sea or Over Land to the most remote and farthest distant quarters of the earth at any time within the compasse of these 1500 yeares' (1589), and Sir Walter Raleigh's 'Discoverie of the large, rich and bewtiful Empyre of Guiana, with a relation of the Great and Golden Citie of Manoa' (1596).

English prose was now established in a variety of subjects, and its subsequent history is one of continuous extension. A medium of infinite adaptability was at the disposal of the English writer.

Sixteenth-Century Drama. And to 1642

Translations of classical plays, particularly Roman (by Seneca), had finally transformed English drama from the Interlude to the play proper. Early playwrights were John Bale (1495-1563) and Sir David Lyndsay, but their work was still crude; and it was the play 'Gorboduc', written by Thomas Norton (1532-84) and Thomas Sackville and acted before Queen Elizabeth in 1562, which marked the beginning of English blank-verse drama. It is a tale of murder, being more a dramatic narrative than a drama since its observation of the rules of Senecan tragedy and the Unities makes it almost actionless.

Then came 'Jocasta' by Gascoigne and Francis Kinwelmerch, an adaptation of an Italian version of the 'Phoenissae' of Euripides. Other tragedies followed quickly, all written on the Senecan model of five acts, with choruses and an excess of rhetorical declamation, their themes being English (legendary) history, Italian intrigues and 'King Leir, and his three daughters, Gonorill, Ragan and Cordella'; and still no great play had been written.

Among the first comic dramatists John Heywood (1497?-1587) was, so far as we have names, the very first. His plays, such as 'The Playe of the foure PP', were little more than Interludes, however, and the first true comic dramatist, using the classical models of Terence and Plautus, was Nicholas Udall (1505-1556), whose 'Ralph Roister Doister' is a blustering farce still capable of amusing sophisticated modern readers and audiences. Then came 'Gammer Gurton's Needle' (published 1575), whose author may have been John Still (1543-1608): it too is a frolic of coarse and ingenuous humour, setting the fashion for the comic drama which reached its Elizabethan climax in Dekker's 'The Shoemaker's Holiday'.

We are now amid the Elizabethan drama with its many creators. Among these were: John Lyly, who wrote, among other plays, 'Sapho and Phao' (1584), 'Endimion the Man in the Moone' (1591) and 'Midas' (1592); George Peele (1558-97), author of 'The Old Wives Tale'; Robert Greene (1560?-92), whose best play was 'The Honorable Historie of frier Bacon and frier Bongay'; Thomas Lodge (1558?-1625) and Thomas Nashe (1567-1601); Thomas Kyd (1558-94), whose 'The Spanish Tragedy' is of special interest to students of 'Hamlet'; and, greatest of all Shakespeare's early contemporaries, Christopher Marlowe

(1564-93).

Perhaps all the dramatists and plays so far named can claim the time only of the literary scholar, but with the name of Marlowe, Elizabethan drama suddenly starts for everyone to whom the theatre matters. He wrote the following plays: 'Tamburlaine the Great', 'The Tragicall History of Dr. Faustus', 'The Jew of Malta', 'The Troublesome Raigne and Lamentable Death of Edward the Second', 'The Massacre of Paris' and 'The Tragedie of Dido Queene of Carthage'. The most popu!ar tragedian of his day, he was also its best poet, for Shakespeare had yet to write his most important plays when 'Faustus' was produced. His characters have neither the individual personality nor the universality of Shakespeare's tragic heroes and heroines, but his sense of theatre, his dramatic energy and, above all, his writing of blank verse are comparable with Shakespeare's at all but his surprising best. Ben Jonson spoke of 'Marlowe's mighty line'; and these lines from the last scene of 'Faustus' show how far in advance both poetically and dramatically he was of the Senecans who preceded him:

> Faustus. Ah Faustus,
> Now hast thou but one bare hower to live,
> And then thou must be damnd perpetually:
> Stand still you ever mooving spheres of heaven,
> That time may cease, and midnight never come:
> Faire Natures eie, rise, rise againe, and make
> Perpetuall day, or let this houre be but
> A yeere, a moneth, a weeke, a naturall day,
> That Faustus may repent, and save his soule!
> *O lente, lente currite, noctis equi:*
> The starres moove still, time runs, the clocke will strike,
> The divel will come, and Faustus must be damnd.
> O Ile leape up to my God: who pulles me downe?
> See see where Christs blood streames in the firmament.
> One drop wou!d save my soule, halfe a drop, ah my Christ.
> Ah rend not my heart for naming of my Christ!
> Yet will I call on him: oh spare me *Lucifer*!
> Where is it now? tis gone: And see where God
> Stretcheth out his arme, and bends his irefull browes:
> Mountaines and hilles, come, come, and fall on me,
> And hide me from the heavy wrath of God.

287

SHAKESPEARE

Shakespeare lived from 1564 to 1616. Little is known of his life, many are the theories about his identity, some people even believing that Bacon wrote the plays with 'Shakespeare' as his pseudonym. The possibility is no doubt fascinating but of less interest than the plays. Probably more words have been written about them than about any other single artistic subject, and more editions published and performances enacted than of the plays of any other dramatist. Shakespeare is, in short, the most famous writer in the whole of Western literature, universally acclaimed, by other writers as well as by the reading public, the greatest dramatic poet of all time. We have put him into his period for the purpose of this short history—to attempt to do more here would be fatuous.

But he was only the best of many successful dramatists who lived and wrote during Elizabeth's reign and until the closing of the theatres in 1642. For the glow of Elizabethan literature lit up the years which followed the queen's death in 1603, and it is customary to include among the Elizabethan dramatists those who wrote their best plays after 1603.

In a diary kept by Philip Henslowe recording fees paid to dramatists from 1597 to 1603, twenty-seven authors are named. Not all of them are important, but Francis Meres, criticizing writers in 1598, particularizes the following as, in his opinion, the best: Michael Drayton, Chapman, Dekker, Ben Jonson, Thomas Heywood, Anthony Munday, Henry Porter, Robert Wilson, Richard Hathwaye(?) and Henry Chettle. Only a few of these matter to us today. (Elsewhere Meres pays generous tribute to Shakespeare.)

Ben Jonson (1572?-1637) wrote a number of satirical comedies which he called 'comedies of humours' (i.e. human types). They include 'Every Man in his Humour', 'Every Man out of his Humour', 'Volpone or the Fox', 'Epicene or the Silent Woman', 'The Alchemist' and 'Bartholomew Fair'. He also tried his hand at tragedy but with small success. Plays about real, hard, brutal life, his comedies present us with the most vivid pictures we have of different Elizabethan types.

George Chapman (1559-1634) wrote comedies too, but his best plays were his tragedies of French History, 'Bussy D'Ambois', 'The Revenge of Bussy D'Ambois' and 'The Conspiracie, and Tragedie of Charles Duke of Byron, Marshall of France'.

Other notable seventeenth-century dramatists were: John Marston (1575?-1634), author of 'Historio-Mastix' and 'What You Will'; Thomas Dekker (1570-1641), the writer of the best comedy after those of Jonson, 'The Shoemaker's Holiday'; Thomas Middleton (c. 1570-1627), whose best plays were 'The Changeling' (in collaboration with William Rowley) and 'The Witch' (not unknown to students of 'Macbeth'); Thomas Heywood (1572?-1650?), whose 'A Woman Kilde with Kindnesse' is one of the best post-Shakespeare plays; Francis Beaumont (1584-1616) and his collaborator John Fletcher (1579-1625), who wrote together such brilliant plays as 'Philaster', 'The Maid's Tragedy' and 'The Knight of the Burning Pestle'; Philip Massinger (1583-1640), author of 'A New Way to Pay Old Debts' and 'The Maid of Honour'; Cyril Tourneur (1575?-1626), whose 'The Revenger's Tragedy' and 'The Atheist's Tragedy' make some of the most grim reading in all English drama; John Webster (1580?-1625?), certainly the best tragedian after Shakespeare with 'The White Devil' and 'The Duchess of Malfi'; John Ford (1586-1639?), who wrote 'The Broken Heart' and ''Tis Pity She's A Whore'; and James Shirley (1596-1666), the last important dramatist before the new drama came with the Restoration.

But these are only the better known of the dramatists and their plays. For it was a prolific age in all departments of literature, in none more than in the drama. In addition to the hundreds of plays written, there were elaborate masques, mixtures of ballet and interlude, for which the best dramatists wrote the libretti: indeed, so much dramatic literature of one sort or another was composed that one feels that some terrible reaction was inevitable.

It came in the shape of the Puritan attack on the stage. With the victory of Cromwell one kind of drama came to an end, and with the Restoration another kind began. Attacks on the drama as immoral had started in the previous century, and when in the reign of James I the acting companies came under royal patronage, the Puritans looked upon the whole context of the theatre with increased antagonism as though it were a royal weapon to be used against them. Eventually, on the 2nd of September 1642, they followed up their constitutional victory with the passing by the Long Parliament of an ordinance closing all theatres. For a time English drama was dead, and when it came to life again it was a new thing.

Seventeenth-Century Verse

During these first forty-two years of the seventeenth century English poetry had gradually undergone a change. As one looks back over the history of any literature one can discern changes in manner and matter occurring almost in a regular pattern. In early times they are easy to detect because of the comparative paucity of the literature and the contrasting expansion of the time involved; but as modern times are approached they become less defined, more subtle, and the process of change spreads over a long period during which one method is almost imperceptibly supplanted by another. Not all the writers at any given time follow the new fashion, think in the new way: what usually happens is that there are some who do follow it, others who pursue the older style, and still others who remain unaffected by either.

So in these forty-two years there were poets like William Drummond of Hawthornden (1585-1649), George Wither (1588-1677), Fulke Greville (1554-1628), Giles and Phineas Fletcher (1588-1623, 1582-1650) and Michael Drayton (1563-1631), who wrote in the established manner of Elizabethan verse, the manner which had been maintained by lyricists like Robert Southwell (1561-95), Samuel Daniel (1562-1619) and Thomas Campion (1576-1620), and anthologized in 'The Phoenix Nest' (1593) and 'Englands Helicon' (1600).

But there were other poets who wrote in a new idiom and imagery, the 'Metaphysicals', as Dr. Johnson nicknamed them.

The poet who led and inspired them was John Donne (1573-1631), who became Dean of St. Paul's. His best poems were 'Songs and Sonets', 'Elegies', 'Satyres' and 'Divine Poems'. One of his love poems alone—'The Message'—will show the difference between this new poetry and the (by then) old poetry of Wyatt and Surrey:

> Send home my long strayd eyes to mee,
> Which (Oh) too long have dwelt on thee;
> Yet since there they have learn'd such ill,
>   Such forc'd fashions,
>   And false passions,

> That they be
> Made by thee
> Fit for no good sight, keep them still.

> Send home my harmless heart againe,
> Which no unworthy thought could staine;
> But if it be taught by thine
> To make jestings
> Of protestings,
> And crosse both
> Word and oath,
> Keepe it, for then 'tis none of mine.

> Yet send me back my heart and eyes,
> That I may know, and see thy lyes,
> And may laugh and joy, when thou
> Art in anguish
> And dost languish
> For some one
> That will none,
> Or prove as false as thou art now.

The poets who followed Donne's modernity were as much a mixture of good and bad as any group of disciples. The best were the religious poets, George Herbert (1593-1633), Henry Vaughan (1622-95), Richard Crashaw (1572-1626) and Frances Quarles (1592-1644); Andrew Marvell (1621-78), especially in his earlier work; and the lyricists, Thomas Carew (1598-1639) and Richard Lovelace (1618-58).

But they had contemporaries who wrote neither in the older way nor quite in theirs, poets like Robert Herrick (1591-1674) and Sir John Suckling (1609-42), whose lyrics, often called *Cavalier lyrics* (i.e. courtly), combine the formal simplicity of the typically Elizabethan song with the colloquial downrightness and startling pointedness of the new poetry. Suckling's famous little *Song* illustrates this combination:

> Out upon it, I have lov'd
> Three whole days together;
> And am like to love thee more,
> If it prove fair weather.

291

> Time shall moult away his wings
> Ere he shall discover
> In the whole wide world agen
> Such a constant lover.
>
> But the spite on 't is, no praise
> Is due at all to me:
> Love with me had made no staies
> Had it any been but she.
>
> Had it any been but she
> And that very Face,
> There had been at least ere this
> A dozen dozen in her place.

We have now moved a long way from Chaucer and entered modern times. Most of the best writers are known to every educated person if only by name, and the mass of preserved literature is beyond detailed record here. From 1650 onwards poems, plays, novels, books of all kinds, begin to pour from the printing-presses, until today the number of new books published every week outstrips the ability of all but the professional bibliographer to register. And I speak now only of those books which merit the registering. To simplify the arrangement of this short chronicle, therefore, each of the main divisions of our literature, verse, prose and drama, will be taken in turn up to the present day; yet even so there cannot be offered more than the merest suggestion of the sustained multiplicity of this literature during the past three hundred years. The purpose of this survey will have been fulfilled, however: that is, to place the writers and their works in time and to give an outline of the development and continuity of English writing.

VERSE

MILTON

Before discussing the next change in poetic style we must turn our attention for a moment to one great poet of the seventeenth century who stood aloof from all other poetry of his time and is, in fact, unique—John Milton (1608-74), Puritan, Latin Secretary to Cromwell, champion of liberty, the next giant of the new world after Shakespeare and Donne.

His early verse included 'On the Morning of Christs Nativity' (which has some affinity with metaphysical verse), 'L'Allegro' and 'Il Penseroso', 'Lycidas', one of our great elegies, a few remarkable sonnets, and 'Comus'. And then came his two epics, 'Paradise Lost' and 'Paradise Regained', and, finally, 'Samson Agonistes'.

'Paradise Lost' is unquestionably the greatest epic poem in English. Very few indeed of the thousands of lines of its twelve books fail to maintain the heroic grandeur of Satan's exhortation to his followers in the first book:

> He call'd so loud, that all the hollow Deep
> Of Hell resounded. Princes, Potentates,
> Warriers, the Flowr of Heav'n, once yours, now lost,
> If such astonishment as this can seize
> Eternal spirits; or have ye chos'n this place
> After the toyl of Battel to repose
> Your wearied vertue, for the ease you find
> To slumber here, as in the Vale of Heav'n?
> Or in this abject posture have ye sworn
> To adore the Conquerour? who now beholds
> Cherube and Seraph rowling in the Flood
> With scatter'd Arms and Ensigns, till anon
> His swift pursuers from Heav'n gates discern
> Th' advantage, and descending tread us down
> Thus drooping, or with linked Thunderbolts
> Transfix us to the bottom of this Gulfe.
> Awake, arise, or be for ever fall'n.

In 'Paradise Lost' Satan, cast down into hell with his followers by God, succeeds in gaining the expulsion of Adam and Eve from the paradise of the Garden of Eden; in 'Paradise Regained', which is in four books, Christ triumphs against the temptations of Satan in the wilderness.

'Samson Agonistes' takes the dramatic form of ancient Greek tragedy with a Chorus. It tells of the close of Samson's life when he was blind (as Milton was himself) and enslaved.

Everything that Milton wrote, in verse and prose, was—is— at the loftiest pitch of sound and sense. His whole artistic life was one of intense devotion to the heroic conception—even his sonnets seem bigger in every way than those of any other poet.

293

His poetry is like Michelangelo's painting and sculpture—on the grand scale; it goes far beyond the normal English appeal to the emotions and the fancy; there is something splendidly remote in it all. As Dr. Johnson said to Hannah More, Milton 'was a genius that could cut a Colossus from a rock; but could not carve heads upon cherry-stones'.

Another unique poet of this time was Samuel Butler (1612-80), whose satire, 'Hudibras', written in the tetrameter couplet, is a galloping attack on Puritanism and all its excess of self-righteousness:

> Free-will they one way disavow,
> Another, nothing else allow.
> All piety consists therein
> In them, in other men all sin.
> Rather than fail, they will defy
> That which they love most tenderly,
> Quarrel with minc'd pies, and disparage
> Their best and dearest friend, plum-porridge.

The next new style of verse-writing, which was now to be used by at least two important poets, first Dryden and later Pope, was not exclusively used by any one poet, and many lyrics and odes were composed by Restoration writers, Marvell's 'Horatian Ode upon Cromwell's Return from Ireland' being perhaps both the best and the best known.

Dryden attributed the credit for introducing the new style to Edmund Waller (1606-87). As a matter of fact, it was not new in English literature, since it was only the decasyllabic couplet in which Chaucer had written his 'Canterbury Tales'; but it did now achieve a new popularity with poets and become the means to a new end.

Waller translated the fourth book of the 'Aeneid' into the couplet, and it was this work which caught the imagination of the poets. Ironically enough, however, it is his short lyrics which have maintained his place in the anthologies—'The Girdle', for instance.

In the seventeenth century the couplet, the heroic couplet as it became called, is seen at its best in 'Cooper's Hill' by Sir John Denham (1615-69), 'The Davideis, a Sacred Poem of the Troubles of David' by Abraham Cowley (1618-67), and the satires of

John Dryden, the Poet Laureate (1631-1700).

With the possible exception of Pope, Dryden is the greatest verse-satirist in our literature. Not all his poems were satirical, for he also wrote elegies, songs, odes, fables and translations (notably of Chaucer), but his best work was in satire, in poems like 'Absalom and Achitophel', 'The Medal' and 'MacFlecknoe' (quotations from which may be read in earlier chapters).

EIGHTEENTH-CENTURY VERSE

Twelve years before Dryden died his successor was born: Alexander Pope (1688-1744). He was the poet of perfect form, even in attack. Like Dryden, he wrote other than satires, his early work being pastoral poems, the elegy 'To the Memory of an Unfortunate Lady', and the tragic love-story 'Eloisa to Abelard'. He also translated Homer's two epics, translations which it became the duty of every educated person of this classical century at least to pretend to have read, and wrote the critical and philosophical poems, 'An Essay on Criticism' and 'Essay on Man'. But, excellent writing though these latter in particular are, his satires are his masterpieces and of these 'The Rape of the Lock' and 'The Dunciad' stand out in especial brilliance.

'The Dunciad' is the greatest attack ever made in literature by one writer on all those other writers whom he despised. In four books, 'the great empire of Dulness' is laid waste in the onrush of heroic couplets, and all the poetasters and sciolists of the day are held up to merciless ridicule. The following lines, taken from the end of the second book, describe the test set to critics to see whether they can keep awake during the reading aloud of two authors' works (eventually everyone present is asleep, of course):

> Three college sophs, and three pert Templars came,
> The same their talents, and their tastes the same;
> Each prompt to query, answer and debate,
> And smit with love of poesy and prate,
> The pond'rous books two gentle readers bring;
> The heroes sit, the vulgar form a ring.
> The clam'rous crowd is hushed with mugs of mum,
> Till all, tuned equal, send a general hum.
> Then mount the clerks, and in lone lazy tone
> Through the long, heavy, painful page drawl on;

Soft creeping, words on words, the sense compose;
At ev'ry line they stretch, they yawn, they doze.
As to soft gales top-heavy pines bow low
Their heads, and lift them as they cease to blow:
Thus oft they rear, and oft the head decline,
As breathe, or pause, by fits, the airs divine.
And now on this side, now to that they nod,
As verse, or prose, infuse the drowsy god.

Although Pope led the poetic world of the first half of the eighteenth century, and although the couplet was the convention of the day, no other poet managed to share his throne except Swift, who had a skill in satirical verse which for sheer invective and cunning has seldom been rivalled. There were alive other poets, however, writing differently: Matthew Prior (1664-1721), though he also wrote the couplet; Ambrose Philips (1674-1749), one of Pope's enemies; Henry Carey (1693?-1743), famous for 'Sally in our Alley'; and James Thomson (1700-1748), whose 'The Seasons', a long descriptive poem in blank verse and four books (Winter, Summer, Spring and Autumn, with a final hymn to nature), stands in contrast with Pope's verse in both matter and manner and was a forerunner of that reaction against the couplet and the subjects of moral didacticism and satire which, gathering momentum in the second half of the eighteenth century, eventually culminated in the 'romantic movement'.

Dr. Johnson's best poems, 'London' and 'The Vanity of Human Wishes', with their lines of memorable advice, were written in the couplet, as too was Goldsmith's 'The Deserted Village', in which, however, a new—or older—note was struck and showed his contemporaries that the couplet need not serve only the fashionable ends.

Inevitably the couplet began to lose ground. No poet could hope to write it better than Dryden and Pope, at least in satire and didactic verse, for with them it had reached its Olympus-top. A change was due, either in the use of the couplet itself or in a new form altogether: it took place in both, but with more effect in the latter, thanks largely to two poets, William Collins and Thomas Gray, who, in spite of smallness of output and an only eighteenth-century romanticism, did point to newer things. Both wrote odes, but it is especially the 'Ode on the Popular Superstitions of the Highlands of Scotland' of Collins (1721-59)

296

that seems to be heralding the days of half a century later:

Ev'n yet preserv'd, how often may'st thou hear,
  Where to the pole the Boreal mountains run,
Taught by the father to his list'ning son
  Strange lays, whose power had charm'd a Spencer's ear.
At ev'ry pause, before thy mind possest,
  Old Runic bards shall seem to rise around,
With uncouth lyres, in many-coloured vest,
  Their matted hair with boughs fantastic crown'd:
Whether thou bid'st the well-taught hind repeat
  The choral dirge that mourns some chieftain brave,
When ev'ry shrieking maid her bosom beat,
  And strew'd with choicest herbs his scented grave;
Or whether, sitting in the shepherd's shiel,
  Thou hear'st some sounding tale of war's alarms;
When at the bugle's call, with fire and steel,
  The sturdy clans pour'd forth their bony swarms,
And hostile brothers met to prove each other's arms.

Gray (1716-71) also wrote odes—'On a distant prospect of Eton College', 'The Progress of Poesy', 'The Bard', etc.—but his best and most popular poem—indeed, the best loved poem from the eighteenth century—is the 'Elegy written in a country churchyard'. Next to this in popularity is the 'Ode on the death of a favourite cat, drowned in a tub of goldfishes'. It was a sign of his artistic independence that when in 1757 he was offered the laureateship in succession to Colley Cibber, he rejected it.

Other poets writing away from all that Pope's imitators stood for were Edward Young (1683-1765), author of 'Night Thoughts on Life, Death and Immortality'; John Dyer (1699-1757), whose 'Grongar Hill' was a favourite with later poets; William Shenstone (1714-63), whose 'The Schoolmistress' was a parody of Spenser's style; Mark Akenside (1721-70,) who used the blank verse decasyllabic line for his 'The Pleasures of Imagination'; and Christopher Smart (1722-71), who wrote his 'A Song to David' in a lunatic asylum.

But as usual these are only the best names of many. The eighteenth century was as fruitful of verse as any other century, even if none of it rose to the pinnacle of possibility; and those who are ready to dismiss its first half as Pope and nothing else

297

would do well to look at 'The Oxford Book of Eighteenth-Century Verse'.

Proceeding through the century we come to yet another new influence, the rediscovery of the Middle Ages with their Gothic architecture and associations of legend. The odes of Gray and Collins had already done something to remind men of them, and then came the excitement of 1760 after the publication of James Macpherson's fabricated prose adaptations of old Gaelic verse in his 'Fragments of Ancient Poetry collected in the Highlands of Scotland, and translated from the Gaelic or Erse language'. The controversy which raged about his old poet 'Ossian'—Dr. Johnson led the sceptics—helped to give the 'poems' and their subjects a wide popularity. The classical eighteenth century was coming to an end. Thomas Percy (1729-1811) joined Macpherson in meeting and creating the demand for the exciting, the adventurous and the emotional, when he published his 'Reliques'; and then one of the strangest personalities in all English literary history flitted across the scene—Thomas Chatterton (1752-70), the 'marvellous boy' as Wordsworth called him, 'The sleepless soul, that perished in his pride'. Inventing a priest, Thomas Rowley, and imitating fifteenth-century spelling and vocabulary, he gave in his pseudo-archaic verse another glimpse of the past to a public sated with the present. But he was unable to conceal his own identity, and it is for his satires and lyrics that we must now account him a true poet even though he reached only his teens.

Others still who were attracted by and turned public attention to the past were the Wartons, Thomas (1688-1745) and more importantly in the second half of the century, his sons, Joseph (1722-1800) and Thomas (1728-90). They brought back to the public mind Dante, Spenser and Milton as opposed to 'Mr. Pope', who was already a figure in history, and they were joined by Thomas Tyrwhitt (1730-86), who recalled to the literary world of fashionable London the perpetual readability of Geoffrey Chaucer.

Two outstanding poets belong to the close of the century: William Cowper (1731-1800), whose personal story is one of the saddest and yet most beautiful in human record: his longest and finest work was 'The Task', but he is known to us all by 'The Diverting History of John Gilpin' and the hymn, 'God moves in a mysterious way', from his 'Olney Hymns'; and

298

Robert Burns (1759-96), one of the supreme lyricists in our language, Scotland's cherished 'Bobbie'.

But both poets lived in exalted times and contemporary with the greatest. For by 1800 the fulness of poetry had returned full cycle and a number of poets were alive who were to take English verse and shape it for the wonder of all subsequent generations.

INTO THE NINETEENTH CENTURY, AND NOW

Chief among these poets were Wordsworth (1770-1850), Coleridge (1772-1834), Byron (1788-1824), Shelley (1792-1822) and Keats (1795-1821), who need only be named in this little history. But anyone who lets them completely overshadow their contemporaries will miss many treasures, for among those contemporaries were William Blake (1757-1827), George Crabbe (1754-1832), Sir Walter Scott (1771-1832), Robert Southey (1774-1843), Samuel Rogers (1763-1855), Thomas Campbell (1777-1814), Thomas Moore (1779-1852), Thomas Hood (1799-1845), John Clare (1793-1864), Thomas Lovell Beddoes (1803-1849), W. M. Praed (1802-39), George Darley (1795-1846) and R. H. Barham (1788-1845).

There were still others of varying degrees of poetic importance, but what other period, before or since, and even including the Elizabethan, could boast so many true and individual poets? Of the great poems of Wordsworth and the others who in modern times would be known as the *Big Five* many are household names—'Tintern Abbey', 'The Ancient Mariner', 'Don Juan', 'Adonais' and 'Lamia'—but of their contemporaries, some of whom survived them to pass into Victorian England the flame of poetry which they had so fiercely fanned into perpetual life, there are works which should be better known and would be if for a while the names of Shelley and Byron, Keats, Coleridge and Wordsworth could be forgotten. Taking the poets in the order in which they are printed above, the following poems can be recommended to all who delight in and profit from important literature: (Blake) 'Milton, A Poem in Two Books'; (Crabbe) 'The Village'; (Scott) 'The Lady of the Lake'; (Southey) 'Joan of Arc'; (Rogers) 'Italy'; (Campbell) 'Hohenlinden'; (Moore) 'Irish Melodies'; (Hood) 'Miss Kilmansegg and her Precious Leg'; (Clare) 'The Rural Muse'; (Beddoes) 'Death's Jest Book'; (Praed) 'The Red Fisherman'; (Darley) 'Nepenthe'; (Barham)

299

'The Witches' Frolic' (from that unique book, 'The Ingoldsby Legends').

So once again poetry was the main occupation. Stylishness and convention were gone, the poets wrote as they were compelled to by their imaginations, using all forms and all words. The old world had been demolished by great events in Europe, and a new world was in the making whose prophets were its poets. It was not their fault if they were largely to remain 'unacknowledged legislators'.

The flame burned on in Tennyson (1809-92) and Browning (1812-1889). Once again, however, they are only the most famous of many. Everyone knows 'The Lady of Shalott' and 'My Last Duchess', but the output of both men was immense and neither can be known merely from a few short poems however excellent they may be. And just as their other and longer works must be read, so, if we are to know the full range of Victorian poetry and not miss individual poems of merit, we must read the works of: Elizabeth Barrett Browning (1806-1861); Matthew Arnold (1822-88); James Thomson (1834-82); the pre-Raphaelites, Dante Gabriel Rossetti (1828-82), William Morris (1834-96), Swinburne (1837-1909) and Christina Rossetti (1830-94); Edward Fitzgerald (1809-93); and the sisters, Charlotte and Emily Brontë (1816-55, 1818-48).

The Victorian period produced literary masterpieces of every kind. It was a long and complex period, dominated by the industrial revolution, political warfare and social reform, scientific discovery and religious controversy; in many ways it was complacent and absurd, in many ways it was turbulent and intellectually brilliant. Behind the aspidistra and the fear of reality lurked genius and an increasing unrest, and, more often than at this point we are apt to think, the lurkers came out in front. Still, or perhaps therefore, its artists did produce masterpieces. In poetry they enriched our history with Tennyson's lyrics, the dramatic monologues of Browning, Fitzgerald's translation of the Rubáiyát of Omar Khayyám, Elizabeth Browning's 'Sonnets from the Portuguese', James Thomson's 'The City of Dreadful Night', the passionate love-lyrics of Emily Brontë, the exquisite artistry of Rossetti and Swinburne, the sad romances of Matthew Arnold.

By now we are almost in our own day. Many poets no longer alive have not yet even been named; many were born in Victorian times who are still alive; and today there is a new poetry being written. To end this survey, therefore, two lists are appended, the first of the better known poets who lived after 1850 and are now dead, the second of some of the better known poets still alive:

(a) Coventry Patmore (1823-96); Gerard Manley Hopkins (1844-89); Francis Thompson (1859-1907); Henry Newbolt (1862-1938); Sidney Dobell (1824-74); George Meredith (1828-1909); W. S. Blunt (1840-1922); Thomas Hardy (1840-1928); Robert Bridges (1844-1930); Lionel Johnson (1867-1902); Ernest Dowson (1867-1900); G. K. Chesterton (1874-1936); Laurence Binyon (1869-1943); A. E. Housman (1859-1936); Rudyard Kipling (1865-1936); W. H. Davies (1871-1940); Edward Thomas (1878-1917); Rupert Brooke (1887-1915); Wilfred Owen (1893-1918); W. B. Yeats (1865-1939); James Elroy Flecker (1884-1915); 'AE' (G. W. Russell, 1867-1935); D. H. Lawrence (1885-1930); Robert Nichols (1893-1945); Hilaire Belloc (1870-1953); James Stephens (1882-1953); Dylan Thomas (1914-53); Walter de la Mare (1873-1955); Roy Campbell (1901-57); Edith Sitwell (1887-1964); Louis MacNeice (1907-64); T. S. Eliot (1888-1965); John Masefield (1878-1967); Siegfried Sassoon (1886-1967).

(Two young poets of great promise were killed in the Second World War: Alun Lewis and Sidney Keyes.)

(b) Edmund Blunden, Robert Graves, C. Day Lewis, W. H. Auden, Stephen Spender, George Barker, Roy Fuller, Laurie Lee, Richard Church, John Betjeman, William Plomer, R. S. Thomas, D. J. Enright, Philip Larkin, Ted Hughes, Vernon Scannell, Thom Gunn, Kathleen Raine, Elizabeth Jennings.

It is to be hoped that these names will not remain only names with those who use this book. Not every poet in the lists can be expected to please, but from their work there will be much to suit all tastes. Some are more important than others, of course: Hopkins matters much more than, say, Blunt, and Lawrence much more than Belloc. Perhaps not one of them can stand alongside the greatest in our literature, but it is a mistake to fix our eyes only on the greatest. Today's modern poetry has its enemies no less than its friends, as all modern poetry has, and not all of it is, we may safely say, scheduled to be recorded in future histories. But the writing of poetry goes on—judging by the number of pieces printed in periodicals there would appear to be more composition of verse at least than ever before—and whether it is to be the Imagists or the Georgians or the Moderns, or none of these, no future poet, historian or critic is likely to look back on the twentieth century as a barren period for English poetry: for however much or little of its poetry he may regard with favour, he will not easily be able to dismiss as insignificant Wilfred Owen, Bridges, Hardy, Yeats, Blunden, de la Mare and T. S. Eliot, to select a mere seven. Meantime those who read poetry are watching for the first signs of the next influence and wondering what will be the major form and directive of the poetry of the second half of the century. To the truly observant watcher there are already one or two clues.

PROSE

THE SEVENTEENTH CENTURY

To return now to the prose of the seventeenth century. Among the earliest and finest examples of it are the sermons preached by Donne as Dean of St. Paul's. He wrote other works in prose, notably 'Biathanatos', a discussion of suicide, but the style of none of them can rival the majestic sweep of the sermons. It must indeed have been an exciting experience to sit in the congregation and listen to words like these:

> It (death) comes equally to us all, and makes us all equal when it comes. The ashes of an Oak in the Chimney are no Epitaph of that Oak to tell me how high or how large it was; it tells me not what flocks it sheltered while it stood, nor what men it hurt when it fell. The dust of great persons graves is speechless too, it says nothing, it distinguishes nothing: as soon the dust of a wretch whom thou wouldest not, as of a Prince thou couldest not look upon, will trouble thine eyes, if the wind blow it thither; and when a whirlwind hath blown the dust of the Churchyard into the Church, and the man sweeps out the dust of the Church into the Churchyard, who will undertake to sift those dusts again, and to pronounce, This is the Patrician, this is the noble flower, and this the yeomanly, this the Plebeian bran? So is the death of Jesabel (Jesabel was a Queen) expressed; They shall not say, this is Jesabel; not only not wonder that it is, nor pity that it should be, but they shall not say, they shall not know, This is Jesabel.

One of the most learned classical scholars and writers of the first half of the seventeenth century was Robert Burton (1577-1640), whose chief work was the curious encyclopaedic book, 'The Anatomy of Melancholy, What it is. With all Kindes, Causes, Symptomes, Prognostickes and Severall Cures of it. In three Main Pertitions with their Sections, Members and Subsections. Philosophically, Medicinally, Historically, Open and Cut up. By Democritus Junior.' It is a sort of pantomimic anticipation of Freud's books on psychoanalysis.

Philosophical works began to multiply in this century, the earliest being Francis Bacon's 'Advancement of Learning' and 'Novum Organum' (in Latin). Bacon (1561-1626) was the best of the late Elizabethan prose writers. Besides his philosophical works he wrote the novelistic 'New Atlantis', 'The Historie of the Raigne of King Henry the Seventh' and the famous 'Essays', the most exact counterpart in English to the essays of Montaigne. As Lord Chancellor of England he has his place in political history also, and as the suspected author of Shakespeare's plays (at least in the minds of the members of the Bacon Society) he holds a unique place in literary controversy.

Political writings also abounded, the book-trade was flourishing—there were no less than twenty-two printing houses situated in London by 1582—and great libraries were founded, such as the Bodleian in Oxford, which was a restoration by Sir Thomas Bodley (1545-1613) of the 'Old Library'. Altogether, the first fifty years of the century saw considerable literary activity other than poetry and the drama.

Milton's prose writings discuss a variety of controversial subjects. Many of them he wrote in Latin, including the celebrated 'De Doctrina Christiana', but the most important and influential were in English. His own marital experience occasioned 'The Doctrine and Discipline of Divorce', an eloquent plea for reason as opposed to the unreasonable attitude of the Church. But this was only one of his demands for individual liberty, of which he was a champion all his life. His most famous tract, 'Areopagitica', is still the classic expression of the case for the freedom of the press. It was published in 1644, and fifty-one years later the press was freed from the shackles of the state's control. Others of his prose works are attacks on royalty and ecclesiastical domination, and a tractate 'On Education'.

Another writer about religion was Jeremy Taylor (1613-67),

chaplain to Archbishop Laud and Charles I and, after the Restoration, bishop of Dromore; his 'The Rule and Exercises of Holy Living' and 'Holy Dying' are famous both for their instruction and their elaborate dignity of style.

The best loved book of the century was also a religious work, John Bunyan's 'Pilgrim's Progress'. Bunyan (1628-88) must be considered as one of the early novelists, for his allegories are stories as well as moralities. Imprisoned from 1660 to 1672 for preaching without official permission, he wrote his best books in his cell: the first part of the 'Progress', 'Grace Abounding to the Chief of Sinners', 'The Life and Death of Mr. Badman' and 'The Holy War Made by Shaddai upon Diabolus'.

Letter-writing was also an artistic occupation in the seventeenth century, as the letters of Sir Henry Wotton (1568-1639), Bacon, and the 'Verney Family' (which were not published until the nineteenth century) amply testify. Histories too were popular, an outstanding one being the Earl of Clarendon's 'The History of the Rebellion and Civil Wars in England'.

To the second half of the century belong certain prose writers of striking individuality, five of whom must be specified in any history of our literature, however short. There was Sir Thomas Browne (1605-1682), author of 'Religio Medici' and 'Hydriotaphia, or Urn Burial', two short books of exceptional interest, psychological and stylistic. The style, classical and splendid yet having a curious idiosyncratic languor, a style which was to be imitated by later writers but by nobody so lovingly as by Charles Lamb, is well illustrated in this passage from 'Religio Medici':

But in eternity there is no distinction of tenses; and therefore that terrible term, predestination, which hath troubled so many weak heads to conceive, and the wisest to explain, is in respect to God no prescious determination of our estates to come, but a definitive blast of his will already fulfilled, and at the instant he first decreed it; for to his eternity which is indivisible, and altogether, the last trump is already sounded, the reprobates in the flame, and the blessed in Abraham's bosom. St. Peter speaks modestly when he saith, a thousand years to God are but as one day: for to speak like a philosopher, those continued instances of time which flow into a thousand years, make not to him one moment; what to us is to come, to his eternity is present, his whole duration being but one permanent point, without succession, parts, flux, or division.

The other four writers were Thomas Fuller (1608-61), author of 'The Historie of the Worthies of England', a sort of guide-book to England and its people, and 'The Holy State and the Profane State', a collection of humorous character-sketches; Izaak Walton (1593-1683), who wrote biographies of Donne, Hooker and others and the second most popular book of the century, 'The Compleat Angler, or The Contemplative Man's Recreation'; Thomas Hobbes (1588-1679), the author of 'Leviathan, or the Matter, Form, and Power of a Common-wealth Ecclesiastical and Civil', which, proclaiming political absolutism and the subordination of the Church to the civil authority, has been one of the most discussed books in the history of English political philosophy; and John Dryden, who has been called the first *modern* prose-writer, so clear, direct and free from medieval and/or Elizabethan traditions is his style. Moreover, he was the first critic of literature in the modern understanding of the word. His works include 'Of Dramatick Poesie, An Essay', 'A Discourse concerning the Original and Progress of Satire', and the Preface to his translation of Chaucer's and Boccaccio's tales.

Two famous diarists lived in this century, John Evelyn (1620-1706) and Samuel Pepys (1633-1703), and at least one other important philosopher, John Locke (1632-1704), author of 'An Essay concerning Human Understanding'. Isaac Newton's 'Philosophiae Naturalis Principia Mathematica' was published in 1687, but was only the most influential of many scientific works written in the days of the founding of the Royal Society.

Apart from 'New Atlantis' and 'Pilgrim's Progress' there were few books written in the century which can be classed as interesting novels. Two books by Mrs. Aphra Behn (1640-89), whose fame rests chiefly on her plays, alone command our respect, 'The Fair Jilt' and 'Oroonoko, or the History of the Royal Slave', which made the public aware of the evils of slavery. It is a tragic tale of British cruelty and negro suffering.

But the English novel was now about to enter upon a career of popularity unparalleled by that of any other literary form.

To Daniel Defoe (1659-1731) must be given the credit of writing the first novel as we understand the word. He wrote many non-fictional works, for he was a journalist, verse-satirist, political pamphleteer and historian; but primarily he was a novelist, even though he did not publish his first tale until 1719, when 'Robinson Crusoe' appeared. Its sequels, 'The Farther Adventures' and 'Serious Reflections during the Life and Surprising Adventures of Robinson Crusoe', have never attained the popularity of the first volume, though this is not surprising when one considers how good that first volume is. Already over sixty, Defoe then wrote an amazing succession of racy pictures of racy life: 'Captain Singleton', 'Moll Flanders', 'Colonel Jacques', 'A Journal of the Plague Year', 'Roxana' and many more. His total output of composition was immense, but, like some other writers, it was his misfortune to write one masterpiece which has overshadowed everything else his active and honest mind created.

AND SO THE EIGHTEENTH CENTURY

Neither in poetry nor in drama was the eighteenth century as productive as the centuries before and after it, but in prose it surpassed the former and can stand comparison with the latter. Its most famous writers, with the exception of Pope and the new poets at its close, all wrote in prose: novelists, philosophers, historians, journalists, letter-writers, ecclesiastics and critics. They included Richard Steele (1672-1729) and Joseph Addison (1672-1719), the creators of 'The Tatler' and 'The Spectator', the characters of The Spectator Club and, in the case of Addison at any rate, some of literature's perfect essays; Jonathan Swift (1667-1745), whose satire, 'Gulliver's Travels', is perhaps the best-known book of the century; Jeremy Collier (1650-1726), author of 'The Ecclesiastical History of Great Britain'; Lady Mary Wortley Montagu (1689-1762), famous alike for her unfortunate relationship with Pope and in her own right as a letter-writer; George Berkeley, the philosopher (1685-1753) whose 'An Essay towards a new theory of Vision' expressed an anti-materialist idealism which was rebuked by Dr. Johnson in a famous incident; the mystic, William Law (1686-1761), author of 'A Serious Call to a Devout and Holy Life, Adapted to the State and Condition of All Orders of Christians'; and the novelists, Samuel Richardson (1689-1751), Henry Fielding (1707-54), Tobias Smollett (1721-71) and Laurence Sterne (1713-68).

Richardson wrote 'Pamela; or Virtue Rewarded', 'Clarissa'

306

and 'Sir Charles Grandison', the first novels of ordinary, middle-class, domestic, sentimental English life. Without the start that he gave to this genre of fiction there might have been no Jane Austen. Then Fielding turned on the sentimentality of 'Pamela' in his 'Joseph Andrews' to write a swift-moving novel and create at least one memorable character, Parson Adams. This success he followed with 'The History of Mr. Jonathan Wild the Great', 'Tom Jones' and 'Amelia'.

Smollett's novels, 'The Adventures of Roderick Random', 'The Adventures of Peregrine Pickle' and 'Humphrey Clinker', and Sterne's 'Tristram Shandy' and 'A Sentimental Journey through France and Italy by Mr. Yorick', all faithful and witty pictures of the new middle-class society of the eighteenth century and of the lower orders who waited upon it, finally made popular the new novel to which Defoe, Richardson and Fielding had devoted so much of their skill, and for which the reading public was obviously so ready.

Four other novelists who belong to this century, one wholly, the others in part, may be mentioned at this point: Horace Walpole (1717-1797), the famous letter-writer, whose 'The Castle of Otranto' initiated a new type of novel, the horrific and melo-dramatic story (described in the sub-title as *Gothic*) of haunted castles, terror and evil; Fanny Burney (1752-1840), whose books 'Evelina', 'Cecilia' and 'Camilla' were the first to make the life of a simple, good girl the story of a whole novel; Matthew Lewis (1775-1818), friend of Byron and author of the most notorious novel of the day, 'The Monk', another Gothic tale of intrigue and horror (its popularity provided its author with the nickname 'Monk Lewis'); and Ann Radcliffe (1764-1823), whose 'The Mysteries of Udolpho', though second only to 'The Monk' in popularity, has since been appreciated as at once the best of these late eighteenth-century thrillers and the limit to which the absurdities could be taken: Jane Austen's 'Northanger Abbey' is a parody of it.

The colossus of eighteenth-century prose was Dr. Samuel Johnson (1709-1784), who is best known to most people as the subject of Boswell's 'Life'. His own output of literary work was large, for besides the novelistic 'Rasselas', 'A Journey to the Western Islands of Scotland', and his newspapers, 'The Rambler' and 'The Idler', he made important contributions to the lin-guistic and critical studies of his age in 'The Lives of the Poets',

307

the Dictionary and the edition of Shakespeare. All are scholarly if opinionated, all are backed by the thundrous authority of a great name, but there are many things in them which we cannot countenance today and which have no more than the interest of a literary curiosity. As for Boswell's biography, which first appeared in 1791 (Boswell: 1740-95), it was the first comprehensive work of its kind, a store-house of information on the cultured life of the day, a portrait, painted with meticulous skill, of a man who in the opinion of some was the biggest humbug who ever passed as an important writer and in the opinion of others was indeed the leader of all that is best in eighteenth-century literary philosophy.

Perhaps the most friendly personality of the century was Oliver Goldsmith (1728-74). We have already met him as a poet and shall meet him again as a dramatist. In prose he wrote one ever-popular novel, 'The Vicar of Wakefield', a large amount of journalism and criticism in 'The Bee', and essays in 'The Citizen of the World'. He must have been one of the most versatile writers in our literature, for he turned his hand to all forms and failed with none. As Dr. Johnson, who, though loving to twit him in company, realized his worth, wrote for his epitaph, 'Nullum quod tetigit non ornavit'—'Nothing which he touched he did not adorn'.

He was one of the circle which centred round Dr. Johnson, the most brilliant collection of individuals to form themselves into an informal society in that or any other century. Other members were Boswell, of course, Edmund Burke (1729-97), the finest orator in English and the author of 'A Philosophical Inquiry into the Sublime and the Beautiful', Edward Gibbon (1737-94), who wrote the most famous history in our language, 'The Decline and Fall of the Roman Empire', and Sir Joshua Reynolds, the painter.

The published letters of these days are not only valuable for the social information which they give, they also show the care which their writers bestowed upon them. Not all letters are intended merely for one pair of eyes, and it is clear that some eighteenth-century letter-writers knew that their correspondence would interest readers whom they themselves could never know. The art of prose can be seen at its most self-conscious in the letters of Horace Walpole, the Earl of Chesterfield, Fanny Burney, David Garrick and Hannah More. Chesterfield, for instance, in his letters to his son had things to say to his generation as well, if not to the future and even to us today:

> The art of pleasing is a very necessary one to possess; but a very difficult one to acquire. It can hardly be reduced to rules; and your own good sense and observation will teach you more of it than I can. Do as you would be done by, is the surest method that I know of pleasing. Observe carefully what pleases you in others, and probably the same things in you will please others. . . . Of all things, banish the egotism out of your own conversation, and never think of entertaining people with your own personal concerns, or private affairs; though they are interesting to you, they are tedious and impertinent to everybody else: besides that, one cannot keep one's own private affairs too secret.

Among the unclassifiable writers of the second half of the century one in particular must be named—Gilbert White (1720-93), who wrote the 'Natural History and Antiquities of Selborne', one of those unassuming, meditative books—like 'The Compleat Angler'—which might have been written at any time.

Philosophical writers not yet named include David Hume (1711-76), Adam Smith (1723-90) and Joseph Priestley (1733-1804), and one religious figure has his place in a history of eighteenth-century literature—John Wesley (1703-91), whose 'Journal' gave Methodism a literary as well as an evangelical appeal.

INTO THE NINETEENTH CENTURY, AND THE PRESENT

As the old century ended and the nineteenth opened, there was no decline in English prose. One might have expected it, so long had prose by then maintained its ascendancy in scope, variety and literary merit. But prose, after all, is not comparable with poetry or drama, since everything not written in verse or dramatic dialogue goes by its name in the categories of literature. Yet that does not mean that it need be artistic—often it means the opposite—and it must be conceded to the eighteenth century as a whole that it was the first century in which English prose sustained a high level of importance.

All the famous poets of the new century wrote prose works: letters of great literary interest, such as those of Keats and

Shelley; critical treatises like Shelley's 'A Defence of Poetry'; critical prefaces like Wordsworth's to the 'Lyrical Ballads'; journals like Byron's; and scrapbooks of literary criticism like Coleridge's 'Biographia Literaria' and 'Table Talk'.

Among the early novels were Mary Shelley's 'Frankenstein' (she wrote others too) and those of Jane Austen (1775-1817). The mere stories of 'Pride and Prejudice', 'Persuasion' and her other novels would not have given Jane Austen the high place she holds in the estimation both of the public and of the literary critics. For they seem to be only love-stories set in the context of conventional middle-class England, a context in which idle, rich people live self-centred lives, dancing and going for rides in carriages. As pictures of this England at the time of the Napoleonic wars they may have some value, but Jane Austen did not plan them as novels of contemporary life: what makes her books so valuable as literature is the intelligence of her whole method. For she made her apparently unimportant people and their apparently unimportant lives interesting to us as only great artists can: in real life most of them—not all, certainly not some of her heroines—would be intolerable, but in her fiction they are delightful. Miss Bates in 'Emma' is the perfect example. They are more than delightful, however: they are also significant. For the point of the immaculate style, the consummate artistry, the ironic wit—the point in all the books is that the good life is not to be had without a proper understanding of reality. The good life is what matters, not excitement, not public importance, not fantasy. Jane Austen had no need to go outside the little world she chose to write about: all the material she wanted was there. Her novels are real novels because they are love-stories in which, eventually, the true partners are found.

Jane Austen's contemporaries may be known only to specialists —Maria Edgeworth (1767-1849), who wrote 'Belinda', 'The Absentee' and 'Ormond', and Thomas Love Peacock (1785-1866), the friend of Shelley, whose 'Headlong Hall' and 'Nightmare Abbey' (its character, Scythrop, is a friendly caricature of Shelley) deserve a better fate; but with the novels of Sir Walter Scott (1771-1832), the most prolific writer since Defoe, the century got into its stride and the novel was on its way to its remarkable future.

Scott's novels and those of the other well-known Victorian and twentieth-century novelists need no detailed specification here. Two lists are therefore given (like those of the poets), of the novelists who have lived since the death of Jane Austen (excluding those already mentioned):

(a) (now dead) W. M. Thackeray (1811-63), Charles Dickens (1812-1870), Charles Kingsley (1819-75), Mrs. Gaskell (1810-65), 'George Eliot' (Mary Ann Evans, 1819-80), The Brontë's: Charlotte (1816-55), Emily (1818-48) (alias 'Currer, Ellis and Acton Bell'), Anthony Trollope (1815-82), Charles Reade (1814-84), R. D. Blackmore (1825-1900), 'Ouida' (Marie Louise de la Ramée, 1839-1908), Wilkie Collins (1824-89), George Borrow (1803-81), George Meredith (1828-1909), Samuel Butler (1835-1902), Thomas Hardy (1840-1928), R. L. Stevenson (1850-94), Rider Haggard (1856-1925), A. Conan Doyle (1859-1930), George Moore (1852-1933), Joseph Conrad (1857-1924), Rudyard Kipling (1865-1936), Arnold Bennett (1867-1931), John Galsworthy (1867-1933), Hugh Walpole (1884-1941), James Joyce (1882-1941), D. H. Lawrence (1885-1930), Virginia Woolf (1882-1941), Mary Webb (1883-1927), G. K. Chesterton (1874-1936), J. K. Jerome (1859-1927), W. H. Hudson (1841-1922), John Buchan (1875-1940), H. G. Wells (1866-1946), Hilaire Belloc (1870-1953), Aldous Huxley (1894-1964), Somerset Maugham (1874-1965), Evelyn Waugh (1903-1966), John Masefield (1878-1967) and Osbert Sitwell (1892-1969).

(b) (still alive) E. M. Forster, Compton Mackenzie, J. B. Priestley, Graham Greene, Robert Graves, Henry Green, Christopher Isherwood, Rex Warner, L. P. Hartley, C. P. Snow, Elizabeth Bowen, Joyce Cary, William Golding, Iris Murdoch, Lawrence Durrell.

Virginia Woolf wrote: ' "The proper stuff of fiction" does not exist; everything is the proper stuff of fiction, every feeling, every thought; every quality of brain and spirit is drawn upon; no perception comes amiss. And if we can imagine the art of fiction come alive and standing in our midst, she would undoubtedly bid us break her and bully her, as well as honour and love her, for so her youth is renewed and her sovereignty assured.' These things English writers have done to her through some three hundred years, and she has changed into ever new youthfulness in their hands. Now she rules the literary world, for good or ill. Defoe, Swift, Fielding, Jane Austen, Dickens, Hardy, these and a score of other novelists of the past are still read and admired and their reputation is certain. But there are novelists

311

still living or only lately dead who may be expected to be of their company different though their conceptions may be. D. H. Lawrence, Virginia Woolf, E. M. Forster and Lawrence Durrell, to select an obvious four, have maintained into our time the high quality of writing and seriousness of intent which are the due of the novel no less than of the poem. In a moment of pessimism Hugh Walpole prophesied that he would be 'read by the tourists', and perhaps he, for one, cannot claim much more than that. If it is the function of the novelist to tell a story well, to entertain, to make the long journey tolerable, then English writers have performed that function; but if Virginia Woolf is right and the novelist can do more, then English writers have done more. No single definition of a *novel* exists: but if it is many things, from the good yarn of 'Treasure Island' to the complex psychology of 'The Waves', and if all the world is its stage, then the English novelists have set out on missions of discovery which have not yet revealed everything.

Returning now to non-fictional prose. By 1800 the book-trade had expanded beyond all measurement, and reading was beginning to rival writing itself as a serious occupation, Reviews and magazines multiplied rapidly; during the nineteenth century the newspaper became everyman's breakfast privilege (*v.* appendix); and the writer, once an isolated figure, became your next-door neighbour.

Early political writers of the nineteenth century included Shelley's father-in-law, William Godwin (1756-1836), whose wife, Mary Wollstonecraft, the authoress of 'Vindication of the Rights of Women' (its title in imitation of the 'Rights of Man' by Thomas Paine, 1737-1809), had died in giving birth to a daugher, Mary, Shelley's second wife. The revolt of America and the French Revolution had sent the precious word *liberty* ringing around the western world, and the writers had taken up the challenge of the common people. Thomas Paine's book (1791-2) had been an answer to Burke's attack on the revolution ('Reflections on the Revolution in France'), and soon many other answers were made. Godwin and his wife were only two of the fighters for political freedom using pens instead of swords: the sordid relationship between him and his son-in-law cannot alter our appreciation of his political writings.

Later writers in this category were William Cobbett (1762-1835), author of 'Rural Rides', and Jeremy Bentham (1748-1832), both of whom, though far less revolutionary than Godwin or Paine, were among the founders of nineteenth-century liberalism.

Among the earlier essayists and critics William Hazlitt (1775-1830) and Charles Lamb (1775-1834) were pre-eminent. Critic of drama and painting, and miscellaneous essayist, Hazlitt is yet most respected as a critic of literature in his 'Characters of Shakespeare's Plays', 'Lectures on the English Poets', 'English Comic Writers' and 'The Spirit of the Age'. Lamb was of course 'Elia' with all that that queer and glorious little name implies. He had written 'The Tale of Rosamund Gray and Old Blind Margaret,' some ineffectual plays, the 'Tales from Shakespeare' (in collaboration with his poor sister, Mary), the 'Specimens of English Dramatic Poets contemporary with Shakespeare, with Notes', a book which did a great deal to restore to the public mind other Elizabethans, and much journalism. And then came the 'Essays of Elia', unquestionably the most peculiarly delightful essays in English literature. One can admire the essays of Bacon and Addison, but one must love or fail to understand those of Lamb, for they are intensely personal, amounting almost to an autobiography. They are romantic writings, full of a strange, learned, very human little man's reflections on a host of topics, and through them there troops a procession of characters not unlike the pilgrims of Chaucer, their guide, philosopher and friend the chief character of Elia.

Other essayists were Walter Savage Landor (1775-1864), who was also a poet—his best prose work was the 'Imaginary Conversations' (1824-9); Leigh Hunt (1784-1859), poet also and editor of 'The Examiner', friend of Lamb, Moore, Byron and Shelley (it was he who introduced Keats to Shelley); and Thomas de Quincey (1785-1859), whose 'Confessions of an English Opium-Eater' and 'On Murder considered as one of the Fine Arts' are unique in both matter and manner.

Religious writers included the great John Henry Newman (1801-90), F. D. Maurice (1805-72) and Charles Kingsley, these last two ranking high as political writers also in the cause of the 'Christian Socialism' which they founded.

Outstanding historians were George Grote (1794-1871), author of 'The History of Greece'; George Rawlinson (1812-1902), the translator of Herodotus; Thomas Carlyle (1795-1881), who wrote the history of the French Revolution and 'The History of Friedrich II of Prussia, called Frederick the Great'; Lord

Macaulay (1800-59), author of 'History of England from the Accession of James II', a tremendous work in five volumes; James Anthony Froude (1818-94); W. E. H. Lecky (1838-1903), appointed Regius Professor of Modern History at Oxford in 1892; and Lord Acton (1834-1902), the corresponding professor at Cambridge.

Carlyle also merits special attention for his books 'Sartor Resartus' and 'On Heroes, Hero-Worship and the Heroic in History'. An uneven writer, and a complex personality, he was capable of outbursts of harsh, hierarchical but entrancing oratory, whose style has come to be known as *Carlylese*:

> 'Call ye that a Society,' cries he again, 'where there is no longer any Social Idea extant; not so much as the Idea of a common Home, but only of a common over-crowded Lodging-house? Where each, isolated, regardless of his neighbour, clutches what he can get, and cries "Mine!" and calls it Peace, because, in the cut-purse and cut-throat Scramble, no steel knives, but only a far cunninger sort, can be employed? Where Friendship, Communion, has become an incredible tradition; and your holiest Sacramental Supper is a smoking Tavern Dinner, with Cook for Evangelist? Where your priest has no tongue but for plate-licking; and your high Guides and Governors cannot guide; but on all hands hear it passionately proclaimed: Laissez Faire; Leave us alone of your guidance, such light is darker than darkness; eat you your wages, and sleep!
>
> 'Thus, too,' continues he, 'does an observant eye discern everywhere that saddest spectacle: The Poor perishing, like neglected, foundered Draught-Cattle, of Hunger and Overwork; the Rich, still more wretchedly, of Idleness, Satiety, and Over-growth. The Highest in rank, at length, without honour from the Lowest; scarcely, with a little mouth-honour, as from tavern-waiters who expect to put it in the bill. Once-sacred symbols fluttering as empty Pageants, whereof men grudge even the expense; a World becoming dismantled; in one word, the CHURCH fallen speechless, from obesity and apoplexy; the STATE shrunken into a Police-Office, straitened to get its pay!'

Literary and dramatic criticism, already raised to the level of creative literature by Dryden, Johnson, Coleridge, Lamb and Hazlitt, now became a professional occupation in its own right, although its best writers—and perhaps this must always be so— were also original writers in verse and/or prose: Macaulay, Matthew Arnold and Swinburne, for instance.

In political propaganda the finest literary work of the second half of the nineteenth century was done by the poet and crafts- man, William Morris (1834-96), who founded the Socialist League, in 'A Dream of John Bull' and 'News from Nowhere'. Yet his work failed in its intent, for it expressed a desire to put the clock of history back and cleanse England of the industrial revolution in days when it was far too late to do that. Morris's dream was beautiful but only a dream; for the clock may not be put back: instead, the new problems had to be faced and, if possible, solved in their own context. This, writers like John Stuart Mill (1806-73), James Martineau (1805-1900), Herbert Spencer (1820-1903) and T. H. Huxley (1825-95) realized. So too in the spheres of sociology and politics did Sidney and Beatrice Webb, the most influential and prolific writers on these subjects who lived into our own century.

Still a host of important writers of prose in the nineteenth century clamours for recognition in these pages: the best of them must be content with inclusion in a short list: John Ruskin (1819-1900), author of 'Modern Painters', 'The Stones of Venice' and 'Sesame and Lilies', critic, sociologist, politician, one of the great stylists; Walter Pater (1839-94), author of 'Marius the Epicurean', the patron saint of the aesthetics; John Morley (1838-1923), historical essayist, biographer, and editor of the first series of 'English Men of Letters'; the linguistic and literary scholars, W. W. Skeat, Stopford Brooke, Sir Edmund Gosse, George Saintsbury, William Ker, A. C. Bradley (best known for his 'Shakespearean Tragedy'), Sir Walter Raleigh and Sir Arthur Quiller-Couch, whose 'On the Art of Writing', 'On the Art of Reading' and 'Studies in Literature' should be read by everyone seriously concerned with books; Lytton Strachey (1880-1932), the biographer of 'Eminent Victorians', 'Queen Victoria' and 'Elizabeth and Essex'; and E. V. Lucas (1868-1938), the essayist and biographer.

Some of these lived into our own times, and they were joined by many more who have distinguished themselves in one or other of the directions of prose. The best of these also must be

315

satisfied with inclusion in a short list: George Bernard Shaw, novelist, writer of long, disquisitive prefaces to his own plays, author of 'The Quintessence of Ibsenism', 'The Perfect Wagnerite', 'The Intelligent Woman's Guide to Socialism, Capitalism and Fascism' and 'Everybody's Political What's What'; H. J. C. Grierson, editor and literary critic; Hilaire Belloc, essayist and historian; G. K. Chesterton, essayist and religious controversialist, editor, journalist, literary critic and biographer; G. G. Coulton and G. M. Trevelyan, historians; Max Beerbohm, caricaturist, essayist and critic, brilliant star of the *fin de siècle* days of 'The Yellow Book' and the Victorian music-hall; Robert Lynd, editor and essayist; Bertrand Russell, philosopher and educationalist; George Orwell, essayist and novelist; Desmond MacCarthy, literary and dramatic critic; Edmund Blunden, essayist and biographer of Leigh Hunt and Shelley; Edith, Sacheverell and Osbert Sitwell, as gifted in miscellaneous prose as in verse; Maurice Baring, essayist, novelist, translator; David Nichol-Smith, who was Merton Professor of English Literature at Oxford, editor and critic; C. S. Lewis, critic and author of 'The Allegory of Love', 'The Screwtape Letters' and 'The Problem of Pain'; Lord David Cecil, critic and biographer of Cowper; I. A. Richards, critic; Philip Guedalla, essayist and biographer; Peter Quennell, essayist and author of 'Byron in Italy' and 'Byron, The Years of Fame'; F. R. Leavis, literary critic; T. S. Eliot, literary critic; Michael Roberts, editor and critic; V. S. Pritchett, literary critic; Aldous Huxley, essayist, biographer, philosopher.

Today we live in a prose age, despite all the significance of contemporary and modern verse. Never have there been more novelists, critics, biographers; and the most famous literary personalities of the twentieth century so far have been writers of prose in one form or another—D. H. Lawrence, for obvious example, in the novel, and Shaw in the drama. As has been observed, the commonest and most popular literary form is the novel: indeed, if in the second half of the twentieth century as many good novels are written as have been written in the first half, then the century may well go down in literary history as *the century of the novel*. But behind that title will lie the mass of prose of all types which the century will also have produced, and from that mass there will surely protrude into recognition many works of lasting value to all who study the art of literature.

DRAMA

We must now retrace our steps once more to the seventeenth century to see how the drama has been faring all this time. It is not such a profitable journey.

During the Protectorate the theatres were closed, although clandestine performances of *drolls* or *droll-humours* were held from time to time (these were either adaptations from, say, Shakespeare or more or less impromptu farces). Sir William D'Avenant (1606-68), who is usually accredited with the first English opera, 'The Siege of Rhodes' (1656), even managed to obtain permission to stage semi-private productions of his own musical plays, and in 1658 he opened the Cockpit Theatre in Drury Lane for this purpose. Perhaps the music made the plays seem less wicked. But so far as the public drama was concerned Cromwell's rule spelt gloom, even death, and perhaps to those eleven years must be attributed the fact that, in contrast with prose and poetry, English drama has never recaptured the prolonged relevance and splendour of Elizabethan times.

But the Restoration did come, both of the monarchy and of the drama to the public stage. New companies were formed, playwrights were freed from the leash, and a new kind of play was inevitable. The tradition of the sophisticated, intriguing, domestic, upper-middle-class comedy was inaugurated, and the stage was set for Sheridan, Oscar Wilde and the modern 'bedroom farce'. There have been a few serious and skilled tragedians since 1660—Dryden, Sean O'Casey, for example—but the poetic power of the Elizabethan and Jacobean tragedy has never since been equalled and no later English tragedian can compare with such foreign writers as Ibsen and Strindberg.

Still, England had had her great dramatists and their plays have never declined in popularity. Throughout the Restoration years and ever since, Shakespeare, Ben Jonson, Marlowe and Webster have remained among the chief claimants on the attention of actors and audiences, and the best actors down the centuries have won their fame for their Hamlets, Shylocks, Doctors Faustus and Volpones.

The most successful of the new plays were those of Thomas Killigrew (1612-83) and D'Avenant, Samuel Tuke's 'Adventures of Five Hours', and Sir George Etherege's 'She wou'd if she cou'd' (1668) and 'The Man of Mode', which introduced into England the *comedy of manners*, the social comedy of the superficialities and stupidities of the well-to-do, so well written in France by Molière (1622-73), whose work was, indeed, the chief influence on the re-established English theatre. Other dramatists were Sir Charles Sedley, Aphra Behn, the first woman to write for the stage, and William Wycherley (1640-1716), among whose plays 'The Country Wife' is one of the few comedies of the time to retain its popular appeal today.

But the best plays were those of William Congreve (1670-1729), Sir John Vanbrugh (1664-1726) and George Farquhar (1678-1707).

Congreve's plays included 'The Double Dealer', 'Love for Love' and 'The Way of the World'. They are all brilliant comedies, sparkling with absurd comic situations, complex in plot but skilfully resolved, their dialogue swift and unrestrained, their people real, as Jane Austen's are, in their own little world.

Vanbrugh wrote 'The Relapse, or Virtue in Danger' and 'The Provok'd Wife', in which characters like Heartfree, Lady Fancyfull and Constant besport themselves in a merry round of love-making and intrigue; and Farquhar wrote 'Love and a Bottle', 'The Recruiting Officer' and 'The Beaux Stratagem', a comparatively open-air comedy in which Aimwell, Lady Bountiful, Mrs. Sullen and others also get involved in the typical Restoration plot.

Minor comic dramatists were Thomas Shadwell (1642-93), the butt of Dryden's satire, Thomas D'Urfey, John Crowne (1640?-1703?), and Colley Cibber (1671-1757), the butt of Pope's satire.

There is much that can be written about this Restoration comedy, for it and against; the best things have been written already, however, by Charles Lamb in his essay, 'On the Artificial Comedy of the Last Century', in which he asserts that criticism of it from the standpoint of our own later morality is not true literary criticism at all: 'When we are among them (its characters), we are amongst a chaotic people. We are not to judge them by our usages.' Unfortunately, however, Jeremy Collier, a clergyman, was a contemporary of Congreve, Wycherley, Vanbrugh and Farquhar and viewed their work with alarm. In 1698 he led the second attack on the English theatre, in his 'A Short View of the Immorality and Profaneness of the English Stage'. Controversy ensued, in which some of the dramatists participated, and gradually lower-middle-class mentality, the main support of puritanism in all its manifestations and the origin of the attack, prevailed. The drama became more polite, more subtle, 'naughty' by suggestion rather than by proclamation, and England had to wait until the end of the nineteenth century before one dramatist, though never naughty in the Restoration sense—in fact, the enemy of everything that the Restoration stood for—refused to be polite no matter how offended people might be. His name was George Bernard Shaw.

Tragedies were also written after 1660, but few of them are important. A new style came into vogue, called *heroic*, the name given to the decasyllabic couplet in which these tragedies, like the satiric poetry of the time, were written. The tragedies of the French dramatists, Corneille (1606-84) and Racine (1639-99), were being translated, but their methods were badly imitated, and exaggeration and ranting—*heroics*—spoilt these new English tragedies. The worst of them were written in the couplet, an inappropriate medium for tragedy, the few good ones in the blank verse line of the Elizabethans.

Among the latter were one play at least by Dryden and one by Thomas Otway (1652-85), perhaps the only two tragedies written since 1642 by Englishmen which can, however remotely, compare with the best Elizabethan: for since that date nearly all the best plays have been comedies.

Dryden wrote some comedies to begin with, including 'Marriage-à-la-Mode' and 'Amphitryon', but they matter little alongside 'Love for Love' or 'The Beaux Stratagem'. His tragi-comedies, such as 'Don Sebastian' and 'Love Triumphant', are also of small dramatic moment.

His first tragedies were written in the heroic manner—'The Conquest of Granada' and 'Aurung-Zebe', both oriental tales —but he realized that the couplet was not the right vehicle for tragedy and turned his glance and then his fine critical mind back to Shakespeare to see how tragedy should be written. With the help of D'Avenant he adapted 'The Tempest'; alone he adapted 'Troilus and Cressida', not, however, with any success; and then he learnt his lesson and wrote the only play of his which gives real dramatic pleasure, 'All for Love, or The World Well Lost', an adaptation of 'Antony and Cleopatra'. Though but a shadow of Shakespeare's play, it does recapture the tragic

319

atmosphere of its great theme and convince us of the truth of its sub-title.

Otway, too, graduated through the rhymed heroic drama and the artificial comedy to the blank-verse tragedy, in which form he wrote his single masterpiece, 'Venice Preserv'd', a tale of agony, treachery and death, much nearer to the Elizabethan drama than the Restoration.

Reference should be made at this point to 'The Rehearsal' (printed 1672), a burlesque of the heroic tragedies and a proof that even in their own day these were realized in their worthlessness. Its composition is attributed to George Villiers, the second Duke of Buckingham (1628-1687), whom Dryden had satirized as Zimri in 'Absalom and Achitophel', but it is thought likely that he collaborated with others. Around a collection of parodies of the typical speeches in these heroic tragedies a silly story is woven, and the whole thing is a clever mockery of contemporary playwrights, including Dryden.

One of the best plays of the eighteenth century was not a play in the strict sense of the word but a comic operetta: Gay's 'The Beggar's Opera' (1728), which is still very popular.

In the drama proper the rest of the century can claim many minor writers but only two important ones. Among the former were George Lillo (1693-1739), whose 'The London Merchant, or the History of George Barnwell' was the first tragedy of ordinary domestic life in prose; Edward Moore (1712-57), author of the comedy 'Gil Blas' and the tragedy 'The Gamester'; and Arthur Murphy (1727-1805), author of the tragedies 'The Grecian Daughter' and 'Zenobia' and the comedies 'Three Weeks After Marriage' and 'The Way to Keep Him', by which he helped Lillo to turn English tragedy away from the verse from which it had hitherto been almost inseparable. But their comedies were better work than their tragedies, and there is no saying but that they were in part responsible for the decline of English tragedy from the poetic intensity with which it must be written if it is to succeed. (It is perhaps significant that the great modern tragedies of Synge and O'Casey are written in the Irish dialect whose prose has the incantatory quality of verse.)

The attack on Restoration comedy—the *artificial comedy*—by Collier resulted, as has been said, in some, at least superficial, cleansing, and the result was what has been called the *sentimental comedy* of writers like Steele in his 'The Lying Lover' and 'The
320

Tender Husband'. But if sentimentality came in, wit went out, and Steele was soon better employed in another direction.

Others besides Steele tried their hand at drama—Dr. Johnson, for instance, wrote a tragedy called 'Irene'—but only two men succeeded in writing plays that were immediate successes and have remained favourites with theatre-goers, and they were both comedians.

Oliver Goldsmith wrote two comedies, 'The Good-Natur'd Man' and 'She Stoops to Conquer' (1773). The former is a worldly-wise and witty telling of the love of young Honeywood for Miss Richland and of Valentine for Olivia: many of its lines have become unacknowledged quotations—'I'm now no more than a mere lodger in my own house'; but 'She Stoops to Conquer' surpasses it in plot, characterization, wit and popularity, as anyone who has read both will readily realize: it is, as it deserves to be, one of the best-liked of all English comedies (yet Goldsmith, like Sheridan, Oscar Wilde and Shaw, was Irish).

The three comedies by Richard Brinsley Sheridan (1751-1816), 'The Rivals', 'The School for Scandal' and 'The Critic', are models of their art, gay, witty, individually characterized and admirably planned. With them, however, the typical English comedy as it had developed from, say, 'Much Ado About Nothing', through the Restoration period and on to Goldsmith, came to an end. Not only were Sheridan's plays too good to be succeeded in their kind, but also the comic social novel had already begun to do the work of this comedy in its own way.

THE NINETEENTH CENTURY AND TODAY

The first half of the nineteenth century was a comparatively bleak period for drama. Old plays were as popular as ever, the theatres were many and full, playwrights abounded, but few original minds were turned to the stage. Most of the poets wrote plays—Byron, Keats, Shelley and Coleridge in particular—but these were not all primarily, or even necessarily, intended for theatrical production: both Shelley and Byron claimed that a drama can exist, can be written, apart from the stage. Being, therefore, dramatic poems rather than plays (like, say, Milton's 'Samson Agonistes'), they cannot be considered here. Mention should be made, however, of Shelley's 'The Cenci' (pub. 1819), which tells the story of the tragic family of Count Francesco

Cenci, his daughter, Beatrice, whom he drove by his passion to plot his murder, and her step-mother, Lucretia, and brothers Giacomo and Bernardo. It is the only one of the dramatic poems written by him and his contemporaries to have been produced in modern times, unsuitable for the stage though much of it is.

But time had separated verse from drama, and it is no wonder that the emphasis in these works was on the poetry and not on the drama. Attempts have been made in recent times to reunite the two, among the successful being the plays of T. S. Eliot and Christopher Fry. Others are W. H. Auden and Christopher Isherwood's 'The Ascent of F6', 'The Dog Beneath the Skin' and 'On the Frontier'; Stephen Spender's 'Trial of a Judge'; Louis MacNeice's 'Out of the Picture'; Norman Nicholson's 'The Old Man of the Mountains'; Ronald Duncan's 'This Way to the Tomb'; and Anne Ridler's 'The Shadow Factory'. Certain radio-plays in verse have also been written, including Patric Dickinson's 'The Minotaur' and Louis MacNeice's 'The Dark Tower'. And while speaking of verse-drama of the twentieth century, we should include Thomas Hardy's 'The Dynasts, An Epic-Drama of the War with Napoleon, in Three Parts', G. K. Chesterton's 'The Wild Knight', and works by Laurence Binyon, John Masefield, W. B. Yeats and James Elroy Flecker.

Charles Lamb tried his hand at play-writing but failed badly, and later Tennyson and Browning, who were not artistically interested in the theatre, joined the throng of forgotten dramatists. Dramatic poems they too may or may not have written, but they certainly did not write plays; for to be a success a play has to be *good theatre*, and the secret of the success of Shakespeare's poetic dramas—and of those of his contemporaries, —lies in the simple fact that in their day poetry and drama (especially tragedy) were united, with the result that, in spite—or because—of writing for the stage, with all its possibilities and limitations, great poetry and great drama were produced.

The first half of the nineteenth century is, then, strewn with the corpses of unsuccessful plays, and even in the second half many a play either never reached the footlights at all or left them quickly, famous though its author was in another context. Indeed, the first thirty years of the second half saw little change in the position. Melodrama and farce had become popular, and T. W. Robertson's 'Caste' (1867) is still good enough to be played seriously in days when gentlemen like Mr. Sweeney Todd are only a joke.

But in the last twenty years a revival occurred. Plays of various kinds were written by a handful of men who did devote their time and talent to the writing of plays intended for the theatre, plays, moreover, of social and human concern or else comedies of fascinating intrigue and wit. Best of the dramatists were Henry Arthur Jones (1851-1929), whose output was immense but is today represented by only two plays, 'The Silver King' and 'The Liars'; Sir Arthur Wing Pinero (1859-1934), who began with farces like 'Dandy Dick' and 'The Magistrate' and then turned to more serious matters in those excellent plays, 'Sweet Lavender', 'The Second Mrs. Tanqueray' and 'Trelawney of the Wells'; and Oscar Wilde (1856-1900), in whose comedies the epigram became for the first time the very heart of the matter. No comedy since Sheridan's can rank with 'Lady Windermere's Fan', 'An Ideal Husband' and 'The Importance of Being Earnest' for witty dialogue, skill in dramatic conception and capriciousness of plot. 'The Importance of Being Earnest' is certainly one of the cleverest leg-pulls in the history of the English stage.

And the revival has been maintained into our century (Jones and Pinero living into it, in any case), most notably by three Irish dramatists, J. M. Synge (1871-1909), Sean O'Casey and George Bernard Shaw.

Synge's 'The Playboy of the Western World', a comedy with an almost tragic atmosphere and some of the supernatural qualities of Ibsen's 'Peer Gynt', and his one-act plays, 'Riders to. the Sea' and 'The Shadow of the Glen' (there is also 'Deirdre of the Sorrows'), do not depend for their effect on characterization, situation and dialogue so much as on the dramatic atmosphere which pervades them and gives to the people and their circumstances their unmistakably dramatic significance. It is an atmosphere of suspense and often of gloom shot through with the impish gaiety of the Irish people and the clear light of the beauty of the human struggle. They are plays about fundamental things, and the language in which they are written has the musical quality of the Irish idiom, befitting the theme as, in the English idiom, only verse could:

323

FERGUS. Will you come this night to Emain Macha?

NAISI. I'll not go, Fergus. I've had dreams of getting cold and weary, and losing my delight in Deidre; but my dreams were dreams only. What are Conchubor's seals and all your talk of Emain and the fools of Meath beside one evening in Glen Masain? We'll stay this place till our lives and time are worn out. It's that word you may take in your curragh to Conchubor in Emain.

FERGUS. And you won't go, surely?

NAISI. I will not. . . . I've had dread, I tell you, dread winter and summer, and the autumn and the springtime, even when there's a bird in every bush making his own stir till the fall of night; but this talk's brought me ease, and I see we're as happy as the leaves of the young trees, and we'll be so ever and always, though we'd live the age of the eagle and the salmon and the crow of Britain.

Sean O'Casey wrote at least three excellent plays, 'Juno and the Paycock', 'The Shadow of a Gunman' and 'The Plough and the Stars'. The case of Republican Ireland against imperial England, and the claim of the poor and the dispossessed on the good things of the world, are put in them with a power and a passion impossible to history-book or political tract. They differ from Synge's plays in their setting and the individuality of their people—there is only one Paycock and only one Joxer—but they too receive their dramatic tension from the dark atmosphere which clings like a fog about these people and their words, and from the bright light of their courage and humour.

Of Shaw it is as unnecessary to speak as of Shakespeare. He was the doyen of the modern theatre, its greatest box-office success, its most notorious iconoclast, its devil and its darling. In the 'Prefaces' to his plays—which, collected into a single volume, comprise a dictionary of belligerent common sense—he probably wrote more about the theatre and the art of drama than any other practising playwright. He practised what he preached, and he preached in his plays and we love it. No better epitaph is needed for him than the motto of a famous aircraft-carrier: *Explicit Nomen*.

But let us be fair to English dramatists even as we praise Irish.

324

They have had an uphill fight all the way: against more than two centuries of almost dramatic still-birth; against the spring into popularity of burlesque, melodrama, farce, pantomime and music-hall; and against what is both the most successful form of public entertainment yet devised and a new art attracting original, creative minds and the best actors—the cinema, which at one time looked like effecting a second closure of the theatres, not because of their naughtiness but because of their deserted auditoria. And now there is television.

Yet there have been some competent and genuine dramatists during the century: J. M. Barrie (1860-1937), John Galsworthy (1867-1933), Arnold Bennett (1867-1931), John Drinkwater (1882-1937), Somerset Maugham, Laurence Housman, John Masefield, St. John Ervine (another Irishman), J. B. Priestley, James Bridie (a Scotchman), Ian Hay, Clemence Dane, A. A. Milne.

One cannot predict permanence for any of them as one can for Shaw. The older dramatists—Shakespeare, Congreve, Sheridan, Synge—are so clearly superior, and it is they who are still the mainstay of our theatres. But today most of our big theatres are given over to other things than plays, to more popular productions: 'musicals', revues, variety shows, circuses and Bingo.

Nevertheless, in the past decade there has been some revival of interest in the theatre, mainly due to the work of several new and exciting playwrights: John Osborne, for example, Harold Pinter, Arnold Wesker, Samuel Beckett. And up and down the country there still are repertory companies and amateur dramatic societies of every conceivable size and kind, all harder at work than ever before. And is there not the Mermaid Theatre in London? And the Royal Court?

Conclusion

So more than a thousand years of literature have been briefly surveyed, and the survey has all the defects of any panorama—the details are not clear, many of the details are not visible. There has been no time for many things; most painfully there has been no time for possible favourites: Edward Lear, the nonsense-poet; T. E. Lawrence, 'Lawrence of Arabia', author of 'The Seven Pillars of Wisdom'; C. E. Montague, critic and novelist; Alice Meynell, gentlest of poets; W. S. Gilbert and his 'Bab

Ballads'; and those American writers who matter when we discuss our own literature—Mark Twain, Emerson, Edgar Allan Poe, Henry James and Ernest Hemingway.

Where, too, are the dialect poems and novels? Where is William Barnes? Where are the books on sport and animals, the children's books, the encyclopedias, the books on art and science? Where are Havelock Ellis, Roger Fry and Neville Cardus? Where is 'Arabia Deserta'? Where are the detective-novels? Where is 'Journey's End'? Where are the books of the late war—'The Nine Days' Wonder' and 'The Last Enemy'? Where are today's magazines and periodicals? Where is the history of the popular song? Where is Richard Jefferies?

For all these omissions—and many more—no excuse is possible but that of the limitations of a short history.

Finally, what can be said of our literature as a whole? Surely that it is one thing, indivisible into periods except for the convenience of record and the necessities of detailed analysis. Be it prose or verse, old or new, great or humble—it is one thing England has many glories, but her literature is her greatest, to preserve which we would be ready to sacrifice most else. In his 'The Hero as Poet' Carlyle imagined foreign nations asking us whether we would surrender India or Shakespeare, and he himself was quick to give our unhesitating answer: 'Indian Empire or no Indian Empire; we cannot do without Shakespeare. Indian Empire will go, at any rate, some day; but this Shakespeare does not go, he lasts for ever with us; we cannot give up Shakespeare.'

With Shakespeare we could all give other names also, aware as we are of the many great writers we can boast. But, the great apart, we are a nation of writers. It was the Irishman, Samuel Lover, who, in 'Handy Andy', said that 'when once the itch of literature comes over a man, nothing can cure it but the scratching of a pen'. Englishmen have indeed suffered very badly for a very long time from that itch, and their scratchings have left on history marks for permanent memory.

Appendix. The Newspaper

Today several daily newspapers are printed in London and sold all over Great Britain: 'The Times', 'The Daily Telegraph', 'The Daily Mail', 'The Daily Express', 'The Guardian', 'The Sun', 'The Daily Mirror', and 'The Daily Sketch'. Some of these newspapers have northern and Scottish editions printed in

Manchester. Others, printed only in the provinces, have the status almost of national newspapers, such as 'The Birmingham Post'. There are countless more—some printed for the evenings only, some printed weekly—serving country and suburban areas and/or special purposes; and to complete a list of all the newspapers—that is all the publications registered at the General Post Office as newspapers—we should have to include the Sunday papers and a host of miscellaneous periodicals. In short, England is well provided with newsprint, and the newspaper is the most widely read publication in history. It has not always been so in the three hundred years of its life.

In Elizabethan times only a few aristocrats with political power learnt the latest news from their own private reporters: the printing-press was not yet intended for the provision of information to the lower orders.

During the seventeenth century pamphlets were occasionally printed giving news, for in 1638 permission had been reluctantly conceded to two printers to publish what was called a *newsbook*. Their first was dated December 20, 1638, and called 'An abstract of some speciall forreigne occurrences brought down to the weekly news of the 20 of December'. Thereafter Royalists and Cromwellians published these books, one of the most famous being 'The Publick Intelligencer'.

There was still nothing resembling a daily newspaper, however, and the most frequent appearance of any *book* was twice a week. The first daily did not come out until 1702: 'The Daily Courant'.

Altogether, great numbers of these *books* were published during the seventeenth century; all are now long forgotten except one, 'The London Gazette', which first appeared in 1665 and still exists to record news of the Court.

The first famous writer to establish a periodical was Daniel Defoe, whose 'The Review' came out in 1704. A new life was given to the newspaper, for it was much more than a newspaper. In 1709 Steele published the first number of 'The Tatler', which was issued three times a week until January 1711: Addison's 'The Spectator', first published on March 1st, 1711, took its place. The newspaper had become literature. In 1713 Steele, who had contributed to 'The Spectator', published 'The Guardian', to which Addison also contributed. Indeed, the two men were almost inseparable, Steele, for example, inventing the characters of 'The Spectator Club' and Addison developing them into the individual personalities they became.

In 1711 the first established provincial paper, 'The Newcastle Courant', was printed. It was followed in 1712 by 'The Liverpool Courier', and many other 'provincials' sprang up, especially in the north.

The newspaper grew and expanded throughout the eighteenth century, both as a disseminator of news and political propaganda and as a literary periodical; and in 1768 the most famous correspondent in English political journalism began writing in 'The Public Advertiser'—'Junius', whose identity has not yet been certified.

In 1785 the best-known of all English newspapers was established: 'The Daily Universal Register', later known as 'The Times'. Thomas Barnes came to it in 1817, and by the time he left it in 1841 it was obviously destined for its long and distinguished career.

'The Morning Post' was started in 1772 and lasted until 1937, when it was combined with 'The Daily Telegraph'. And still another product of the eighteenth century was 'The Morning Chronicle', which continued until 1862 and numbered among its writers the young Charles Dickens.

During the nineteenth century the newspaper's public changed with the material conditions of the industrial revolution. Education spread and a new reader came into existence—'the man in the street'. What had been written for and read by only a comparatively select few came gradually to be written for and read by the people as a whole. Scores of new papers were started, many of which, such as the evening 'The Pall Mall Gazette', have long been defunct. But some did last: 'The Daily Telegraph', first published in 1855, and 'The Daily News', which Dickens edited for a while and which later absorbed 'The Daily Chronicle' of 1877 to become 'The News Chronicle'.

As the century came to its close the truly 'popular press' came into its own with the publication of 'The Daily Mail' in 1896; and four years later 'The Daily Express', and twelve years later still 'The Daily Herald', brought into almost every home in the country the most influential reading-matter that has ever come from a printing-press.

The newspaper is a complex publication and 'big business'. Anything and everything are in it: advertisements, photographs, articles, essays, verses, serial stories, short stories, jokes, puzzles and strip-cartoons. Above all today, it is a powerful weapon of political propaganda. Never before has its reader had such an obligation to himself and to society to read critically: it is his duty to know who owns the newspaper he reads, to understand its 'platform', and to look at the different points of view, the different presentations of even the same item of news, put forward in other papers. The days of disinterested journalism—if they ever existed—have gone.

APPENDIX B

The English Language

I trade both with the living and the dead, for the
enrichment of our native language.

(DRYDEN.)

Teutonic. Germanic and Old Norse. Old English

WHEN the Jutes, Angles and Saxons invaded and conquered
southern Britain in the fifth and sixth centuries, they found a
Celtic people speaking a language different from their own, a
people who had lived under Roman rule for a long time and
spoke both their own Celtic tongue and, to some extent, Latin.
But apart from place-names, only a very few Celtic words (called
loan words) survived the invasions—Otto Jesperson, the great
etymologist, gives *ass* and *brock* among about a dozen—and so
far as we can tell, the civilization and the language of Celtic
Britain disappeared. Certainly nearly all linguistic traces of the
Roman occupation disappeared, and it was not until the Norman
invasion of 1066 and, still later, the spread of the Renaissance to
England that the Latin of ancient Rome came to swell the
English language. Some Latin *loan words* are traceable to the
period subsequent to the Christianization of the country about
A.D. 600, words connected with the new religion: e.g. *cugele*
(=cowl, L. *cuculla*), *regol* or *reogol* (=monastic rule, L. *regula*);
and a few, such as *wine* (L. *vinum*), date even earlier.

We have, therefore, to consider our language as, in the main,
no older than the time of the invasions of the fifth century. The
invaders spoke dialects of the Germanic branch of the Teutonic
group of languages, itself only one branch of the Aryan or
Indo-European family, which included Persian, Greek and
Latin. Our *parent language* was thus predominantly Germanic in

character. Later, the coming of the Danes added the Scandinavian or Old Norse branch of the Teutonic group, and two forms of 'English', both closely connected, however, existed in the country simultaneously, the Norse prevailing in the northern half where the Danes had chiefly settled, and the Germanic in the southern. But when eventually the kingdom of Wessex became the centre of government under King Alfred, West-Saxon, as it is called, became the literary language of the country, and it is in this that most of the early Old English manuscripts which have been preserved were written.

The general name of *Old English* was given by Grimm to the language of England before 1066, and that name has persisted. The historian Camden had mistakenly called it *lingua Anglosaxonica*; King Alfred was more modern with his *Englisc*. *Old English* gradually merged into *Middle English* (also Grimm's term) during the twelfth century, and Middle English lasted until towards the end of the fifteenth century and the invention of printing.

Cnut, the Danish king who ruled England from 1014 to 1035, first achieved the union of the whole country, but in spite of this the competition between Germanic and Norse words still continued, the latter being more and more often successful in ousting older Germanic synonyms. There is a famous passage in Caxton's 'Eneydos' (1490) which illustrates the struggle which went on: it concerns the established word *ey* and the Scandinavian *egg*:

And certaynly our langage now used varyeth ferre from that whiche was used and spoken whan I was borne. . . . And that comyn englysshe that is spoken in one shyre varyeth from a nother. In so muche that in my dayes happened that certayn marchauntes were in a shippe in tamyse, for to have sayled over the see into zelande. And for lacke of wynde, thei taryed atte forlond, and wente to lande for to refreshe them. And one of theym named sheffelde, a mercer, cam in-to an hows and axed for mete; and specyally he axed after eggys. And the goode wyf answerde, that she coude speke no frenshe. And the marchaunt was angry, for he also coude speke no frenshe, but wolde have hadde egges, and she understode hym not. And thenne at laste a nother sayd that he wolde have eyren. Then the good wyf sayd that she understod hym wel. Loo, what sholde a man in thyse dayes now wryte, egges or eyren. Certaynly it is harde to playse every man, by cause of dyversite and chaunge of langage.

Egg won, of course, and, similarly, the Old Norse verb *to die* ousted the older *sweltan* and the pronouns *they, them, their* ousted *hie, hem, hir, hem* surviving, however, in the abbreviation *'em*.

The Norman Conquest. Middle English. French

In 1066 England succumbed to yet another foreign invasion, by the Norman French, and so a further foreign influence was to be exerted on our language. Gradually and slowly—for communications were then eight hundred years slower than they are now—the influx of French words began, until it reached its climax between 1250 and 1400.

The invaders, the new rulers, were Normans, and so the Northern French dialect was the first to be absorbed into English. Moreover, they were originally *Norse men*, so that many of the new 'English' words were once again of Norse origin.

Later, with the accession of the Angevins in the twelfth century, the Central French dialect became the dominant influence, and thus it came about that two French dialects left their mark on our language. The same word was absorbed twice, in two forms and with some change of meaning. Differences of spelling, for instance, were that in Central French *gu* (and later *g*) was used for the Northern *w*, *ch* was used for *k* or *c*, and *s* was used for *ch*; and so we have from Norman French such words as *warden, wage* and *catch,* which originally were the same as the Central French *guardian, gauge* and *chase*.

Inevitably English absorbed thousands of French words, connected especially with food and cooking, law, government, property, rank, war, trade and relationships, just those departments of life of which the ruling classes were in control. For after the conquest the French language virtually supplanted English in such departments. The English peasantry were little affected by it, and Robert of Gloucester recorded in his 'Chronicle' (*c.* 1300) that 'lowe men' held to 'hor owe speche ʒute' (ʒ is the old runic letter *yok* equalling *z, y,* or *gh*), but in all those spheres where the direction of a country's life is governed and its literature is written, French, and not English, was used. Until about
332

1385 it was taught in all schools even to the exclusion of English. But by then the reaction back to the native language had begun and, according to John of Trevisa (1326-1412), 'in all þe gramer-scoles of England children leveþ Frensch and construeþ and lurneþ in Englysch'. (þ is the old runic letter *thorn* equalling *th*, still seen in the form of Y in inn-signs, though it is now pronounced as if it really were our modern Y.)

The conquest had taken place three hundred years earlier, however, and French had enjoyed a long reign. The Chancellor's speech opening parliament was not written in English until 1362, and for these three hundred years there had not been any memorably great English literature. Much had been written in English, but Chaucer (*c.* 1340-1400) was the first truly great writer to use his native language and to establish it as the literary medium it has since been. It was a very different language from that of 'Beowulf' and showed the tremendous change which French had effected. Still, it was English, however transformed. One of Chaucer's successors, Hoccleve, was not uttering words of fulsome praise when he called him 'the firste fyndere of our faire langage'.

The supremacy of the West Saxon dialect, the dialect of King Alfred's court, had, of course, been ended by the conquest, and when men returned to English generally—when, that is, the government rejoined the common people and the country returned to a single language—numerous dialects were in being, none of them assuming dominance over the others. But there were three strong competitors for leadership: the Northumbrian, which had held sway before Alfred's time, the West Saxon and the Mercian or Midland; and as it was in the last of these three that Chaucer wrote, the language of London, it assumed a literary supremacy which eventually led to its general recognition as *English*.

And so England had its own language again, with French a vital element in it. Sometimes the native synonym survived: *help* and *love*, for example, were and are more commonly used than *aid* and *charity* except in special contexts. Sometimes, too, the French equivalent came to be used with a different connotation from that of the surviving native word. It was Sir Walter Scott in 'Ivanhoe' who observed that the names of several animals are English when they are alive—*ox, cow, calf, sheep, swine, boar, deer*—but French when they are dead and served up on a

333

table—*beef, veal, mutton, pork, bacon, brawn, venison.* But more commonly the incoming French word became a new English word. So French commercial terms poured into English, especially during the fifteenth century: the word *commerce* itself is originally French (from Latin). And we are still incorporating French words, *beret* being a recent example. Often we retain the original spelling and pronunciation: *café, soupçon, rendez-vous, encore, faux pas;* yet all these words are now classed as English.

We go on incorporating French, no less than other foreign, words and expressions because they name things and situations for which, in spite of the richness of our own language, we have no adequate terms: the following short selection of commonly used French expressions will show how much the French language has contributed already to English in this way: *nom de plume, bête noire, double entendre, coup d'état, fait accompli, pièce de résistance.*

Latin

Closely associated with our vast incorporations of French is the even vaster Latin element in our language, for many Latin words came in by way of French and in their French spelling. So we have *honour*, spelt with the French *u* (the Americans retain the original Latin spelling, *honor*, taken over from England in the seventeenth century).

During the Renaissance in England, and generally throughout the sixteenth century when so many Latin terms came into English, either directly or by way of Italian, many originally Latin words which we already had from French were remodelled so as to be in accordance with their Latin spelling, though we retained their existing pronunciation. *Subtle, debt* and *doubt* are examples.

Comparable with the twofold absorption of the same French word outlined above are the Latin *doublets* in English, pairs of words each of which was incorporated at a different stage, spelt differently and usually having a different meaning, though both were exactly the same word in Latin. One form is indirectly from Latin—and usually through French—the other is a later incorporation direct from Latin. Examples abound: *dainty—dignity, guest—hostile, reason—ration, tavern—tabernacle, arch—arc, loyal—legal, amiable—amicable, mayor—major, pale—pallid.*

334

As has been said, the Roman occupation is little traceable in our language, and it is impossible to say exactly when Latin began to be widely anglicized. But even before the eleventh century foreign clergy who had come to English monasteries were adapting *Latinisms* into their translations of Latin works. Coming in with French too, Latin constitutes a large part of the new vocabulary of Middle English; and it was of course the language of the church and the law.

By the time of the Renaissance, therefore, it was no stranger. Not until the latter part of the fifteenth and during the sixteenth centuries, however, did it become the chief direct contributor to our vocabulary. Then learned Englishmen outside the walls of monasteries wrote in Latin as well as in English: Sir Thomas More wrote his famous 'Utopia' (1515-16) in Latin, and, a good deal later still, Bacon—and Milton—wrote in both languages with equal skill. The new interest in classical Latin authors, the study of Italian literature, the 'new learning' which characterized the earlier sixteenth century in particular, led native writers to adapt Latin terms on an unprecedented scale, so that by now, as the lists of prefixes and suffixes in another appendix show, a very big proportion of our vocabulary has a Latin origin. Consider only some of the words which we have gained from one Latin word, *manus* (=hand): *manual, manipulate, maintain, amanuensis, manage, manufacture, manuscript, mandate.*

Sometimes the new Latin equivalent ousted the native word as Danish words had ousted Anglo-Saxon: *to contradict,* for instance, supplanted *to gainsay,* which has not disappeared but has long been archaic. And we have numerous examples of another kind of doublet, a Latin word existing alongside a native word which was originally synonymous with it: *horticulture* and *gardening,* for example. The Latin word is usually looked at askance as 'learned' and verbose, and although it may fairly merit the former epithet, it is verbose only when the native equivalent is still synonymous. Such a style of writing as that of Sir Thomas Browne, Dr. Johnson and Charles Lamb, to name only three writers, is peculiarly Latinate. Johnson's preference for the Latin word has even led to the coining of the term *Johnsonese,* which is seldom a term of approval. But all these writers knew what they were doing, and it is in the hands of lesser men that *Johnsonese* is an evil; for unless a writer is the master of his vocabulary and bends Latinisms no less than the

335

simplest native words to his own purpose, then *Johnsonese* can become Euphuistic pomposity, what has been called an 'inflated turgidity of style', the using of, say, *sanguinary* instead of *bloody* or *agricultural occupation* for *farming*.

Without Latin our language would be immeasurably less expressive; yet there is danger in too much. Lecky, the historian, said of Gladstone that 'he seemed sometimes to be labouring to show with how many words a simple thought could be suppressed or obscured': if expression degenerates as much as that it becomes merely jargon.

Finally, we have retained Latin expressions in their original spelling in the same way that we have retained French and for the same reason: for instance: *status quo, sine die, magnum opus, lapsus linguae, alter ego, ex cathedra, deus ex machina, a priori, sub rosa, per se, de facto, de jure.*

Greek

Greek too has played an enormous part in the formation of our present language. The Reformation encouraged its study, and in 1516 Erasmus published the Greek New Testament. During the sixteenth century Greek literature was hardly less avidly read by scholars than Latin, and many of its words were anglicized. Learned rulers like Henry VIII and Elizabeth were influential in fostering the movement towards the new and rich culture offered by the great authors of ancient Athens and Rome; and statesmen and poets like Wyatt, Surrey and Sidney were its leaders. A new literary vocabulary came into being, and it is from its literature that a country gains much of its language. Lyly's 'Euphues, the Anatomy of Wit' (1578) and 'Euphues and his England' (1580) were aimed at the reform of education and manners along classical lines, and their diction and style, though both extravagantly pedantic, did much to popularize the new Grecian and Latinate vocabulary.

There is less Greek than Latin in the English of everyday usage, but, again as the lists of prefixes and suffixes show, it does constitute a large element of our language. In science and politics it has given many of our words: *biology, astronomy, therm,* the word *politics* itself, *democracy*; and it is in such spheres, technical and professional, that it is seen at its most active and influential.

Other Languages

Having considered the contributions made by French, Latin and Greek, it may be as well at this point to look briefly at the contributions made by other foreign languages to what we possessively call English. Almost every other language on earth has contributed something to the formation of our own—and, in its turn, English has contributed much to many other languages: the word *gentleman*, for example, is well on its way to becoming international.

From Africa we have the names of animals like the *gorilla* and the *chimpanzee*; from Arabia words like *harem, coffee* and *algebra*; from Australia: *kangaroo* and *boomerang*; from Holland: *spool, hawker, skipper, yacht, laager* and *commando*; from Egypt: *gipsy* and *oasis*; from modern Germany: *kindergarten, waltz* and *blitz*; from Hebrew: *cherub* and *jubilee*; from Italy: *piano, macaroni, stanza, sonnet* and *allegro*; from Malaya: *bamboo*; from India: *wallah* and *pukkah sahib*; from Mexico: *tomato* and *cocoa*; from Persia: *bazaar, caravan* and *chess*; from Polynesia: *taboo*; from Russia; *steppe, bolshevik* and *mazurka*; from Spain: *negro, desperado, grandee, renegade, banana, armada* and *cargo*.

From other countries and foreign place-names we have the names of imported commodities: *champagne, gin* (from Geneva), *china, japan, cashmere, port* (from Oporto) *morocco, fez, jersey* and *italics*.

All these examples are chosen at random from thousands of words.

Roman names are seen in those of all English towns ending in *-chester* (=-caster); similarly the Danish word for *town* is seen in our suffix *-by*, as in *Grimsby*; and some Celtic words still exist in the names of Welsh and Scottish towns: *Llandudno*, for instance, means the church of St. Tudno.

Proper Names

But there are many other sources of our huge vocabulary than other languages. Original proper names, both of actual people and of fictitious characters, have provided us with antonomasia, abstract nouns and descriptive phrases. A mean person we call a *Shylock*, and a treacherous man a *Judas*. *Dunce* was the nickname given by sixteenth-century reformers to the pedantic disciples of Duns Scotus, the medieval scholar. A *lazar* is called

337

after Lazarus. Then we have *doubting Thomas*, a *Don Juan*, a *slave* (=Slav), and the recent example of *Hitlerism*. We speak of *raising Cain*; Guy Fawkes gave us *guy* both as a noun and as a verb; the verb *to tantalize* was adapted from the name of poor Tantalus who never touched what he reached for; *to bowdlerize* was invented from the name of Dr. Bowdler who published his expurgated 'Family Shakespeare' in 1818, 'in which nothing is added to the original text, but those words and expressions are omitted which cannot with propriety be read aloud in a family'; Dr. Spooner gave us *spoonerisms* and Mrs. Malaprop *malapropisms*; Atlas gave us our book of maps; the St. Audrey lace sold at old fairs gave us the adjective *tawdry*; Don Quixote's fantasies were *quixotic*; the Magi were *magic men* or *magicians*; Plato's ideals were *platonic*; Shaw's wit was *Shavian*; H. G. Wells's pictures of the future were *Wellsian*; and the Marquess de Sade's delight in cruelty was *sadistic*. Instances could be multiplied almost, one feels, indefinitely.

Slang

It often happens that what one age or country considers slang becomes the standard terminology of another, for slang is so widely used that it eventually settles down to win the respect that is due to old age. The classic example of this is the Latin slang word for *caput* (=head)—*testa* (=pot), which became the French *tête*. In English we have also reversed the process and adapted a non-slang original for our own slang: the Mexican word *vamos* meaning *let us go* has become our *vamoose*; and the Spanish *sabe usted?* meaning *do you know?* has become our *savvy?*

We live now in an age of slang, and almost daily our colloquial vocabulary is being enlarged. Many of the words and phrases will sooner or later be formalized and have only a history as slang. Such apparently indispensable colloquialisms as *scram* and *O.K.* are already well on the way to such recognition. The American language, the richest store-house of slang the world has yet had, is making an incalculable contribution to the English of the future in this direction. Not only are we fast adopting American idiom—using *to check up on* for our own *to check* and *to face up to* for our own *to face*—but we are also finding ready use for indigenous American slang words and phrases. For rich though English already is we still come up against moments when, it would appear, only an American slang term seems to express what is in our minds. This is of course the origin of all slang in general use, the creation and adoption of a brief expression in an emergency. And this is why new slang words and phrases are continuously being invented.

There has been published 'The American Thesaurus of Slang: A Complete Reference Book of Colloquial Speech', compiled by Lester V. Berrey and Melville van den Bark, and it is a most fascinating book. A new language has been and is being developed across the Atlantic which, both for itself and for its influence on the future of our own language, repays study. Mr. Desmond MacCarthy, in a review of this book, quoted some colourful examples of this new language in an imaginary letter home by an American airman stationed in England:

> I blew into this big smoke Thursday from—but I must clam up about where I left the tin bird. And here I am pen-pushing to you in a plush lobster palace, or so you'd think it from the out-of-sight prices. Yet all the dish-juggler chucked at us was a splash of red noise, a slab of crippled beef on a load of hay, and a plate of wop-worms. This may call itself a swell dine-wine-dancery but I've eaten better at a quick and filthy in my time.

Nor is this new language restricted to colloquial speech, for much modern American literature—the novels of Ernest Hemingway, for instance—is written in an idiom based on it, a literary idiom far removed from our own. One day perhaps, therefore, the most sedate of Englishmen will call his equivalent of an aeroplane a *tin bird* and will announce with all the solemnity left to him that he and his wife are going to have dinner in a *dine-wine-dancery*.

Service slang has, naturally enough, spread into civilian life since 1945, and perhaps our selfsame Englishman will not think it amiss to call himself *browned off* or to go for a holiday near *the drink*

Not all of us wish for such a change, but perhaps there is nothing we can do to stop it; and if the prospect frightens us, then we can always console ourselves with the assurance that we shall not be there either to read or to hear the American English of tomorrow. So let us return to yesterday.

Animals

The whole animal world has provided us with words and phrases, similes and metaphors. Common examples are: *mouse-like, currish, elephantine, sly as a fox, busy as a bee, hungry as a wolf, book-worm, horse-sense, dogged, sheepish, to ape, to gull, to fox, to monkey with, to crow over, cocky, to hen-peck, cock of the walk, to make a bee-line for, gooseflesh, to go on a wild goose chase, calf-love,* and the metaphorical use of *chameleon* and the mythical *phoenix* and *chimera*.

Quotations

Authors have naturally contributed much to the enrichment of speech and writing both with their images and with their neologisms. Lewis Carroll gave us the new word *chortle*; the nonsense-names of Edward Lear, *Jumblies, Dong* and *Pobble,* have become household terms; Dickens gave us *Pickwickian* and *gamp*; Shakespeare and Milton, most generous of contributors, have enabled us to speak of *caviare to the general, yeoman service, out-Heroding Herod* and *Pandemonium*; and from the Bible we have *the patience of Job, Jezebel* and *to raise Cain*. These from among a legion of possible examples.

Originally these words, names and expressions were quoted, but eventually they passed into current and unquoted usage, with the result that today people use them without knowing their original context. As Dr. Johnson said, 'Every quotation contributes something to the stability or enlargement of the language.'

Abbreviations

New words have become established which are really only abbreviations. So *wig* has supplanted *periwig, cab* has taken the place of *cabriolet, chap* of *chapman, squire* of *esquire, curio* of *curiosity, cinema* of *cinematograph,* and *bus* of *omnibus*; and such symbols as £. *s. d.* and *e.g.* do not have full forms so far as the non-Latin scholar is concerned—indeed, their full forms are so obsolete as not to exist any more in practical usage.

Many abbreviations remain as separate words only in slang: e.g. *pub, prep, vet* and *super*.

The technical names for this loss of letters and syllables and the consequent development of new words are *aphesis* (loss of letters at beginning) and *apocope* (loss of letters at end).

Other Forms of Growth

Verbs have been created from nouns by a process known as *back-formation* or the removal of the noun-suffix. So *to beg* was made from *beggar*, *to edit* from *editor* and *to resurrect* from *resurrection*.

Echoic or onomatopoeic words have been invented to describe noises or states of motion. Common examples are: *bang, cackle, sizzle, ping-pong, flabbergast, jog, buzz, squelch* and *wobble*.

New situations create words. To *camouflage* dates only from the 1914-18 war; *black-out, fighter-bomber, Bevin-boy, Hitlerism, Quisling* and *blitz* are of still more recent origin. *Blitz* is an interesting example of the misappropriation which often occurs in this connection. In German it means *lightning* and the word *blitzkrieg* means *lightning war*, i.e. a war of swift movement. The air-raids on London were a part of this swift-moving war, but since to the Londoner they were primarily noisy and destructive affairs the word *blitz* has come into English to mean any noisy and destructive attack.

We have thousands of compound words, that is, single words composed of originally separate ones. *Husband* originally meant *house-dweller* (*husbonda*, the first word *hus* being the modern *house*); *daisy* was the *day's eye*, a *holiday* was a *holy day* and *Christmas* is *Christ's mass*. Change of pronunciation can be seen to have accompanied the combination: the first syllables of *husband, holiday* and *Christmas*, all pronounced short now, were originally long, as, of course, they still are as separate words.

Then we can construct new words at will by merely hyphenating existing words. *Fighter-bomber* is a modern instance. *Blue-eyed* and *swallow-tailed* are two further recent examples of this *parasynthetic formation* as it is called.

Almost any two parts of speech can be found united in the creation of new words. Preposition and verb are common components: *undertake, upset*. If the preposition is prefixed the resulting single-word verb has a different meaning from that of the original verb followed by the same preposition as a separate word: *to look over* is not the same as *to overlook*. So richly variable is English. Two nouns make up *bookcase*; a present participle and a noun make *writing-table* and *dining-room*; an infinitive and a noun make *tell-tale*; and an adverb and a gerund make *well-being*.

Prepositions follow verbs to create new expressions: so *to give up* is different from *to give* and *to put through* is different from *to put*.

We have many *hybrids*, or words whose parts have different national origins. So of *trusteeship* the first syllable, *trust*, is Scandinavian, *ee* is a French suffix, and *ship* is Saxon. A modern hybrid is *television*, of which *tele* is Greek and *vision* is Latin. *Radiogram* and *fundrome* are still more recent concoctions.

Many corresponding adjectives illustrate the etymological complexity of our language; for whereas their nouns are of native origin, Germanic or Scandinavian, they are Latin. Thus the adjectives corresponding to *son*, *town* and *eye* are *filial* (L. *filius*), *urban* (L. *urbs*) and *ocular* (L. *oculus*).

Change of Meaning

A curious phenomenon of all language is the degeneration of meaning which many words suffer. It is a sign of that development and change which characterize a living organism: it is curious only in the direction which that development takes. But contexts vary and fashions change, and words assume new implications and gradually new meanings. So our word *villain* originally meant farm-labourer (L. *villa*), *silly* meant innocent, *cunning* meant knowledgeable or skilful (*to con*=to know), *lewd* meant of the laity, *nice* meant ignorant (L. *nescius*), and *knave* meant boy or servant (cf. German *knabe*).

A still commoner phenomenon is mere change of meaning, not necessarily degeneration. There is, for instance, so much difference of meaning between Elizabethan English and modern that a special Shakespeare Dictionary has had to be compiled. Sometimes the difference is only slight, though still enough to give a phrase another sense than the modern; but often the difference is complete. When Shakespeare used *presently* he meant *immediately*.

But meanings die reluctantly, and many words retain their older significance in special associations. *Fast*, for example, which used to mean *firm*, is still used with that sense in such expressions as *to stand fast*, *hard and fast*; *board* meaning first the table on which food was placed and then the food itself is still found in *board and lodging*; *meat* still has its original meaning of *food* in *meat and drink*; and the old negative *nil* (not the Latin negative=nothing) is still seen in *willy-nilly* (=will I, nil I).

Pronunciation and Spelling

There are two characteristics of our language which make it peculiarly troublesome to foreign students and irritating to those who like things straightforward and logical: our pronunciation and spelling.

So many different languages have combined to make English, and so long has the process of haphazard assimilation gone on, that uniformity of pronunciation has been impossible. Certain changes can be traced, such as the dropping of the final *e* and the medial *gh* in the fifteenth century (both of them were pronounced by Chaucer), but even they were not dropped suddenly and by everyone. Usually two pronunciations have coexisted, some people holding firm to the established one and others adopting the new until eventually the latter prevailed.

During the eighteenth century, in which scholars tried to formalize the language, many books were written which aimed at the standardization of pronunciation. Dr. Johnson tried to standardize it in his dictionary; in 1780 Thomas Sheridan published his 'Dictionary of the English Language' with the same intent; and in 1791 James Walker's 'A General Idea of a Pronouncing Dictionary of the English Language' was published.

But all efforts were in vain, and our pronunciation, like our spelling, has remained chaotic. The two are inseparable in the chaos and depend upon each other in a crisis: it is, for instance, only the pronunciation which makes this sentence tolerable: *Though he brought a bough large enough to put through the trough.*

It is from rhymes in verse that we gain our surest knowledge of how words used to be pronounced. In Elizabethan times the verb *speak* was often pronounced *spake* and rhymed with *break*. This *ay* sound in words like *speak*, *meet* and *mead* continued into the eighteenth century, and we find Swift rhyming *speak* with *break*. Sometimes, indeed, *speak* was spelt *spake*.

But the modern pronunciation is also met in Elizabethan verse, and the two pronunciations existed side by side for a long time until at last the old *spake* dropped out of fashion, to survive only in dialect.

Shakespeare also rhymed *past* and *waste*, for *past* was pronounced *paste*; and elsewhere we find *taste* rhyming with *past*, showing that our modern pronunciation also existed, for *taste* then had the short *a* of the Old French *taster* and the Italian *tasto*.

That *do* was pronunced *doe* in the eighteenth century is seen when Pope rhymes it with *show* (it is still so pronounced in *don't*), and the grammarian Cooper tells us in 1685 that it was pronounced both as it is today and as *doe*. The historical pronunciation is *doe* (OE *dōn*).

Among the evidence that the noun *wound* was pronounced like the past tense of *to wind* in the eighteenth century is Pope's rhyming it with *bound*; and this pronunciation can still be heard in one way of saying the archaic oath *zounds* (=God's wounds).

The pronunciation of the final *g* of the present participle is a comparatively recent innovation, and when we scoff at the *huntin', shootin', fishin' crowd* we are pronouncing as our ancestors did. We see *doing* rhymed with *ruin* in the eighteenth century and Swift rhyming *picking* with *chicken*.

Examples of different pronunciation from our own abound: we see *love* rhymed with *remove*, *join* with *line* and *wand* with *land*.

The irregularity of our spelling also is due to the careless mixture of languages which makes English. It too has changed through the centuries, as the quotation from Caxton illustrates: indeed that quotation shows that spelling was even more chaotic in the past than it is today.

Gradually vowels and consonants either dropped out altogether or were altered (*thorn*, for example): the diphthongs *æ* and *œ* are fast dropping out now. The old *a* of words like *ham* (=home) and *stane* (=stone) were eventually changed to *o*, though they still survive in dialect, at least in pronunciation. So the old *u* of, say, *hus* became *ou*, though, as we have seen, it too survives in words like *husband*.

Words already incorporated from French had their spelling remodelled according to Latin orthography after the Renaissance, *doute*, for instance, becoming *doubt* and *suttle* becoming *subtle*.

Numerous other changes occurred in time, and we have our chaos still. Letters are used which are not pronounced—*h* in *honour*, *b* in *debt*, *p* in *psychology*, *n* in *hymn* and so on; and, surest sign of the confusion. we have many homographs, homo-phones and homonyms.

Attempts at Reform

It is no wonder that there has been and still is much agita-tion and much suggestion for reform. In our day Bernard Shaw was the doyen of the would-be reformers. In his will he left money to be spent on the establishment and teaching of a new alphabet which would have forty-two letters 'capable of noting with sufficient accuracy all the sounds of spoken English without having to use more than one letter for each sound'. His own surname, for example, contains only two sounds but requires four letters to spell them; and other words containing only two sounds require still more letters. Shaw claimed that his alphabet would not only spell all words of two sounds with only two letters, i.e. would ensure *phonetic spelling*, but would also save millions of years of time now spent in the use of our 'ancient twenty-six letter Phoenician alphabet'.

But there have been many attempts to purify English in one direction or another, and all have either failed or had a merely limited success.

In the sixteenth century writers aware of the changes which the language had been undergoing began to ask what was *good* English. Sir Philip Sidney found it in the cultivated speech of the Court, and his view was widely held by aristocrats. But other writers concentrated on the more linguistic aspect of the question and began to advocate *pure* English as contrasted with Euphuism and the classical diction which had become so fashion-able. Richard Mulcaster (1530?-1611), a schoolmaster at Merchant Taylors' and St. Paul's, was one of the leaders of the purists. Three others were the *Cambridge purists*, Sir John Cheke (1514-57), Thomas Wilson (1525?-81) and Roger Ascham (1515-68), who strove to maintain such purity as could by then be preserved by opposing the further importation of foreign words and the use of what they called 'inkhorn' terms and 'aureate' vocabulary.

Earlier Caxton, who by introducing printing into England had done a little to standardize vocabulary and spelling, had thought it advisable to omit 'the rude and old englyssh, that is to wete certayn wordes which in these days be neither usyd ne understandyn'. So the old *icleped* declined in favour of

345

called, ich became *I, wone* became *dwelt* and *hiʒt* gave way to *named*.

Among the more successful popularizers of simple and native English were the various translators of the Bible. First translated by Nicholas Hereford and John Purvey, who worked with Wyclif (1320-84), and later by Tyndale in 1525 and Coverdale in 1535, and then as the Authorized Version in 1611, its unaffected simplicity and continuous use of the native as distinct from the 'learned' word did exert a considerable influence on the popular vocabulary, especially in the Puritan days of the seventeenth century. The English language was introduced into the Church after the Reformation, and the itinerant preachers who maintained the tradition of Wyclif did much to keep the general use of the language among the people free from classical importations.

In his 'Grammatica Linguae Anglicanae' (1685) Cooper spoke of the difficulty of learning English because of the lack of a generally adopted grammar. The absence of modern grammatical logic was responsible for such phenomena in Chaucer, Shakespeare and later writers as the use of a plural subject followed by a singular verb, and vice versa, and of double negatives, comparatives and superlatives. Today *more better* is a very bad solecism. Even as late as the eighteenth century cultured speech as seen in novels admitted expressions like *you was* and the double negative, but although some writers, among whom was Goldsmith, protested against the would-be maker of rules— Goldsmith saying that 'rules will never make a work of discourse eloquent'—most scholars were agreed that some control was desirable.

So in the latter half of the seventeenth century and in the eighteenth a 'better English' movement grew up, whose influence is proved in Dryden's statement: 'I live in an age where my least faults are severely censured'. Dictionaries were compiled as practical guides through the maze of new and new-fangled words. Thomas Blount's 'Glossographia' was published in 1656; 'The New World of English Words' by Edward Phillips, Milton's nephew, in 1658; Nathan Bailey's 'Universal Etymological English Dictionary' in 1721; and Dr. Johnson's Dictionary in 1755. Addison included 'A Dictionary for the Explanation of Hard Words' and a 'Spelling Book' in Leonora's library.

Among the abortive campaigns to establish the language was

that led by writers like Gabriel Harvey, Dryden and Addison for an English Academy. Italy had had its Accademia della Crusca in the sixteenth century and France its Academie in 1635. Something like these, however, was set up in England also. For in the seventeenth century the influence of the new scientific thinking was being felt, and in 1662 the Royal Society was inaugurated, it being conditional upon its members that they should write in a clear and 'naked' style approaching mathematical plainness. In 1664 it appointed a committee 'for improving the English tongue' which included its historian, Thomas Sprat (1635-1713), the diarist Evelyn and the poets Dryden and Waller. That committee was the nearest England came to an Academy.

During the eighteenth century there were many books aimed at reform. There were Swift's 'Treatise on Polite Conversation' and 'Proposal for Correcting, Improving, and Ascertaining the English Language'; Dr. George Hickes's collection of Anglo-Saxon texts in 'Linguarum Veterum Septentrionalium Thesaurus', which encouraged the study of English literature; Lindley Murray's 'English Grammar' (1795); and Isaac Watts's 'The Art of Reading and Writing English' (1721), which summed up their common message in this couplet:

Let all the foreign tongues alone
Till you can spell and read your own.

Since then there has been no relaxation of the efforts made by grammarians, lexicographers and philologists to educate the people to write and speak 'correctly'. Today we have professors of philology, etymologists, elocutionists, teachers and popular writers all bent on the same purpose. Books like Sir Arthur Quiller-Couch's 'The Art of Writing' and Professor Quirk's 'The Use of English', not to name many a holiday-reading paperback, and the general extension of education and the influence of the BBC's use of *King's* (or *Queen's*) *English*, have all had their effect, so that even if our pronunciation and spelling are chaotic most people know that the chaos exists, and, in fact, the chaos itself is, paradoxical though this may sound, standardized.

And still the attempts at simplification go on. The most notorious recent attempt has been Basic English, which reduces the vocabulary to a mere 850 essential words, only eighteen of

347

these being verbs. But it is intended primarily for foreigners and to be an international language.

Whether or not the English language is destined to be basic we cannot know, but there have been attempts to simplify, codify and regularize it before, all futile, so futile indeed that all would-be reformers should have learnt by now that no living language can live in a straitjacket. By all means let those who use the English language avoid slovenliness and verbosity. Everyone who speaks and writes should speak and write exactly, keeping his words free from jargon, Euphuism, the cliché. The grammarians have done and are doing useful service and it cannot be denied that there is still too much lumber in the attic.

But English is like an old and stately mansion. It has more rooms than we think, and it is easy to lose one's way in its long twisting corridors. It stretches and rambles, and there is still too little communication between the right wing where the cultured live and the servants' quarters. Guests are perhaps too frequent and they sometimes forget to wipe the mud off their boots when they come in; but their laughter echoes down the corridors, and, on the whole, their ghosts are friendly. It would be a poor house without them.

Moreover—and to drop the metaphor—the English language is the common property of one of the largest societies of people in the world and is already destined to be the closest approximation to an international language we may expect to know. For all its weaknesses it does possess the strength to sustain such a privileged position.

Elizabethan English

The following list shows the meanings which some common modern words had in Shakespeare's day, and how considerably they differ from those of today:

admire:	to wonder;
advertisement:	information; advise, counsel;
battle:	a body of troops in battle-formation;
clip:	surround, embrace;
composition:	recompense; agreement; consistency;
conceit (noun):	conception, idea; apprehension;
defeat (vb.):	destroy, defraud;
enforce:	to violate;

equal (adj.):	just;
faithful:	convinced;
favour:	countenance, face;
free (adj.):	innocent; magnanimous;
generous:	noble;
humorous:	eccentric; moist;
invention:	imagination; plan;
jewel:	plaything;
jump (vb.):	to agree; to risk;
liberal:	wanton, gross; free-spoken;
luxury:	lechery, lust;
merely:	utterly;
modern:	everyday, ordinary;
naughty:	good for nothing, bad (applied to adults);
obsequious:	funereal; dutiful towards the dead; obedient;
obscene:	unseen;
owe:	own;
peculiar:	private;
practice:	trickery, intrigue;
prevent:	to anticipate; to escape, avoid;
read:	to guess (read a riddle);
regiment:	rule;
sad:	sufficient, drab-coloured, serious;
secure (adj.):	free from care;
strict:	narrow, tense, close;
success:	result, outcome;
tall:	goodly, gallant;
treaty:	proposition, negotiation;
virtue:	ability; essence;
wink:	to sleep; to close the eyes.

Etymology

Reference has been made in this appendix to etymology, the 'branch of linguistic science concerned with the formation and meaning of words'. The yet more technical name for the study of the meaning of words is *semantics* or *semasiology*. It is a most fascinating study, full of surprise and amusement no less than of intellectual interest, as the following list of the origins of some of our words will show:

349

alarm: comes from the Italian war-cry, *All' arme!*;

bathos: is a Greek word transcribed into English lettering meaning depth, borrowed by the poet Pope to signify what he called 'the art of sinking in poetry';

cabal: comes originally from the Hebrew *quabbalah*=tradition; later used in sense of *political machination* and was especially applied to Charles II's 'Committee for Foreign Affairs', five of whose members had names the initial letters of which spelt cabal: Clifford, Arlington, Buckingham, Ashley (=Shaftesbury), Lauderdale;

candidate: from Latin=a person dressed in white;

carouse: from German *gar aus*=quite out, i.e. empty your glass;

chaos: is a Greek noun transcribed and from a Greek verb meaning to gape or yawn, i.e. a vast formless void: so *chasm*;

fellow: is the OE word *feolaga*=a partner: =an idle companion: =man: original meaning still seen in *fellowship*;

hoax: is a corruption of the dog-Latin *hocus pocus* (seventeenth century);

jeopardy: is from French *jeu parti*=even game;

jewel: is a diminutive of Latin *jocus*=plaything, cognate with French *jeu*, or is the Old French *joel*, possibly from Latin *gaudium*=joy;

nincompoop: is a corruption of Latin *non compos mentis*;

precocious: is from Latin *praecox* (=*prae*+*coquo*) =cooked too early;

rival: from Latin adjective *rivalis*=of a brook or river: came to refer to neighbours who got water from the same stream, and was then used in Roman law in contests between people about their rights in this matter;

salary:
is the Latin *salarium*, a slang word for the money given to a Roman soldier to buy salt (*sal*);

scene:
is from a Greek word=tent: =booth: =structure in Greek open-air theatre as background of stage or orchestra: = any view; cf. original meaning in 'behind the scenes';

shamefaced:
=shamefast, *shame* originally=modesty, *fast*=steady, confirmed: became corrupted to present form and assumed to mean showing shame in one's face;

silly:
is the OE *saelig*=blessed, innocent: = simple: =foolish;

tattoo (military):
from the Dutch *Tap toe*=drinking-house shut, i.e. a signal for the troops to go to their quarters;

tide:
is cognate with the German *zeit*=time, as in Christmastide, Whitsuntide, Eastertide: =periodical rise and fall of the sea;

treacle:
is from a Greek word=of a beast: =a remedy for a bite by a wild animal: = any remedy: =remedy in form of syrup;

villain:
is from the Latin *villa*=estate: a farm-labourer: =a term of contempt: =a scoundrel.

Dialects

It will have been observed from this brief and general survey of our language that there has never been a single, universal form of English, that it has at least been separated into Northern, Midland and Southern forms (this is of course true of all languages); and though today there is a *Standard English* pronunciation and vocabulary which prevails from Land's End to John o' Groats, we are all familiar not only with such major deviations as the Scotch and Welsh inflexions but also with the difference between, say, a Yorkshireman's way of speaking and a Cockney's. And it is not only a matter of pronunciation—certainly not of *provincialisms* such as the Cockney's *type* for *tape*—but of vocabulary as well: words are commonly used in the Colne valley which

351

the inhabitants of Camberwell will never use.

The differences between dialects go back to very early times when there was little intercourse between the inhabited parts of the country and hence very little chance for words of special local attachment to spread; and these differences persist because, as yet, the mass of the people of one area still live in geographical separation from the rest of the country. But whereas in early times the differences were primarily linguistic, by today we have several forms of dialect. The regional form is still the most prominent, but we also have a clear contrast between the general dialect of the countryman and that of the town-dweller, between the dialect of the uneducated and that of the educated, even though they live next door to one another, and, to a smaller extent, between the dialects of the old and the young. (In a sense, jargon too is a form of dialect, and there are what may be called *professional dialects*.)

These are gradually disappearing, however, and *Standard English*, which was originally the Court Dialect of London in the fourteenth and fifteenth centuries, will, we may assume, eventually be spoken by everyone. Whether or not primitive dialectal words as distinct from dialectal pronunciation will also disappear is something about which it would be dangerous to prophesy. But this at least may be said: if they do, English will be a poorer language in quality no less than in quantity.

The following is a short list of some of these dialectal words which it would be a pity to lose:

Frisgig (Lancashire)=a silly young woman;
Nesh (Midlands)=weakly, oversensitive;
Clarty (Northern)=muddy;
Pightle (Yorkshire)=small field;
Dimpsy (West Country)=twilight;
Luggy (Yorkshire)=*Cotty* (Midlands)=tangled (but of the hair only).

All these are still in common usage: for other examples readers are referred to Ivor Brown's 'Book of Words'.

(One of the best short books on the vast subject dealt with in this appendix is Otto Jesperson's 'Growth and Structure of the English Language', published by Basil Blackwell, Oxford.)

APPENDIX C

Surnames

As the word implies, surnames are extra names, extra, that is, to first or *Christian* names. Being additions they are of course not as old as first names, and we need only look at, say, the Bible, to realize that there were no surnames two thousand years ago. The Bible, indeed, shows the origin of all surnames, for even in those far-off days when the population of Galilee was so small it was found necessary to distinguish somehow between people who had the same (first) name. Thus the two disciples of Jesus who were called James were distinguished as the sons of Zebedee and Alphaeus, Simon Peter was distinguished from Simon the Zealot, and Judas the son of James was distinguished from Judas Iscariot. In other words, the distinction was made by naming the father or by some reference to the sect to which a man belonged. Nicknames were also used.

To turn, then, to ourselves. The same need to distinguish between people with the same name arose wherever a settlement was made, and so gradually throughout history the ways of doing this increased and what we now know as surnames came into being. It was a slow process going on simultaneously all over the country.

There are four main methods by which the necessary distinctions were made, four main origins, therefore, of our modern surnames. Not every surname can be accounted for by them, and the origins of many baffle even the experts. A glance through a London telephone directory is enough to convince anyone what a hopeless task would confront the man who attempted to compile a definitive dictionary of surnames. For people of every nationality have settled in England and brought their names with them. Thousands of Englishmen are offended if they are told that they have *foreign-sounding* surnames; but they have, for their ancestors were foreigners—as were everyone else's.

Still, the majority of English surnames can be accounted for in one or other of the following ways:

Patronymic or Baptismal

Clearly the first source of second names was the first names of parents, particularly of fathers. As in the Bible, men were distinguished from one another by being called sons of their fathers. At first one James would be called the son of, say, Peter: James the son of Peter. Later, this method was considered clumsy, and the word *son* was suffixed to the father's (or mother's) first name: Robertson, Johnson, Peterson, Phillipson, etc. Later still, the suffix was abbreviated to the single letter *s*, and nearly all surnames that end with *s* are patronymics: **e.g.** *Roberts, Peters, Jones, Phillips.*

Further methods were adopted. The parent's own first name was merely repeated as a surname, and almost every male Christian name is a modern surname: *John, George, Walter.*

Then the nickname form of the parent's first name was also used, either alone or with the addition of the suffix *son* or *s*. All the following surnames, for example, mean *son of Robert*: *Dobbs, Hobbs, Hobson, Hopkins, Hopps, Hopkinson, Robins, Robinson, Robson.* And all the following mean *son of Isabella*: *Ibb, Ibbs, Ibson, Ibbott, Ibbotson.*

Some common patronymic or baptismal surnames:

Jowett, Gillot, Gillottson (from Juliana);

Tillot, Tillottson (from Matilda);

Richard, Richards, Richardson, Hicks, Hickson, Higgs, Higson, Higgins, Dickens, Dix, Dixon, Dicks, Dickson, Dickinson (all from Richard);

John, Johns, Johnson, Jonson, Jenkins, Jenkinson, Jennings, Jack, Jacks, Jackson (all from John);

Thomas, Thom, Thoms, Thomson, Thompson (from Thomas);

Simpson, Simmonds, Simmons, Simkins, Simon, Simons (from Simon);

Peter, Peters, Peterson, Perkins, Parkinson, Perks, Parks, Person, Perrin, Piers, Pierson, Pears, Pearson (from Peter);

Nichols, Nicholson, Cole, Collett, Collins, Collinson, Collison (from Nicholas);

Hugh, Hughes, Hutchins, Hutchinson, Hutchison (from Hugh);
Gibbon, Gibbons, Gibbs, Gibson (from Gilbert);
Henries, Henryson, Hawkins (from Henry);
Phipps (from Phillip);
Atkins, Atkinson (from Adam);
Hodge, Hodgson, Hidgson, Dodge, Dodgson (from Roger);
Wilson (from William);
Davies, Davison (from David).

Topographical

The second source was the locality in which a person lived. Any name of a place or neighbouring feature, any short phrase which would describe the spot where he or she lived, was made use of to provide a second, distinguishing name. Thus we have surnames which were originally names of towns and villages, and even the names of foreign countries have been used to distinguish one—presumably immigrant—John from another. Points of the compass, mountains, hills and so on—all have been used in this way. Especially interesting are the suffixes which characterize these topographical surnames. For instance, many people have a surname which ends with the word *bottom*, and both they and other people consider such a suffix rather regrettable. But the word has nothing to do with that part of our anatomy on which we sit. The correct spelling is *botham*, of which *bottom* is only a corruption, and the word means the hollow at the foot of a slope. So the common surname *Higginbottom* (or *Higginbotham*) means that one Richard was distinguished from another by being called, literally, the "little Richard who lived in the hollow at the foot of the slope".

Other common suffixes are:

-white or -thwaite	=a clearing;
-royd	=a clearing;
-thorpe, -throp, -trop	=a village;
-ett (not the diminutive, which is seen in, say, *Jowett*)=-head	
	=upper end of;
-brigg, -brick	=bridge;
-ham	=home;
-ton	=town;
-ley	=lea;

355

| -ay, -ey | =hedge, enclosure; |
| -by | =town; |

So *Murgatroyd* means that Margaret (and so her children) lived in a clearing; *Birkett* means that, say, John Birkett lived at the upper end of the birch trees; and William Hazlitt was that William who lived at the upper end of the hazel trees (-itt here=ett).

Other topographical suffixes are self-explanatory: -dale, -end, -side, -gate, etc.

Some topographical surnames:

Underhill, Bywater, Underwood, Townsend, Akenside (=at the side of the oak trees), *Downham* (village name), *Sutcliff* (at the south cliff), *Whitaker* (the white acre), *Nokes* (=atten okes =at the oak trees), *Nash* (=at the ash tree), *Schofield* (the school field), *Ford, Hill, Tree, Stone, Bridges, Castle, Wood, Field, Meadows, Chester, Manchester, Cheshire, Wells, Mills, Wolfendale* (=dale of wolves), *Cliff, England, France, German, French, Marsh, Beaverbrook, South, Cross, Church, Towers.*

Occupational or Official

A third source of surnames was the nature of the work done by an individual. In early times many people were employed in great households and on great estates, and their work gave rise to many surnames. Thus *Waddup=Waddoup*, a name given to those who were in charge of the wardrobes where hung the countless robes of their aristocratic employers. *Spencer* means the man in charge of the buttery (the suffix, *-er*, being the normal agent-suffix). *Grainger* means the keeper of the grange. Many surnames which end in *man* mean *servant of* the name preceding it: e.g. *Human*=servant of Hugh.

So all the titles of the various people who moved and had their being in courtly circles, from the highest to the lowest, eventually became common-or-garden surnames: e.g. *King, Prince, Page, Falconer, Fowler, Chamberlain, Lord, Baron, Knight, Duke, Butler, Marshall.*

But the vast majority of occupational surnames originated merely from the work done irrespective of its nature, and in this category too there are some interesting suffixes:

-herd: e.g. *Calvert*=calf-herd, the man who looked after the calves; *Coward*=cow-herd; *Stoddart*=stoat-herd;

-monger: e.g. *Ironmonger*;

-maker: *Candlemaker*;

-hewer: *Stonehewer*;

-smith: *Smith, Blacksmith, Arrowsmith*;

-wright: *Arkwright* (=maker of meal-bins), *Wainwright* (=wagon-maker);

-man (cf. *supra*): *Denman=Swinnart*=swine-herd; *Bridge-man* (=person who looked after bridges);

-er: *Tucker=Fuller*=walker on cloth;=*Walker*=the man who stamped on cloth to press it; *Parker; Fletcher*=the arrow-maker; *Kisser*=the maker of thigh-armour; *Dyer; Napier;*

-ster: *Brewster, Baxter* (=baker), *Webster* (=maker of webs); *Lister=Litster=Dyer.*

Some occupational surnames:
Butcher, Baker, Mason, Farmer, Clerk (Clark), Collier, Wheelwright, Tolman, Cartwright, Shepherd, Bellringer, Cooper (=barrel-maker), *Fisher, Carter, Taylor, Hunter, Hunt, Painter, Carpenter, Palfreyman* (=man who looked after horses), *Spicer, Mercer* (=clothes dealer).

Occupational and patronymic names were sometimes combined: e.g. *Clerkson, Parsons.*

Nicknames

Finally, it was possible to make the necessary distinction by adding nicknames to the first names. Almost any descriptive adjective could be placed before *man: Longman, Whiteman, Goldman, Richman.* The original French suffix *-et(t), -ot(t)* was imitated in its diminutive use: *Bunnett*=bon-et-on=good little one. Other diminutive endings were also used: *-ing, -kin(s).* So Bunting=Bunnett.

Names of animals, birds, flowers and so on were liberally used; descriptive compounds such as *Younghusband* were invented; anything from shape and age to the colours of the rainbow was seized upon for the purpose. E.g. *Wild, Golightly, Lightfoot, Hare, Hogg, Lamb, Fox, Swift, Kidd, Bacon. Peacock* (=Pocock), *Finch, Goodman, Bellamy* (=good friend), *Wagstaff, Shakespeare, Long, Young, Bland, Proud* (=Prout), *Noble, White, Smallbone, Rainbow.*

The suffix -cock is common in these sobriquet surnames. It was originally used to describe the scullery-boy or the apprentice, who was cheeky and lusty, and then it came to mean anyone who was like a scullery-boy in behaviour. Usually it was suffixed to a nickname: *Badcock* (Bartholomew), *Maycock* (Matthew), *Hitchcock* (Richard), *Hancock* (Hans).

The patronymic suffix was also combined with the nickname of the parent: so *Patterson*=son of Patty=Matty=Martha; *Dickens*=son of little Richard.

There are some very strange examples of this fourth type of surname: e.g. *Fear* and *Death*.

Reference has been made to the London Telephone Directory: it may amuse readers to try to discover the origins of the following surnames taken at random from that book: *Bennum, Arbeid, Dullaert, Kelshaw, Ionn, Hoaen, Heraty, Conkie, Munro*. Perhaps their origins are not so obscure as their spelling suggests: after all, *Jenkins* means only *son of little John*.

APPENDIX D

Prefix and Suffix

A PREFIX is a letter or group of letters placed in front of an existing word to form a new word. A suffix is a letter or group of letters added to the end of an existing word for the same purpose.

Many of these letters exist as words in their own right in their original languages, and some are words in their own right in English too (e.g. *graph*). Conversely, many of the words to which they have been added do not exist as separate words in English, though these also have an independent existence in their original languages.

Thousands of new words have been introduced into English by the use of prefixes and suffixes, and we may add hundreds of new words to our own vocabulary if we become familiar with their meanings.

The following abbreviations are used in the lists:

adj(s).	=	adjective(s)	OE	=	Old English
dimin.	=	diminutive	OF	=	Old French
fem.	=	feminine	orig.	=	original
F	=	French	part.	=	participle
G	=	Greek	plur.	=	plural
intrans.	=	intransitive	trans.	=	transitive
L	=	Latin	T	=	Teutonic
nos.	=	numbers	vb(s).	=	verb(s)

Prefix

a-(T)	=on: aboard.
(L)	=away from: avert.
(G)	=not: atheism.
ab-, abs- (L)	=away from: abduct, abstract.

ad- (L)	=to: advertise; and becomes assimilated to the following consonant: accept, affiliate, aggression, allocate, announce, appendix, arrears, assign, assimilate, attend.
after-	=the English preposition: afternoon, afterthought.
al-	=all: almighty, alone, always.
ambi- (L)	=both: ambidextrous.
amphi- (G)	=both: amphitheatre, amphibious.
an- (G)	=not (=a- followed by vowel): anaemia, anarchy.
ante- (L)	=before: antecedent, antedate.
anti- (G)	=opposite, against: antichrist, anticlimax; (=ant- before vowel, anth- before aspirate): antacid, anthelion.
apo- (G)	=from, away: apology, apostle. (becomes aph- before aspirate in G): aphorism.
arch-, arche-, archi- (G)	=chief, leading: archbishop, archetype, architrave.
auto- (G)	=self: autobiography, autograph; (becomes auth- before aspirate in G): authentic.
be- (OE)	=weak form of accented *by* (bygone, bylaw); orig. meaning is *about*: before, bespatter, bejewel; idea of thoroughness: bedrug, bescorch; makes intrans. vbs. trans.: bemoan, bestraddle; forms vbs. from nouns and adjs: befriend, befoul, beguile; forms adjs. in -ed from nouns: beflagged, bewigged.
bi- (L)	=twice: biennial, bicycle.
bio- (G)	=life: biography, biology, biophysics.
bis- (L)	=twice: biscuit.

360

by- =the English preposition: bystander.

cata- (G) =down, away, wrongly, fully, according to: catalogue, cataclysm;
(becomes cat- before vowel, cath- before aspirate in G): categorical, cathode.

circum- (L) =around: circumference, circumnavigate, circumstance.

cis- (L) =on this side of: cisalpine, cismontane.

contra- (L) =against: contradict

counter- =English form of *contra*: counteract.

cum- (L) =with, and seen only in assimilated forms thus:
co-: co-operate;
cog-: cognate;
col-: collateral;
com-: companion;
con-: concentric;
cor-: correspond.

de- (L) =down: descend;=away: deduce;
used to emphasize: denude;
used as negative: decentralize.

deca- (G) =ten: decasyllabic.

demi- (L) =half: demigod.

di(s)- (G) =two: dis(s)yllable, dimeter.

dia- (G) =through: dialogue, diarrhoea;
(becomes di- before vowel): dielectric.

dis- (L) =away: distract, displace; (by assimilation) different;
used as negative: disagree, disinfect.

dys- (G) =bad: dyspepsia.

e-, ex- (L) =out: eject, extract; (by assimilation) eccentric, effluent, effort, effusive, etc.

en- (L, F) =on, in: enamour, enlighten;
(becomes em- before *b* and *p*): embark, employ.

361

epi- (G)	=at, upon: epigram, epitaph; (becomes eph- before aspirate in G): ephemeral.
equi- (L)	=equal: equilateral, equinox, equivocal.
eu- (G)	=well: eugenics, eulogy, eupeptic, euphemism.
extra- (L)	=outside, beyond: extramural, extra-ordinary, extravagance.
for- (OE)	=away, from: forget, forgive; sense of prohibition: forbid; sense of abstention: forgo, forsake; for emphasis: forlorn.
fore- (OE)	=before, in front: forearm, forecast, foreknow, forerun.
gastro- (G)	=stomach: gastronomy.
geo- (G)	=the earth: geography, geometry, geology.
helio- (G)	=the sun: heliograph, heliotrope.
hemi- (G)=semi- (L)	=half: hemisphere, hemistich.
hepta- (G)	=seven: heptagon.
hetero- (G)	=other, different: heterodox, hetero-geneous.
hexa- (G)	=six: hexagon, hexameter.
holo- (G)	=whole: holocaust, holograph.
homo- (G)	=same: homograph.
hydro- (G)	=water: hydrolysis, hydroplane.
hyper- (G)	=over, in excess; hyperaesthesia, hyper-bole, hypercritical, hypermetric(al).
hypo- (G)	=under: hypocrisy, hypodermic, hypo-stasis, hypothesis.
in- (L)	=in, into, on, against: incubate, invade; (by assimilation) illuminate, immerse, irradiate, irrigate; (becomes im- before *b* and *p*): imbibe, impose.

362

in- (I.)	=not: independent, indirect, ingratitude; (by assimilation) illiberal, immobile, irresistible; (becomes im- before *p*): impossible; („ ig-, „ *n*): ignoble.
inter- (L)	=among, between: intercede, interlude, interrogate.
intra- (L)	=within: intramural.
intro- (L)	=to the inside: introspection.
iso- (G)	=equal: isosceles, isotherm.
macro- (G)	=large, long: macrocephalic, macrocosm.
mal-, male- (L, F)	=bad, ill: malcontent, malefactor, malevolent.
man-, manu- (L)	=by hand: mandate, manufacture, manuscript.
mega- megalo- (G)	=great: megaphone, megalomania.
meta- (G)	=with, after (+idea of change): metabolism, metaphor.
micro- (G)	=small: microcosm, micrometer, microphone, microscope.
mid- (OE)	=middle: midsummer.
mis- (OE)	=wrongly: misfit, mislead, misprint.
mis(o)- (G)	=hate: misanthropy, misogamy, misogynist.
mono- (G)	=sole, single: monologue, monotonous; (becomes mon- before vowels): monarchy.
multi- (L)	=many: multiform, multiplication.
ne- (OE)	=not, and loses final *e*: none, nor.
neo- (G)	=new: neolithic, neologism, neophyte.
non- (L)	=not: nonconformist, nonsense.
ob- (L)	=in the way of: object, obverse, obvious; (by assimilation) occur, offer, oppose.
oct-, octa-, octo-, (G, L)	=eight: octagon, October, octogenarian, octosyllabic.

off-	=English preposition: offset.
omni- (L)	=all: omnipotence, omniscient.
on-	=the English preposition: onlooker, onset.
ortho- (G)	=straight, right: orthodox, orthography, orthopaedic.
out-	=the English adverb: outlook, out-manoeuvre.
over-	=the English preposition: overlook, overseer.
palim-, palin- (G)	=again: palimpsest, palinode.
pan-, panto- (G)	=all: panacea, pandemonium, panegyric, pantheism, pantomime.
para- (G)	=beside, beyond: paradox, parasite.
penta- (G)	=five: pentagon, pentateuch.
per- (L)	=through: pervade; sense of completely: perturb; sense of evil: pervert.
peri- (G)	=about: perimeter, periphrasis, periscope.
phil-, philo- (G)	=love: philander, philanthropy, philology, philosophy.
phono- (G)	=sound: phonograph, phonology.
poly- (G)	=many: polygamous, polygon, polytechnic.
post- (L)	=after: posthumous, postpone.
pre- (L)	=before: precaution, precede, prefect, prehistoric.
pro- (L)	=in front of, on behalf of: proceed, produce, pro-British.
proto- (G)	=first: protoplasm, prototype.
psych-, psycho- (G)	=the mind: psychiatry, psychological, psychotherapy.
quadri- (L)	=four: quadrilateral; (before vowel) quadrangle.
quinqu- (L)	=five: quinquagesima, quinquireme.

re- (L)	=back, again: rebel, refer, research, rewrite.
retro- (L)	=backwards: retrogression, retrospect.
se- (L)	=apart: seclude.
semi- (L)	=half; semicircle, semiquaver.
sex-, sexi- (L)	=six: sexennial, sexisyllabilic.
sub- (L)	=under: subject, submarine, suburb; (by assimilation) succeed, suffix, suggest, suppose, surrender.
super- (L)	=over, above: superabundant, superstition.
sur- (F)	=on: surcharge, surface.
syn- (G)	=with, together: synagogue, synchronize, synonym; (by assimilation) syllable; (becomes sym- before b, m and p): symbiosis, symmetry, sympathy, symphony.
tele- (G)	=far: telegraphy, telephone, television, telescope.
tetra- (G)	=four: tetrahedron; (before vowel) tetrarch.
trans- (L)	=across: transfer, translate, transport; (sometimes becomes tra-): traverse.
tri- (G, L)	=three: triangle, trident, triplicate.
un- (OE)	=negative: unlikely, untrue.
under-	=the English preposition: underpay, underprivileged.
uni- (L)	=one: uniform, unison, universe.
up-	=the English preposition: uprising, upwards.
vice- (L)	=instead of: viceregent, viceroy.
well-	=the English adverb: well-being.
with- (OE)	=against: withdraw, withhold, withstand.

Suffix

-able	=the English adjective: agreeable, indispensable.
-ac, -acal (G)	=forms nouns and adjectives: maniac, maniacal.
-acious (L)	=adjectives: fallacious.
-acity (L)	=abstract nouns: perspicacity.
-acy (G, L)	=abstract nouns: fallacy.
-age (L, OF)	=aggregate of: cellarage; function: baronage; action: breakage; cost of using: cartage.
-ain (F)	=adjectives: certain.
-al (L)	=adjectives: general, usual.
-an (L)	=adjectives: anglican, Lutheran.
-ana (L)	=sayings of or about: Shakespeariana.
-ance, -ancy (L, F)	=nouns of quality or action: resistance, constancy.
-ant (L, F)	=adjectives and nouns: defiant, executant.
-ar (L)	=agent or doer: beggar.
-archy (G)	=rule: autarchy, hierarchy, monarchy, oligarchy.
-arian (L)	=member of a sect: trinitarian, vegetarian.
-ary (L)	=nouns and adjectives: actuary, exemplary.
-asm, -ast, -astic	=-ism, etc. (q.v.).
-ate (L)	=nouns, adjectives and verbs of state: primate, intestate, participate.
-atic (F)	=nouns and adjs.: fanatic, lymphatic.
-ation (L)	=abstract nouns: agitation.
-cide (L)	=kill: fratricide, suicide.
-cracy (G)	=rule: autocracy, aristocracy, democracy.
-craft	=the English noun: woodcraft.
-cratic (G)	=adjs.: autocratic, aristocratic, democratic.

366

-cy (L)	=abstract nouns: captaincy, infancy.
-dom (OE)	=nouns of rank and condition: kingdom, serfdom.
-ean (-aean, -eian, G, L)	=belonging to, like: Herculean, Achaean, Bodleian.
-ed (T)	=adjs. and past tenses and parts.: married.
-ee (F)	=person affected: addressee, employee.
-eer (L)	=person engaged in: auctioneer, electioneer.
-en (OE)	=past part.: spoken; dimin.: chicken, maiden; old fem.: vixen; old plur.: oxen; adjs.: golden; vbs. from adjs.: deepen, moisten.
-ence, -ency (L)	=abstract nouns of quality or action: independence, fluency.
-ent (L)	=adjs. and nouns: independent, intent.
-eous (L)	=of the nature of: aqueous, ligneous.
-er (T)	=agent or doer: caller; comparative: bigger; vbs.: wander, waver.
-ern (T)	=adjs.: southern.
-ery (F)	=nouns: drapery, archery, brewery, popery.
-esce (L)	=verbs of inception: coalesce.
-escent (L)	=adjs. of inception: opalescent.
-ese (L)	=adjs. of locality: Japanese; forms of language: Johnsonese, journalese.
-esque (F)	=after the manner of: Dantesque.
-ess (F)	=feminines: countess; abstract nouns: duress, largess.
-est (OE)	=superlative: biggest.
-et (F)	=dimin.: bullet, sonnet.
-ete (G)	=nouns naming participants: aesthete, athlete.

367

-eth (= -th, OE)	=ordinal nos.: thirtieth.
-etic (F)	=adjs.: aesthetic.
-ette (F)	=dimin.: cigarette, etiquette.
-faction (L)	=abstract nouns=making: satisfaction.
-fer (L)	=carry: transfer, refer.
-ferous (L)	=adjs.=carrying: coniferous.
-fic (L)	=making: terrific.
-fication (L)	=abstract nouns=making: purification.
-ful	=full: awful, wonderful.
-fy (L)	=make: Frenchify, horrify.
-gram, -graph, -grapher, -graphic, -graphy (G)	=write, writer, written, etc.: radiogram, autograph, biographer, geographic, autobiography.
-head, -hood (T)	=nouns of condition: Godhead, boyhood, parenthood.
-ia (G)	=abstract nouns and plurals: militia, regalia.
-ial (L)	=adjs.: ceremonial, venial.
-ian (L)	=adjs.: Christian.
-ible (L)	=-able: credible, intelligible.
-ic, -ical (L)	=adjs. and nouns: satiric, music, comical.
-ice (L)	=abstract nouns: avarice.
-ician (F)	=one skilled in: musician.
-id (L)	=adjs. and nouns: fluid, pyramid.
-ier (F)	=-eer and -er: collier.
-il, -ile (L)	=adjs.: civil, agile.
-ing (T)	=present part.: doing; dimin.: farthing.
-ion (F)	=nouns of condition: communion, union.
-ior (OF) (L)	=agent or participant: warrior; comparative: superior.
-iour (F)	=agent or participant: saviour.
-ious (L)	=adis.: pernicious.
-ise (L)	=nouns: franchise; verbs: chastise.

-ish (OE)	=adjs.: impish.
(F)	=verbs: perish.
-ism (G, F)	=abstract nouns: communism, fascism.
-ison, -son, -ition (OF)	=abstract nouns: comparison, ambition.
-ist (G, L, F)	=personal nouns: communist, theorist
-ister (OF)	=agent: minister.
-ite (G, L, F)	=adjs., nouns and vbs.: Shelleyite, dynamite, unite.
-itious, -icious (L)	=adjs.: ambitious, suspicious.
-itous (L)	=adjs.: calamitous.
-ity, -ety (L, F)	=abstract nouns: scarcity, dubiety.
-ive (L)	=adjs.: active, restive.
-iz(s)ation (L, F)	=abstract nouns: realization.
-iz(s)e (G, L, F)	=verbs: realize, specialize.
-kin (OE)	=dimin.: lambkin, Perkin.
-kind (OE)	=race, type: mankind, womankind.
-le (OE)	=nouns: handle; adjs.: brittle; vbs.: twinkle; dimin.: bramble.
-lence, -lent (L)	=abstract nouns and adjs.=full of: pestilence, turbulent.
-less	=the English word: hopeless.
-let (OF)	=dimin.: streamlet.
-like	=the English word: warlike.
-ling (OE)	=dimin.: darling, gosling.
-loger, -logic, -logical, -logist, -logy, -logue	=speak, study, etc.: astrologer, psychological, apologist, biology, monologue.
-long	=the English adj.: headlong.
-ly (OE)	=adjs. of quality: kingly; advbs.: quickly.
-mania (G, L)	=madness: megalomania.
-ment (L)	=nouns of action or result: atonement, fragment.
-meter, -metry (G)	=measure: gasometer, geometry.
-most	=the English adj. for superlatives: inmost.

369

-nd (L)	=gerundive nouns and adjs.: dividend, moribund.
	=participial nouns: fiend, friend.
-ness (OE)	=nouns of state: goodness.
-o-	=used to adapt first word to suffix and in double-barrelled words: psychology, Franco-British.
-ock (?)	=dimin.: bullock, hillock.
-oid (G)	=having form of: asteroid, rhomboid.
-oon (L, F)	=nouns: balloon, spittoon.
-or (L)	=agent or participant: actor, donor.
-ory (L)	=nouns of -or: factory, oratory; adjs.: compulsory.
-ose (L)	=adjs.=abounding in: bellicose, jocose.
-osis (G)	=nouns of condition: apotheosis, meiosis, neurosis.
-ot (F)	=dimin.: chariot, parrot.
(G)	=personal nouns: idiot, patriot.
-otic (G)	=adjs. of -osis: neurotic.
-our (F)	=abstract nouns: colour, humour.
-ous (L)	=adjs.: tremendous.
-phil, -phile, -philous, -phily (G)	=love: Anglophile, bibliophily.
-phobe, -phobia, -phobic (G)	=fear: Anglophobe, hydrophobia, claustrophobic.
-phone, -phony (G)	=sound: gramophone, telephony.
-phore, -phorous (G)	=carry: semaphore, phosphorous.
-phyte (G)	=grow: neophyte.
-ry	=-ery: Jewry, poultry.
-scope, -scopic (G)	=see: telescope, telescopic.
-ship (T)	=nouns of status or skill: craftsmanship, headship.
-sion (L)	=nouns of condition: cohesion, tension.
-som, -some (OE)	=adjs.: quarrelsome, lissom.
-ster, -stress (OE)	=agent: brewster, gamester, seamstress.

370

-teen (OE)	=addition of ten: thirteen, etc.
-ter, -ther (L)	=distinction and comparison: further, other, alter.
-th (OE)	=ordinal nos.: eleventh; nouns=ness: breadth, truth.
-tion (L)	=abstract nouns: attention.
-tomy (G)	=cut: anatomy, dichotomy.
-tude (L)	=state: altitude, solitude.
-ty (L, F)	=abstract nouns: loyalty, plenty.
(OE)	=tens: twenty, etc.
-ule (L)	=dimin.: globule, granule.
-ure (F)	=abstract nouns: aperture, failure, seizure.
-ward(s) (OE)	=direction: outward, forwards.
-ways, -wise	=English words: sideways, clockwise.
-wright (OE)	=workman, maker: playwright, wheelwright.
·y (OE)	=adjs.: milky, thorny; dimin.: Johnny, hanky, lassy.
(F)	=nouns: army, treaty.

Index